POSTMILLENNIAL POP
General Editors: Karen Tongson and Henry Jenkins

Puro Arte: Filipinos on the Stages of Empire
Lucy Mae San Pablo Burns

Spreadable Media: Creating Value and Meaning in a Networked Culture
Henry Jenkins, Sam Ford, and Joshua Green

*Media Franchising: Creative License and Collaboration in the Culture
Industries*
Derek Johnson

Your Ad Here: The Cool Sell of Guerrilla Marketing
Michael Serazio

Looking for Leroy: Illegible Black Masculinities
Mark Anthony Neal

From Bombay to Bollywood: The Making of a Global Media Industry
Aswin Punathambekar

A Race So Different: Performance and Law in Asian America
Joshua Takano Chambers-Letson

Modernity's Ear: Listening to Race and Gender in World Music
Roshanak Kheshti

MODERNITY'S EAR

Leviathan. © 2015 Anish Kapoor / ARS, New York / DACS, London

Modernity's Ear

Listening to Race and Gender in World Music

Roshanak Kheshti

NEW YORK UNIVERSITY PRESS
New York and London

NEW YORK UNIVERSITY PRESS
New York and London
www.nyupress.org

References to Internet websites (URLs) were accurate at the time of writing.
Neither the author nor New York University Press is responsible for URLs that
may have expired or changed since the manuscript was prepared.

Library of Congress Cataloging-in-Publication Data
Kheshti, Roshanak.
Modernity's ear : listening to race and gender in world music / Roshanak Kheshti.
pages cm. -- (Postmillennial pop)
Includes bibliographical references and index.
ISBN 978-1-4798-6701-1 (cl : alk. paper) -- ISBN 978-1-4798-1786-3 (pb : alk. paper)
1. World music--Social aspects. 2. Sound recordings--Social aspects. 3. Music and race. I.
Title.
ML3916.K54 2015
780.9--dc23
2015014812

New York University Press books are printed on acid-free paper,
and their binding materials are chosen for strength and durability.
We strive to use environmentally responsible suppliers and materials
to the greatest extent possible in publishing our books.

Manufactured in the United States of America

10 9 8 7 6 5 4 3 2 1

Also available as an ebook

For Diego

CONTENTS

ACKNOWLEDGMENTS

This project has shifted shape as a result of so many life forces that have put pressure on it and breathed life into it, molding and imprinting upon it over its many years of gestation. While I am single-handedly responsible for all excesses and shortcomings contained within these pages, the book would not have been possible without contributions big and small made by many people I encountered on the meandering and long yellow brick road of its development.

At Indiana University, I was incredibly fortunate to have had as undergraduate advisors Robyn Wiegman and Carol Greenhouse without whose ardent support I would never have pursued my doctorate. Their brilliance so impressed me and their outstanding mentorship taught me so much about the teacher I wanted to grow up to become. I was materially supported by the McNair scholars program there, which enabled me to discover my love of books and research.

At UC Santa Cruz, I was privileged to be in the company of other graduate student misfits who found a home at that odd city on a hill. Afsaneh Kalantary, Ulrika Dahl, Mika Court, Bahiyya Maroon, Alejandra Castaneda, Kale Fajardo, Scott Morgensen, Shiho Satsuka, Kami Chisholm, James Todd, Alejandra Kramer, Roya Rastegar, and Allison Sampson-Anthony provided me companionship and moral support, and gave me the gumption to take the countless leaps of intellectual faith evident in this book. I am grateful for the training I received by my brilliant and uncompromising graduate professors and mentors, including Jackie Brown, Lisa Rofel, Donald Brenneis, Anna Tsing, Bob White, Susan Harding, Diane Gifford-Gonsales, Triloki and Annapurna Pandey, Teresa de Lauretis, David Hoy, Donna Haraway, James Clifford, Angela Davis, Anjali Arondekar, Luis Chude-Sokei, and David Marriott. My mentors Nancy Chen and Gina Dent gave so generously of their time, mentorship, feedback, and nurturing. I have tried to emulate in my own mentorship Nancy's compassion and methodical organization. And from Gina I have learned so much about the political project of intellectual work. Gina joined my committee at a critical juncture, changing the course of my career forever. I am eternally grateful for all the years of unwavering support I have received from her.

And while my day job involved training in critical, feminist, psychoanalytic, and anthropological theory, I trained at night in sound. I have learned so much from my band mates, collaborators, and the musicians I encountered in the early aughts. The time spent with Sam Tsitrin and Sara Cassetti in the Ebb and Flow had a particularly great impact on this project. The hours and hours spent rehearsing, recording, and performing trained me in ways to do the thinking I do in this book that I was completely unaware of at the time. I am also grateful to our manager, Joyce Williams, and producer, Christian Hanlon, with whom I spent many hours in the studio engaging, debating, discussing, and theorizing on the subject of sound.

I grew immensely in the UC President's Postdoctoral Fellowship program and am grateful to Kimberly Adkinson and Sheila O'Rourke who have worked tirelessly to make our success as fellows possible. While a fellow in the Department of Gender and Women's Studies at UC Berkeley, I was accepted with open arms by the entire faculty—Barrie Thorn, Trinh T. Minh-ha, Mel Chen, Charis Thompson, Juana Maria Rodriguez, and Minoo Moallem—but most importantly, was taken under the wing of the inimitable Paola Bacchetta whose sharp-witted, critical mentorship equipped me with the skills necessary for survival in the academy. GWS staff Eileen Andrade and Althea Cummings were incredibly supportive and enabling of me during my very important time there. I am also grateful to the posse of students who surrounded Paola with whom I learned and shared—Marlon Bailey, Fouziyha Toughi, Huma Dar, Matt Richardson, and Zakkiya Jackson.

My work has benefited from engagement by audiences and workshop participants over the years, to whom I am grateful. These include participants at: the 2001 Diaspora Studies Workshop, UC Santa Cruz Feminist Studies, the Feminist Theory and Music 8 Conference at CUNY, the EMP/IASPM Conference at NYU, Northwestern University Performance Studies, UC Berkeley Theater and Performance Studies, UC Berkeley Gender and Women's Studies, UCLA Thinking Gender, FemTechNet, UC Berkeley Anthropology, The Cultural Studies Association, the American Studies Association, the American Anthropological

Association, and the International Association for the Study of Popular Music. I was fortunate enough to participate in the Future of Minority Studies Mellon summer institute on queer theory at Cornell University where I delighted in generous and generative engagements with Jacqui Alexander, Minnie Bruce Pratt, Chandra and Satya Mohanty, Eng Beng Lim, Christina Hanhardt, Stacy Macias, Micaela Diaz-Sanchez, Ernesto Martinez, Caroline Tushabe, Andy Smith, Gabeba Baderoon, Irmary Reyes-Santos, Chaitanya Lakkimsetti, Hiram Perez, Erica Lorraine Williams, and Nadia Ellis. That time helped to crystalize the previously gelatinous components of queer analysis in my work.

I am privileged to be on the faculty in the Ethnic Studies Department at UCSD, a community that has enabled me to grow and prosper, and allowed for my thinking to thrive. I am grateful for the intellectual support of my colleagues Ross Frank, Yen Le Espiritu, Curtis Marez, Shelley Streeby, Kalindi Vora, Kirstie Dorr, Patrick Anderson, Sara Clark Kaplan, Fatima el Tayeb, Jillian Hernandez, Adria Imada, Daphne Taylor-Garcia, Mattie Harper and Dayo Gore, and the support I've received from across campus from Tara Javidi, Lisa Lowe, Lisa Cartright, Jann Passler, Joe Hankins, Meg Wesling, Sara Johnson, Babak Rahimi, Dennis Childs, Danny Widener, Boatema Boatang, Martha Lampland, Lisa Yoneyama, Elana Zihlberg, and the late Rosemary George.

Without the support of my undergraduate research assistant Kelly Chung and graduate student researcher Marilisa Navarro I would have never been able to organize all my research data. And I am forever indebted to Sara Mameni who took great care to proofread and format every word of the final version of the book and engage in close readings of texts of my choosing on a moment's notice. I have greatly benefited from a community of intellectual buddies working in sound who have given to me generously over the years, including Deborah Vargas, Kevin Fellesz, Barry Shank, Shana Redmond, Deborah Wong and Ines Casillas. I would also like to thank the archivists and librarians who have helped me locate materials: Sara Cassetti, Ann Hoog at the American Folklife Center at the Library of Congress, and Laura Elizabeth Smith at the Archives of Appalachia at Eastern Tennessee State University. I also want to thank Charlotte Frisbee and Deborah Wong for separately entertaining my questions regarding women's participation in the early formative period of the Society for Ethnomusicology.

Various people have read through iterations of this project and provided feedback, including members of my postdoctoral writing group Ines Casillas, Marlon Bailey, Sora Han, and Fouzhiya Toughi as well as Amy Sara Carroll, Jillian Hernandez, Patrick Anderson, Deborah Wong, Kalindi Vora, Kirstie Dorr, Kamala Visweswaran, and numerous anonymous reviewers, to all of whom I am grateful for critical feedback. Thanks to Anitra Grisales who provided the highest quality editorial services at impressive speeds without which I could not have completed the project as expeditiously as I have, and to indexer Alex Wescott. And I am grateful to my amazing NYU Press team, especially Eric Zinner, Alicia Nadkarni, Dorothea S. Halliday, the designers, and anonymous reviewers. Thanks especially to Karen Tongson for getting behind the project early on.

With Sora Han I have discovered the great joy of intellectual camaraderie. She has walked alongside the development of this manuscript and then book, having read almost every draft of every chapter along the way; having leaned so heavily on her in its production, I cannot quantify Sora's contribution. While she cannot be blamed in any way for the book's deficiencies, its strengths would be featherweight if not for her acumen and insight. Sora has stimulated my thinking and helped me to ground my claims in ways that helped them to cohere while also encouraging my audacity when necessary. For this commitment I am eternally grateful.

I thank all my interlocutors at Kinship Records including my coworkers and the label's artists. I have chosen to employ pseudonyms to protect the identity of my friends, informants, and interlocutors but I hope that they each will recognize the immense ways that my time with that organization has functioned to critically inform this research. I am also grateful for being included in a world music listening salon and for its participants' willingness to participate in my research. I thank especially DJ "David Philips" for his generosity and openness to my inquiries.

The life of the mind is a labor- and resource-intensive enterprise and would be impossible without the love, care, and material support of my friends and family. I am grateful for the reproductive labor of Rachel Tolentino and her staff at the SDSU Children's Center as well as the staff at the UCSD ECEC (Marisela, Leslie, and Leonor) as well as the teachers and staff at Maria Montessori school (Ms. Yar, Ms. Myers, Ms. Pink, and Ms. Walters) who have provided outstanding care for my son Diego, allowing me the peace of mind necessary to complete this book. I thank Judy and the late Joe Cassetti, Tracy Whelpley, Todd Whelpley, Kathy Carbonetti, Ben Wickey, Lydia Wickey, Mark Whelpley, and Janell Horton who have given me shelter and love and seen this entire project from inception to completion.

My parents Mohammad and Najibeh and my brother Babak, his partner Mark, and their son River have all given me the wings with which I have soared through this process (in particular, my mom, who provided much needed reproductive labor while I completed this project). My love of music grows organically from a natal knowledge of music's generativity in a community organized around music as a means of belonging. From this I learned to seek and find shelter in communities of sound and did so on that night at that fateful performance where I met my "native informant" Sara Cassetti. I am grateful to Sara for the years of material and affective support that has made it possible for me to complete this work, which would most certainly not be what it is today without her acoustic acumen which has guided me and my musical ear for over two decades. I dedicate this book to our son Diego who daily reminds me of the endlessness and possibilities of play, music, joy.

By the late 1990s, when I officially began research for this project, I was accustomed to a soundscape out of sync. Having been steeped in the syrupy sweet tea of the American southeast—a sweetness that covered over the bitterness of the civil rights dream deferred—growing up I learned that the public sphere was no melting pot and music was most certainly not a utopian domain of color-blind integration. This was no "audiotopia."[1] Instead, there was a perpetual dissonance at every threshold, like the one on the dance floor when the DJ crossfades either too soon or too late, causing the beat to go out of sync and leaving everyone with no idea where the song will go. This out-of-sync soundscape AKA Music City USA™ consisted for me of classical Azerbaijani music played on cassettes in the family room, out of sync with the Persian pop played at social functions, out of sync with the New Wave playing on my Walkman, out of sync with the 1990s country music pouring out of trucks, pumped through speakers at fast-food chains, heard on every single station on both AM and FM bands in Nashville. It was a soundscape consisting of multiple rhythms, melodies, and scales—out of sync, with different time signatures—cacophonous.

Make no mistake about it: the Nashville of today, boasting residents like Jack White (of White Stripes fame) and Nicole Kidman, bears no resemblance to the city of my youth. As Barbara Mandrell's 1981 Billboard chart topper (written by Kye Fleming and Dennis Morgan) declares, "I took a lot of kiddin', 'cause I never did fit in, now look at everybody tryin' to be what I was then." Mandrell's song implies that then, as now, the insiders rejected the fad that is Nashville for a "realness" to which perhaps the seasonal or ironic recent transplant was not privy. In Mandrell's time this fad could have been indexed by Robert Altman's 1975 cult classic *Nashville*, whereas today it could be the ABC television serial by the same name. These televisual and filmic representations actively disavow the Nashville of my youth as well as that of today: a city segregated between red, black, white, yellow, and brown, including multitudes of immigrants and their generation 1.5 children.

Research for this book unofficially began back in the day, perhaps in the summer of 1985 as Ricky Scaggs's "Swinging" was rocking away in my head. Though not the biggest fan of country music, I could not seem to escape the genre or that tune. It was actually Parvaneh, my cousin and idol, whose own fondness for the hooky melody blasting from her white Pontiac Grand Am on our way to the mall, made it seem OK to the eleven-year-old me, who needed constant approval from her on all things cool. Or maybe it was in 1990, when I spent the summer working as a sweeper at Opryland USA, the now defunct country music theme park that boasted the superlative "Home of American Music" (see Figure P.1). Patrolling the theme park, where I had previously spent my adolescent summers in a kind of poor man's summer day camp, now brushing half-smoked cigarettes into my long-handled dustpan while wearing the park's official sweeper uniform with pride, I studied the parkgoers and revue performers with the maturity of an alienated sixteen-year-old. Just another opportunity to revel in the mind-blowingly ironic American microcosm that was *the* "Home of American Music." Although fascinating in all its hyperbole, the deracinated definition of American music as 1980s and 1990s country struck me as disingenuous and wishful. This was a wish that explicitly excluded me, a new immigrant, by virtue of its structural exclusion of African and Native American music. This willful disavowal of the centrality of race to American music inspired my interest in studying the centrality of race and gender in popular music.

But the needle abruptly scratched across the LP of the commonsenseness and commonplaceness of a soundscape out of sync when I discovered Asian underground music in the late 1990s. It was not so much my identity that pulled me toward this emergent genre but my fascination with the seemingly disparate sounds, which should have been out of sync but were mixed together beautifully. This coming-into-consciousness took place at the moment of my first encounter with Paul Gilroy and his theses on music, race, diaspora, colonialism, and belonging. Armed with these utopian ideals, I headed *into the field*, which was for me a record company I will call Kinship Records, a company whose ethos seemed to embody the very idealism I had just discovered in the form of sonic hybridity.[2] The needle once again scratched, however, this

Figure P.1. Opryland USA, the now defunct country
music theme park that boasted the superlative,
"Home of American Music."

time across the LP of my naïveté and idealism, when I very quickly col-
lided with a racial and gendered division of labor not only inside the
organization, not simply on the production and distribution end of this
industry, but also in the consumption of the music, in the way it was
listened to and heard.

In the following work I present a form of theorizing on multiple registers. On the one hand, I employ a way of knowing that has grown organically from my historico-political-cultural circumstances. It is a way
of theorizing that Barbara Christian has named through her notion of
"a race for theory":

> [P]eople of color have always theorized—but in forms quite different
> from the Western form of abstract logic. And I am inclined to say that
> our theorizing (and I intentionally use the verb rather than the noun) is
> often in narrative forms, in the stories we create, in riddles and proverbs,
> in the play with language, since dynamic rather than fixed ideas seem
> more to our liking. . . . My folk, in other words, have always been a race
> for theory—though more in the form of the hieroglyph, a written figure
> which is both sensual and abstract, both beautiful and communicative.[3]

As Christian deciphers above, there are forms for and ways of theorizing that result from a lifetime of learning, not necessarily from the
published text but from the marginalia scribbled along its borders, a

learning that happens out of necessity based on exclusion from formal systems of knowledge production, a learning that results from being on the receiving end of various systematic phobias and isms, a learning that is facilitated through community, alienation, and environment. The theorizing capability of the marginalized, legible in forms like literature, music, art practice, dance, movement, affect, and sexuality, are forms that are decidedly more accessible and vernacular than scholarly.

In the spirit of Barbara Christian's naming of *our* theorizing as a theorizing that takes shape and form in ways that have historically been illegible to "the Western form of abstract logic," yet audible and legible to *our* folk, I theorize through the medium that I have always understood best—sound. Playing by ear throughout this book, I objectify the problems of the contemporary world music culture industry, the racialized and gendered fantasies through which the industry has formed, the development of systems of knowledge around these fantasies, and the capacity to both produce knowledge against the grain of these formations and to submit to their pleasures in a queer utopian practice of listening, all through an engagement with sound.

I theorize in this book through sound not in an effort to exemplify a subaltern reading practice, and not to legitimate it by translating into discourse an undervalued way of knowing with the body, at least not first and foremost.[4] Instead, I employ the survival strategy *playing by ear* in order to read the world music culture industry as the institution that has attempted to harness that very reading practice and rebrand it as a commodity. In the same way that I *played by ear* when I would sit for hours in my bedroom working out top-40 radio hits on the dime-store Bontempi air organ I had somehow acquired, I now deploy *playing by ear* as a performative, rather than mimetic, method/ology—as a performative listening praxis where one listens with the body. This performance praxis produces forms that fall under the general rubric of what musicologist Lars Lilliestam calls "un-notated music," or music that is conveyed by using means other than notation, which is essentially all musical traditions except Western music, in other words, world music.[5] Playing by ear is one of the tropes through which I elaborate my methodology of *listening*, which I also refer to as *aurality*—a sense perception-cum-survival strategy—in a reading of the commoditization of this very sense perception/survival strategy. I do this while at the same time tracing a genealogical lineage through that very thing that Christian calls the "Western form of abstract logic," with which she is at odds. I do so in order to argue that any compound capable of corroding Western philosophy's ossifications lies within its own history, within its own "marginalized discourse"; it requires a radical form of interdisciplinarity that takes liberally from these seemingly opposed historical formations. While some of the Western philosophical theories that I deploy in this book may be the "theory" against which Christian writes (what she calls "New Philosophy"), these forms enable for me modes of engaging—*auralities*, or ways of listening—comparable to the way Christian describes literature: "In literature I sensed the possibility of the integration of feeling/knowledge, rather than the split between the abstract and the emotional in which Western philosophy inevitably indulged."[6] Thus, I present to you listening as a reading practice of listening, rooted in listening as a mode of survival and resistance, routed through listening as methodology, to listening as object. While I make the case that sensibilities like listening, which have been imagined by some as the means to cultivating intersubjective identifications with the subaltern, have been absorbed into the culture industry, folded into its business model, and instrumentalized for modern self-making, I chart this emergent mode-of-perception-cum-business model with the utopian aim of tracing the simultaneous formation of a queer utopian practice of listening. I trace a parallel formation of an ethical listening praxis that opens up a set of possibilities that continue to be emergent, a practice of listening through which the listener relates differently to pleasure. This emergent queerness is in the same vein as that which the late Jose Esteban Munoz read: "QUEERNESS IS NOT YET HERE. Queerness is an ideality. We may never touch queerness, but we can feel it as a warm illumination of a horizon imbued with potentiality. We have never been queer, yet queerness exists for us as an ideality that has been distilled from a past and used to imagine a future."[7] Just as queerly, this book reads a past to imagine a future mode of relating differently, wishing for what Native Hawaiian scholar Manu Meyer calls "a radical remembering of the future."[8]

This is a book about sound, that theorizes through sound, that occupies sound, that builds upon what I have been learning from sound my entire life. I have cultivated this practice in the context of ethnographic fieldwork at a world music record company, in my own performance practice, and through the analysis of recording techniques used throughout the twentieth century. In this book and in the social worlds I study, sound is a social formation that is constituted by struggle and struggled over; one that is both overdetermined semantically and yet manifold in its semiotic possibilities. Its sublimity penetrates epidermal, discursive, and geographic barriers—changing and being changed by these movements and reverberations. It is this movement and the transformations that sound, its producers, and its listeners undergo in collisions with productions of and absorptions of sound that I exposit below.

Introduction

Having become all ears for this phonograph dog, you transform yourself into a high-fidelity receiver, and the ear—your
ear which is also the ear of the other—begins to occupy
in your body the disproportionate place of the "inverted
cripple."
—Jacques Derrida, *The Ear of the Other*

Like a loyal pet delivering a newspaper, or fresh kill, I went to Jon
Cohen, the president of the world music record company where I was
a new intern with what I thought was a novel discovery resulting from
my keen analytical capabilities; he rebuffed my excitement with a dead-
pan, thoroughly unimpressed reaction. "Most of our listeners *are* [white]
women," he said to me after I brought to his attention the counterintuitive discovery I had made: a majority of the people in the company's
consumer database were self-identified white women.[1] Jon's matter-
of-fact response caught me off-guard since I believed this data to be
unrepresentative based, if nothing else, on my own anecdotal evidence
(I was one of those listeners but not a white woman, and I knew of many
others). Failing to register the significance of this interaction at the time
(I never found it noteworthy enough to even write about in my field-
notes), it took me many years to understand its significance.

Time after time, I returned to this scenario in memory unable to inte-
grate it logically into any larger narrative I could tell; it was simply paradoxical. How could the president of a world music company claim that
most of their listeners were white women? I was incredulous. Cohen,
like any music industry executive, understood as truism what I found to
be utterly confusing and assumed to be just plain wrong, until I began to
dig a little deeper. It is this paradox that now rings like a bellwether organizing the movements made throughout this book. This white woman's
aural trace appears in shadows and mirrors, and while *Modernity's Ear*

is not about *her*, she has made the chapters in this book resonant. The music produced by Kinship Records is made for her, whether or not she in fact consumes it. It is her *aurality* that preempts the logic of the Kinship Records sound. Let me explain.

Kinship Records is a pseudonym for the San Francisco-based, world/electronica record company where I worked as an intern, then marketing department employee, from 2002 to 2004.[2] I was initially drawn to Kinship as the label that published several artists I was interested in working with in conjunction with my ethnographic research. In the late 1990s and early 2000s, the label was known for releasing hybrid world music that blends classical styles and instruments from around the world with what they call "modern production values." While numerous record companies were promoting this kind of music at that time, Kinship was unique in its promotion of music made collaboratively by diasporic artists from the global South and American and European producers and DJs. For this reason, I found my demographic discovery and Cohen's reaction unexpected. How was it that this music, which I initially heard as by and for diasporic subjects, was in fact being made for white women?[3] Sure, a few white women frequented the late, great DJ Cheb I Sabbah's Tuesday night residency at Nicky's BBQ where I first heard this music, but most of us regulars were South Asian, Middle Eastern, and African diasporics and expats who flocked to this weekly event in the Lower Haight district of San Francisco where we could dance away the Tuesday doldrums. If anything, given the genre's history of orientalist racial fetishism, I could have understood better if the majority of listeners were thought to be white men, but I could not understand the "fact" that they were white women, until I got to know *her aurality* better.

I encountered that white woman regularly over the following ten years as an apparition in the archives and as fantasy in the form of "the ideal listener" for whom the record label produced its sounds. She appeared in proxy form as the host of a radio show: the naïve-yet-enthusiastic correspondent I call Nancy Dayne with whom Cohen would share his world music expertise on a weekly basis. It is her imagined listening capacity, her *aurality*, that is fetishized by the record company most of all and the more I explored the world music industry's history, the more I could hear her aurality archived within it. What I ultimately came to understand about the paradoxical truism "Most of our listeners *are* [white] women" is that it has functioned as the fantasy forming the basis of the world music industry's desire for the last century. *Her aurality* motivates the industry at the level of hardware, sound, and affect design. I've stopped asking myself whether or not she is real because she has become mythologized to the point of reification; she is the topos of the American world music industry.

The Feminization of Listening

This is a book about the important biopolitical role that listening to the sounds of the other has played in the twentieth and early twenty-first centuries in the United States. It is a book about the vast world music culture industry (WMCI), in both its academic and commercial guises. It is a book about bodies as sites through which the other's sounds resonate, and the deeply libidinized practice of listening that American consumers have been trained in through the technological developments and epistemic transformations of the last hundred years. I argue throughout this book that the production of the WMCI is intimately tied to the formation of what many scholars have identified as the twentieth-century feminization of listening.

Listening came to be constructed as a feminized practice through its increasing domestication by the gramophone industry and the ascension of the bourgeois woman, the target market for the machine's home use. As Theodor Adorno wrote of it, "It is the bourgeois family that gathers around the gramophone in order to enjoy the music that it itself—as was already the case in the feudal household—is unable to perform. . . . The diffuse and atmospheric comfort of the small but bright gramophone sound corresponds to the humming gaslight and is not entirely foreign to the whistling teakettle of bygone literature."[4] In arguing that "the gramophone belongs to the pregnant stillness of individuals," Adorno highlights the gendered temporality of listening that always awaited a future site for becoming.[5] The domestication of the practice of listening to recorded music shifted the labor from musical performance to performative listening, a concept I discuss in chapters 5 and 6. In chapter 1 I focus on the preponderance of white female sound collectors, or "songcatchers," in the earliest period of field recording. They worked as comparative musicologists collecting for the Bureau of American Ethnology (and later for the Works Progress Administration, as well as the Smithsonian Institution) from the 1890s through the 1940s, and indexed their futurist political desires in the aurality with which they recorded. I examine the domestication of sound both among collectors and among listeners as a process that brought Native and African American noises under discursive control, rendering them legible "phonographic subjects." This practice fed the desires of feminized, domesticated listeners who not only sought exotic sounds on the phonographs that replaced the pianos in their parlors, but also a new domesticated other on whom the white female listener had a social leg up.

The world music industry is haunted by the specter of this white female sound collector, her technological medium of choice—the phonograph—and the recorded other that she brought under discursive control during the industry's genesis. Barred by jealous male colleagues from professing in the musical disciplines at the university level, her aurality found a home in the practice of salvage recording for the Bureau of American Ethnology. Not only was she willing and able to perform these salvage recordings, but being closer in social ranking to her subjects than her white male colleagues, she was seen as best suited for the task.

The salvage recordings made by female comparative musicologists became foundational for not only what would evolve into ethnomusicology after World War II but also became the business model of the burgeoning music industry, which had by the turn of the century established offices in every major city around the world and conducted recordings in many minor ones at that. As Pekka Gronow has chronicled, "By 1905 [the Gramaphone C]ompany had already made recordings in most European and Asian countries, including such remote localities as Helsinki, Tiflis, and Rangoon. At the same time, Victor's engineers toured South America and the Caribbean. The two companies obviously tried to penetrate every possible market from Tibet to Bolivia."[6] Gronow reveals that the music industry has from its inception been global in scale; that the music industry, even at its most nascent, incipient moment of becoming, was always a *world* music industry.

These conditions of becoming for the genre inform how world music is heard and how it structures the listener's relationship to recordings as well as the culture industry that produces and disseminates them. Generic developments through the twentieth century represent this industry's nimble capacity to respond to local markets and to rebrand its own archive in response to a demand that the industry itself helped to produce. In its inception, the industry managed all aspects of the commodity chain, from hardware (the phonograph) to software (the recorded voice, the field recording, the studio recording) and presented audiences with both folk/traditional and modern versions of themselves. All this infrastructural work paid off: As Gronow goes on to calculate, by 1926 this global music industry raked in profits of $70 million in record sales alone.[7] Just as the film industry did for vision during this same period, the global music industry satisfied a yearning for a developing imaginary that I name the "aural imaginary" in chapter 2, linking faraway places with local subjects whose senses of themselves as moderns were contingent upon their fantasies of these aural others. The burgeoning music industry's profitability stemmed precisely from its globally expansive reach and its capacity to satiate the nostalgic desires of the newly displaced and dispersed immigrant populations for those imagined communities, those homelands left behind, and to reinforce their position as moderns. By beginning with the context of white, female sound collector as one genealogical strand for world music, its culture industry, and its listenership, *Modernity's Ear* traces the white woman's racialized-gendered desire for the aural other as that which has produced the modern listening self. I map the co-constitutive nature of this formation, arguing that this fantastical white female listener begot the (just as fantastical) modern listener.

World music has been instrumental in the formation of a twentieth-century cosmopolitan subject constituted alongside and through technologies and systems of knowledge production. The very term "world music" time-stamps the emergence of the cosmopolitical subject in search of a little bit of everything from everywhere as a way of indexing her own adaptive capabilities in a rapidly transforming world. Scholars quibble over the exact provenance of the term "world music." Some have attributed its origins to a marketing meeting held by a group of British music executives in 1987.[8] Others, like Steven Feld, have identified its origins among 1960s academics who sought to celebrate the world's musical diversity.[9] Across these differences of opinion, the focus on the world music genre and marketing categories as the brainchild of specific academics or industrialists works with the assumption of "if you build it they will come." I see the genre formation and the debates over its boundaries as symptomatic of a larger structuring logic that desires not only "ethnic sounds" but also racialized and gendered bodies. In this study, world music represents an aurality that is formative of the racialized, gendered, and classed subjectivities of listeners, as well as performers, in the context of an emergent late modernity. Furthermore, I locate the genre's formation much earlier, linking it to the epistemic projects of settler colonialism and salvage ethnography contending that the academic study and commercial production of ethnic music are identical twin formations born as a national necessity at a particular techno-historical moment. Thus, I conceive of ethnomusicology and its commercial doppelganger, *world music*, as forming one culture industry, what I call the world music culture industry (WMCI). This single industry is characterized by a brokering—whether in exchange for actual or symbolic capital—in racialized gender. Ethnomusicology, its predecessor comparative musicology, and the world music genre trade in an economy of sound that is driven by desire that produces racialized and gendered fantasies and relations. This economy stages particular encounters within the recording, archiving, and listening event that constitute power relations that imagine and produce a pleasure-in-listening through fantasies of sonic racialized gender, the focus of chapter 4.

Kinship Records and other world/electronica record companies succeed in the marketplace because they function as interlocutors in a historical moment when cultural commodity exchange is in very high demand. The ascendancy of the record company coincides with the neoliberalization of the marketplace, offering equal footing to musical explorers and multicultural subjects who seek representations of themselves there. Kinship filters, packages, remixes, and represents various cultures to audiences in nonthreatening, legible ways. Thanks to the hybrid formula they promote, consumers are not alienated either by dissonant sounds, unfamiliar scales, and rhythmic structures, or by foreign time signatures, as every effort is made to take the work out of listening to the sounds of other cultures, leaving only pleasure and satisfaction to be enjoyed by the consumer. Difference is offered as an object to be enjoyed by consumers not only within the privacy of their own homes but, as I argue in chapters 2, 4, and 5, as an object to be incorporated into the self. By building a brand around the experience of cross-cultural musical collaboration, Kinship has distanced itself from debates of cultural appropriation waged over the last thirty years. Instead, musical hybridity is offered with promises of adapting the listener to a rapidly changing, multicultural world. As I discuss in chapter 4, hybridity's shadowy doppelganger—miscegenation—interpreted as undesirable racial noise, is carefully hedged against through mixing and production work, as well as other framing devices like packaging and liner notes.

I argue in chapter 1 that early twentieth-century white female comparative musicologists left *aural traces* on their recordings that index the social positionality these figures occupied in their first encounter with the *aural other*. Akin to point of view in visual studies, her aural trace now informs the way the record company imagines its contemporary listener (despite the questionable empirical nature of this wish). I pursue the uncanny encounters world music stages in fantasy and the pleasure-in-listening that occurs when bodies interact in the context of what I call "the aural imaginary." My location of this site of encounter within fantasy and the unconscious in no way limits how these processes matter or take material shape. In chapters 4 and 5 I argue that sound contributes to the materialization of bodies and figures bodies as gendered and racially marked within the listener's aural imaginary. Sound is therefore not only a vehicle in the communication of difference in world music but also contributes to the production of difference by materializing bodies in the imaginary of the listener. I develop this theory of materiality through the concept of "invagination" while considering the ear's symbolic work alongside that of the vagina's and contending with how both reproductive orifices overdetermine the gendering of sexual processes. Through a retooling of the Freudian concept of "incorporation," I examine not only the ways in which racialized and gendered sounds are fetishized and how the culture industry capitalizes upon this through the promotion of a *libidinal economy* or economy of desire, but the simultaneous ways in which Kinship has distanced itself from legacies of fetishism and appropriation, for which the genre was scorned throughout the nineties and aughts.

As Penleric insists to Bledsoe in the 2000 Maggie Greenwald film *Songcatcher* that I read in chapter 1, people down the mountain will want to buy mountain music because they are driven by a desire for an affective relation with the way the other's music "makes you feel." *Modernity's*

Ear theorizes the desire for the other in sound as a means of constituting the listening self and the particular culture-industrial harnessing of this systematic process. If we consider the historical structuring of listening as a feminized practice and take the example of the female comparative musicologists I discuss, we must ask how and why mass culture, and in particular phonograph recording and listening, became her entrée into the public sphere. This opens up an opportunity to read a rather queer context of power play. Here, the female comparative musicologist, as the paradigmatic feminized listener, achieved her newly won agency through the seemingly masculine practice of the phonographic subjectivation of the Native American as her necessary inferior. What I would more specifically term the *white feminization of listening* thus comes at a cost: the racialization of recorded sounds by an upwardly mobile female masculinity.[10] The modern practice through which the white bourgeois woman achieved agency—listening—structured her as the phonographic subject's superior, both in social standing and in racialized, gendered standing. And it is the titillatingly disruptive qualities of this "queer power play" that the WMCI has harnessed for profit. While the form of pleasure brokered by the WMCI is a feminized, invaginated, incorporative pleasure, it is nevertheless motivated by a phallic desire; I map in the following chapters how this positions the listener vis-à-vis the "aural other."

"Listening is a directed, learned activity: it is a definite cultural practice," writes Jonathan Sterne. "Listening requires hearing but is not simply reducible to hearing."[11] Sterne associates this turn toward listening in modernity with the development of "audile technique" or "a set of practices of listening that were articulated to science, reason, and instrumentality and that encouraged the coding and rationalization of what was heard."[12]

Listening is distinguished from hearing as a faculty of perception that is learned, and that is historically and culturally variable. But it is no mere faculty at Kinship; instead consumers are referred to as listeners, understood as subjects by way of their faculties of aural perception. By specifically addressing listeners' ears and staging interactions with the aural other there, the ear is constructed as the site of agency production. I focus not only on listening but aurality because of the significance ascribed to the ear and on the biopolitical instrumentalization of listening as an "audile technique" promoted by the WMCI that has had material consequences with raced and gendered implications.

What is the history of the WMCI's imaginary and fantasized ideal listener—that white woman between her late twenties and early forties—and how has an entire industry been structured around fantasizing about her fantasies? What you have before you is a critical examination of the WMCI and its racialized and gendered fantasies of sexuality in sound. In so many respects, this is a partial story about world music, Kinship Records, and the culture industry. Other stories, less amplified in these chapters, explore the varied meanings ascribed to these commodity forms by counterpublics and the ways in which artists have resisted the efforts of the industry to colonize sonic representations. Take, for example, the fact that many of the artists with whom I worked at Kinship Records participated in transnational networks of musical exchange, performing their music in sites beyond the well-worn paths traveled by first-world musicians. Live musical performance is an entirely distinct experience that elicits different meanings than those experienced on record. I have chosen not to explore live performance and the various manifestations of cultural exchange that transpire under those circumstances.

Ethnographic fieldwork performed within a capitalist organization presents a shift in the axis of power between ethnographer and subject. The ethics of ethnographic representation take on a particular form in the context of this book, as I am obligated to uphold as much as possible the anonymity of the events and subjects presented here. My methodology was partly inspired by a deeply rooted investment in moving beyond an analysis of world music that looks only at lyrical text and charismatic musical personalities, or listens only to musical style. This is not a musicological study of style, notation, or score. Rather than performing a textual analysis of lyrics or the transcription of a song into text, I attempt to practice an analysis of the sounds that I encountered through fieldwork experience and within American popular culture. The characters, companies, newspaper articles, and events I describe were inspired by actual people, real businesses, press clippings, and lived experiences, but as the author, I have taken great liberties in the re-presentation of this material, employing pseudonyms throughout.

My methodology grew out of the limitations presented by "studying up" or working with elites, statesmen and -women, aristocrats, capital-ists, and other members of society who sit more comfortably in social hierarchies. I analyze the world music industry as both a site of cultural production as well as a site that promotes the accumulation of capital through aurality, the spatial production of acoustics, and the embodied specificity of sonic phenomenology. I ask: What does a song's staging of space and time, with its movement through the stereo spread, tell us about not only the performer but also the listener? What about the levels of sounds in the mix, the presence and distance attributed to various sounds, and the timing through which sounds enter and exit the song? How can all this be considered alongside the relevance of the album packaging and copy, which work to curate the experience of hearing the music? These texts narrate a story about the artists, collaborators, the record company, and the historical context in which the album was released, but they also tell us about who they imagine we are and how a cultural logic is structured in that imaginary.

Because sound is not the *lingua franca* of the academy, I have struggled with the untranslatability of certain sonorous ways of knowing. Perhaps in response to a similar limit point, Fred Moten asks, "What happens in the transcription of performance, event, ritual? What happens, which is to say, what is lost in the recording? . . . What is the proper form of my endeavor?"[13] On the way to developing his improvisational method, a method that occupies the space of the break, that theorizes in the meter of jazz, he writes, "Sound, suspended brightness, unrepresentable and inexplicable mystery of (music is the improvisation of organization) ritual is music: principled (*archic*) (spatial) organization that constitutes a kind of nonverbal writing: transparent or instrumental, uninflected by the transformation of a buzz-grown extension, bending whistle, hummm."[14] In the spirit of such an ethical magnetism toward the form I work within, I echo Moten's call to poesis and improvisation in writing about/with/through/in and of sound. Taking heed of Moten's response of poesis to the call of music, I render here an attentiveness to and an ethical awareness of sound's form and remain leery of the limits of translating between sound and words. And while I make no promises of poetics in prose, I do *play* with language and form and struggle with translation through neologizing. This practice indexes the radical queer ethical drive that motivates the project, the "playing by ear" that I describe in the Preface. While I chronicle in the following pages how queer and feminist modes of relating and materializing have been coopted by the culture industry, it is ultimately with the aim of imagining another horizon of possibility for a utopian, feminist, queer aurality, a liberationist praxis akin to "playing by ear," one that brings the listener and sound into a copresence of becoming together, one that does not reify heteronormative logics of pleasure and power but exists in a state of play, an ontology that can imagine a different imaginary order.

* * *

The chapters in *Modernity's Ear* are organized around the particular ways in which sound's form is instrumentalized and utilized by the world music culture industry writ large to produce racialized and gendered encounters in the listening event. The familiar tropes deployed in the critical examination of world music—hybridity, appropriation, identity, authenticity, orality, and field recording—are upended in six chapters that reread these formations instead as miscegenation, incorporation, *signifiance* (loss of self), aurality, and refusal. This reorientation toward the embodied encounters and subjective outcomes staged by the WMCI enables me to critically engage the utopian claims about music that motivate this very study. This is the tautology on which the book revolves: motivated by a utopian drive toward listening to uncover the cooptation of the utopian drive toward listening by the WMCI. Along the way I discover the complex workings of desire and fantasy in bolstering the discourse of adaptability and fitness within multiculturalism, finding that even in the imaginary site of fantasy, racialized and feminized bodies are put to work in constituting that more highly adaptive, modern cosmopolitan listener. Gender and race have an exchange value within the world music marketplace way beyond what I initially thought. Yes, there are actual musicians exploited for their labor and grossly underpaid in comparison to the profits collected by producers and record companies. But preceding that context of exploitation, that political economy, is another economy of flows—a libidinal economy—in which the conditions of possibility for political economic exploitation are formed.

While the book is a critical examination of the ideological structuration of listening in the world music culture industry spanning its history from comparative musicology at the turn of the twentieth century through the contemporary ubiquity of world music, the concluding chapter offers an alternate and parallel history of listening to the other in modernity through an examination of recordings made of and by Zora Neale Hurston in various recording expeditions between 1935 and 1939. This contrapuntal Epilogue focuses on recordings that I argue offer an alternative listening relation to the one I chronicle in the other five chapters, one that is as firmly rooted within modernity but refuses the social structuration and symbolic formations that I map in the WMCI. This concluding chapter presents a different origin story of recording than the one I chronicle in the book, offering the starting point for the liberationist genealogy that the book wishes for.

In chapter 1, "The Female Sound Collector and Her Talking Machine," I revisit the scenes of phonographic recordings made by white female Bureau of American Ethnology comparative musicologists of Native Americans. In addition to consulting archival materials and auto/biographical accounts, I look to the 2000 Maggie Greenwald film *Songcatcher* as a prism through which to historicize the merging of comparative musicology and the phonograph industry. This chapter sets the stage for the following five chapters by making the case that a figure like *Songcatcher's* main character Lily Penleric represents both a female-masculine entrepreneurialism and a commitment to ethnographic knowledge production and that her particular way of perceiving these Native American phonographic subjects—what I term her aurality—has been captured as a trace in the recording process. I argue that the "aural trace" of the conditions of phonographic production is as audible as what I call "the aural other." The world music culture industry is in the business of selling both.

In chapter 2, "Listen, Inc.: Aural Modernity and Incorporation," I perform close readings of transcriptions of a nationally syndicated, travel themed radio show—to which Kinship Records president Jon Cohen was a regular contributor—and of the recent popularity of the "Afro-Indie" genre, which is understood as those African-derived musics in U.S. indie rock. This chapter develops the concept of "aural imaginary" as that mechanism through which the aural other is instrumentalized in the constitution of a listening self not simply through appropriation but through incorporation into the subject. I read sound as a representational medium but more specifically narrow in on sound's capacity to materially structure social relations, formations, and actors. I argue here that the WMCI, as represented in Kinship Records, has disassociated itself from the shunned and taboo practice of cultural appropriation and has assumed a new business model, what I call "aural incorporation." Aural incorporation represents that means by which listeners structure racialized sounds to which they may have no birthright into their origin narratives, laying claim to various musical traditions as their own. In this chapter I chronicle these as biopolitical tactics employed by the WMCI.

In chapter 3, "Losing the Listening Self in the Aural Other," I deploy Julia Kristeva and Roland Barthes's term *signifiance* to further theorize the desire that drives the listener to world music. This is a desire that works counter to signification or processes of identification. It explores the theme of subjective transcendence testified to by many listeners of world music through *signifiance* in order to theorize the loss of the self (which Barthes opposes to identification). Through several case studies from fieldwork as well as through the close reading of a song from the Kinship Records release *Arabian Journeys*, I examine the production processes that choreograph the "loss of the self" in sound.

In chapter 4, "Racial Noise, Hybridity, and Miscegenation in World Music," I critically read the ethos of cross-cultural collaboration promoted by this culture industry through the trope of musical hybridity. By theorizing the links between hybridity and miscegenation and their relationship to Darwin's theory of natural selection, this chapter interrogates the heterosexual imperative at work in musical tropes of cross-fertilization and chronicles the gendered division of sonic labor. I begin by surveying work on music and cultural mixing (e.g., syncretism, hybridity, fusion), insisting upon an analysis of the sexual implications at the heart of these metaphors and interrogating their heterologic as a holdover of eugenicist practices of "artificial selection."

In chapter 5, "The World Music Culture of Incorporation," I discuss how the blurring of the lines between commerce, industry, and knowledge production has been the legacy of the world music culture industry. Desire and yearning for the sounds of the other has helped to structure modern, so-called ultramodernist, and popular music forms in dynamic and aesthetic tension, continuing into the contemporary moment. This structure of desire has helped to train first-world listeners and music producers to listen for racialized gender and to structure their own listening subjectivity vis-à-vis, and often in opposition to, this alterity. But thanks to incorporation, the commodity chain has been delinked. The listener, now also in part the producer, aurally lays claim to sonic traditions and constitutes a key site of production. This chapter critically engages a long history of both Marxian and Freudian theorizing on fetishism in an effort to understand a recent shift to what I call the WMCI's post-fetishization of traditional sounds, which coexists alongside the fetishism to which we've grown accustomed.

In the Epilogue, "Modernity's Radical Ear and the Sonic Infidelity of Zora Neale Hurston's Recordings," I examine a collection of recordings made by Zora Neale Hurston where she breaks from ethnographic convention to develop a performance methodology in which her own body and voice are employed to represent the African American musical traditions of the South. I juxtapose this practice against the practice of "phonographic subjectivation" I establish in chapter 1—that process whereby the comparative musicologist brings the previously unintelligible sounds of the Native American into discourse through phonographic recording and archiving. "Modernity's Radical Ear" is a contrapuntal endnote, a "feminine ending" that functions as a "dominant" to the tonic processes I map in the previous chapters.[15]

1

The Female Sound Collector and Her Talking Machine

LILY PENLERIC: Nowadays phonographs they only cost about $10 and
I think that soon everyone is going to have one. I was thinking that
we could make cylinders of mountain music and sell them.
TOM BLEDSOE: [Laughs] Who the hell'd buy 'em?
LP: Oh, I think everyone would. . . . I know they would, Tom. The way
the music makes you feel, of course they would . . .
—*Songcatcher*

"This is not just a musicologist's dream; it's our dream too," writes film
critic Peter Rainer in his review of Maggie Greenwald's film *Songcatcher*
(2000), which follows fictitious turn-of-the-century comparative musicologist Lily Penleric in her pursuit to record and archive Appalachian
music.[1] Although it may have been more enjoyable as an "all-music
movie," Rainer opines, the audience would have missed Penleric's
first encounter with "mountain music," stating "we would have been
deprived of seeing [actress Janet] McTeer's eyes widen when [her char-
acter] Lily first realizes what a time machine of sounds she has entered
into."[2] It is Penleric's discovery, recording, and then ultimate mass production of Mountain Music that Rainer reads as a collective dream, as
"our dream."

With her phonograph recorder in tow, Dr. Penleric canvasses the
mountain hollows to perform what Balladeer Viney Butler (Pat Carroll)
refers to as "song catching," and what Butler's resistant grandson Tom
Bledsoe (Aidan Quinn) refers to as "song stealing." As a cold, stiff, uppity Victorian woman (who represents "a gentler but no less determined
feminism" for another film critic) Lily Penleric stands in sharp contrast
to the folksy, passionate, and gregarious mountain people.[3] *Songcatcher's* narrative elicits identification with the mountain people, whose sole
(and soul) possession—their ballads—the musicologist has come to
steal, or at the very least appropriate for her own gain.

For the critic, *Songcatcher's* collective dream is portrayed through an imagined history of poor-but-proud Appalachians actively maintaining cultural ties with their—and hence "our"—Scottish and Irish origins through the singing of ballads long thought to be extinct, even in Great Britain. Like many collective American fantasies, this dream narrates an origin story evacuated of the troublesome Native and African American figures one would expect to see represented in turn-of-the-century Appalachia since Abolition had only taken place a little over thirty years before and the Great Migrations had only just begun.[4] Native American struggles over tribal land occupied by the mountain people were in progress at the time (and continue to this day), but the absence of Native Americans is particularly striking because the actual practice among turn-of-the-century comparative musicologists was to phonographically record *their* music and languages almost exclusively.[5]

Our collective origin fantasy values the mountain folk pride and possessive individualism and resistance to the uppity professor's solicitations, a pride not even the most noble of savages was imagined to exhibit. *Songcatcher* represents "our dream" because it *does not* represent the systematic work of actual comparative musicologists recording at the turn of the twentieth century. The popular imaginary cannot fathom Native resistance to song collectors who, with the help of various gifts and commodities, were thought to be easily cajoled into recording sessions. The actual origins of comparative musicology among Native Americans is disavowed and displaced onto a fantastic tale that imagines "our" deracinated musical origin story.

This fantasy of sound collecting fulfills a particular twenty-first-century wish among American filmgoers that reimagines the practice of "songcatching," or musicological song collecting, as originating within and for the archiving of Anglo-American culture. This fantasy is perpetuated by the claim made by numerous film critics that *Songcatcher's* Penleric is loosely based on folklorist Olive Dame Campbell's ballad-collection expeditions among Scottish and Irish Americans in the Appalachians at the turn of the twentieth century. However, there is a critical distinguishing feature between Campbell and Penleric. While the phonograph is absent in Campbell's work, in contrast Dr. Lily Penleric is dependent upon it.[6] Despite the technological distinction between the ballad transcriptions Campbell made among white Appalachians and the phonograph cylinder recordings that numerous female comparative musicologists created of dozens of Native American tribes, one feature remains consistent between the dream represented in *Songcatcher* and the collective national fantasy that the Bureau of American Ethnology promoted at the turn of the century: The songcatcher is a white female figure. *Songcatcher's* Penleric is an archetype of the upper-class, white, female comparative musicologist spurned by her male university colleagues and banished to "Indian country" to practice her craft, a profile that describes many early comparative musicologists.[7]

In one of *Songcatcher's* final scenes, a determined Penleric descends a bumpy Appalachian mountain road by horse and buggy—this time accompanied by Tom Bledsoe, her new beau, and Slocumb, her adopted child. The Scots-Irish songs believed to have been lost to history that she "discovered" in the Appalachian mountains, and then spent the better part of a summer recording onto wax cylinder and transcribing onto paper, had recently burned in a fire set by arsonists.[8] To add insult to injury, a jealous male colleague sent her a letter announcing that he would be continuing her recording and transcription project, relegating her to the role of research assistant. Thus, what Penleric thought would surely secure her tenure in the university music department would instead contribute to another male colleague's career advancements, her very success leading once again to her demotion. Penleric's group then unexpectedly encounters an oncoming coach carrying colleague Reese Kincaid (Michael Harding), whom she assumes has been sent to replace her. In the film's final plot point, Kincaid informs her that he has come to offer his services as her assistant. Penleric is nevertheless resolute in her decision to descend the mountain and begin a new life as mother to Slocumb and wife to Bledsoe. She has decided to abandon her academic career in exchange for an entrepreneurial one selling mountain music to people down the mountain, whom she believes will buy her cylinder recordings because of "the way the music makes you feel."[9]

The final scenes illustrate what ethnomusicologist Kay Shelemay has described as the blurring of the lines between the objectives of early ethnomusicology and the popular recording industry. "During the phonograph era, the recording activity of early ethnomusicologists could not be easily differentiated from that of the commercial record industry by either the technologies used or by musical content. Both used the same Edison crank-wound phonographs that had appeared in 1896; they were fairly cheap ($40) . . . and portable."[10] And today ethnomusicological recordings sit side by side at the Smithsonian Institution with commercial recordings like those produced by Folkways Records founder Moses Asch, illustrating that the academic and commercial arms make up one culture industry. Dr. Lily Penleric functions as a prism through which we can understand "our" collective "dream" of songcatching, and how this has manifested and materialized in the formation of the genre of world music and the world music culture industry. This history of recording as remembered by a contemporary American filmmaker establishes a context for understanding the desire for recordings of folk or "archaic" musics, and the raced and gendered origins through which they came into being.

The social worlds that produced these audio archives are central to their commodity forms in circulation, and by that I don't mean that these are documents of folklife. Rather, they are chronicles of the comparative musicologist's race and gender, in contrast with that of the indigenous bodies against which she was defined and structured. Whether in the imaginary retelling of this period through the figure of Lily Penleric or the historical practice of musicologists like Frances Densmore and Alice Fletcher, these figures index and facilitate the world music culture industry's origins. Their work represents the genesis of not only racialized and gendered sounds on record but also a racialized and gendered yearning for these recorded sounds and the social contexts of their production.

I begin in this chapter with the recording practices of early comparative musicologists and ethnomusicologists in order to think through the phonograph as an instrumentalized technological medium, literally an *instrument* of modernity. In the process of being recorded onto a phonographic cylinder, thus passing through *modernity's ear*, the other is brought under a form of discursive control. I begin with this turn-of-the-century phenomenon filmically represented at the new millennium in order to understand how the world music culture industry's ideal listener—the white woman—has been positioned to listen for, desire, and structure herself in relation to the subjectivities of racialized and gendered recording artists, performers, and listeners in contemporary world music.

The Feminization of Comparative Musicology

In a 1936 survey collected for the American Council of Learned Societies, anthropologist George Herzog identified the six most important comparative musicology pioneers in the study of "primitive music," four of whom were women who had been elbowed out of academic institutions and went on to work as song collectors for the Bureau of American Ethnology (BAE): Alice B. Fletcher, Natalie Curtis-Burlin, Frances Densmore, and Helen Heffron Roberts.[11] Their structural role is reiterated on the Library of Congress American Folklife Center webpage on American women song collectors: "Women were among the earliest collectors of ethnographic materials in this country and around the world. . . . Women collectors at the beginning of the twentieth century were pioneers in the field of ethnographic documentation and traveled to places where they encountered situations that were unusual for women at that time."[12]

The phonograph emerged as the preeminent tool in ethnographic research, alongside the white female comparative musicologist as its technician. While women played an important role in twentieth-century American ethnography and folklore in general,[13] it was specifically white women with comfortable class standing who were initially recruited to make phonograph recordings for the BAE. They were enlisted as technicians of the "talking machine" which was believed to have "revolutionized the study of ethnic cultures" during a period in which native peoples were thought to be experiencing cultural loss and extermination.[14] This machine was employed to "salvage" what were thought to be rapidly disappearing Indigenous languages and musical performance practices, and female songcatchers were seen as ideally suited to perform the task of savior. Through her figure we can trace a desire for cataloguing, recording, and archiving the music of the racialized, gendered other and in doing so we trace the structuration and instrumentalization of her desire in the WMCI. This raced and gendered practice of recording and archiving music brought the other into the popular imaginary and spawned the idea of world music and the culture industry that has formed around it. The white, female songcatcher also used the "talking machine" to ventriloquize her entrée into the popular imaginary.

The Sonic Industrial Revolution

Professor Lily Penleric first retreats into the Appalachian Mountains to visit her sister, who has helped establish a school there. She is surprised to discover that the poor, mostly white residents are custodians of an archaic repertoire of Scots-Irish ballads that had never been heard in the United States, much less transcribed or recorded. Penleric ascends the mountain with her phonograph recorder and wax cylinders, despite their burdensome weight, presumably in the hope of making such a discovery. As she reveals later in the film, she was lured as well by "the way the music makes you feel," an affective state that the film constructs as contrary to her own stodgy, Victorian existence. A key scene in the film features her phonograph and its introduction to the local balladeer Deladus Slocumb (Emmy Rossum), whose entire repertoire she is about to painstakingly record.

The scene begins with an extreme close-up of Penleric's hands on the phonograph as she inserts a wax cylinder onto the recording shaft. The camera pans out to establish the recording event, illustrating Penleric's handling of the awkward, heavy talking machine and the phallic power of the recording device (Figure 1.1).

Penleric begins to turn the machine's crank as Slocumb is encouraged by her on-looking teachers to sing loudly into the horn. The awkwardness of the setting and the novelty of the instrument are reminiscent of the recording scenes illustrated in photographs of early ethnomusicologists, the most famous being that of Frances Densmore and Blackfoot Mountain Chief sitting in a staged recording scene (see Figure 1.2). And just as in that famous photograph, the comparative musicologist commands the phallic object masterfully and the more recognizable playback horn is mistakenly attached to the phonograph instead of the smaller recording cone. Slocumb leans into the horn and begins producing repeated takes of every song in her repertoire only to collapse, exhausted on her bed, begging Penleric for a break.

Figure 1.1. Close-up of Lily Penleric's hands on the phonograph as she inserts a wax cylinder onto the recording shaft in *Songcatcher*.

The "sonic industrial revolution," as I call it, gave rise to the world music culture industry through a Fordist efficiency in sound recording and playback, as well as a synchronization of the well-established colonial coalition between science, industry, knowledge production, and governmentality, but in the service of sound reproduction. Under the auspices of "salvage," the industrialization of sound production and recording streamlined the extraction of the remaining value thought to be held by Native Americans: their affect in the form of cultural production and music. So too came the imposition of form and discursive structure. In *Form in Primitive Music*, comparative musicologist Helen Heffron Roberts complains that the lack of form in Indian music makes its transcription particularly challenging, "So far as can be known, the Luiseño, Catalineño and Gabrieliño peoples had no established scale norm or norms on which their songs were based and in accordance with which their musical instruments were tuned."[15] Figures like Roberts determined which Indian sounds qualified as music verses, sound, noise, and language, and how they were to be sonically represented in the archive. This distinction between music and language is semantically and semiotically quite significant within Western systems of classification. The perceived lack of sonic form in Native American music symbolized for the comparative musicologists their discursive and epistemological formlessness; phonograph recordings were instrumental in imposing both this lacking material and symbolic form. I understand the imposition of form through the production of sonic representation as ethnomusicological "effects," producing what I call *phonographic subjectivity*. By building on Jacques Lacan's critique of the symbolic order, of the work of language as producing the "effect" of subjectivity, I conceptualize phonographic subjectivity as the process by which Indigenous bodies—and in the world music context, racialized and gendered performers—are subjected to and made subject through phonographic recording techniques.

By fusing the discursive technologies of phoneme and grapheme, the world music culture industry developed recording to produce the "effect" of phonographic subjectivity. Two basic linguistic concepts are brought together in the creation of a commercial product that both *writes* and *reproduces* sound in a logocentric reductionism in which a formation much like Lacan's symbolic and imaginary are both at work. Not only does the phonograph fuse the phoneme and the grapheme in the production of a recording but in playback mode it enables a repetition of that originary fusion, but with a difference: As a playback medium, it requires a listener who encounters it within a new contact zone, the listening event. This is a context where different temporalities and social actors (who were not present at the original recording event) can be brought together.

When rewritten phonetically [pen-lyric], Greenwald's choice of name for her heroine illustrates precisely her archetypal role.[16] The imposition of forms like musical notation, transcription, and *logos* are represented by the neologism and proper name Penleric [pen-lyric] and sums up the work of comparative musicology. The comparative musicologist-cum-listener—the pen lyricist—is she who subjects the other to the phonographeme. The symbolic system of the modern aural imaginary is the logic of form imposed by the ethnomusicologist who, as Roberts confesses, cannot identify a preexisting standardized formal structure and must find that structure or impose that norm through a phonographic recording, thereby transforming Indigenous sound from sacred or functional performance to archival object.

When passed through the "talking machine," Indians were rendered legible, brought into language, organized, and catalogued. This is much like the technique made famous by Sigmund Freud and coined by Josef Breuer's patient Ana O. (Bertha Pappenheim) as the "talking cure," a method that articulated the patient's various repressed traumas, harnessing them to "signifiers" (as Lacan put it) and thus diffusing their power.[17] Just as in the psychoanalytic "talking cure" where unconscious psychic processes are brought under the control of language through speech, we can imagine a parallel *talking machine cure* for bringing the unintelligible "people without history," and the hitherto unknowable truths hidden in the mysteries of their cultural unconscious, under the control of speech through the systematic and wide-scale practice of phonographic recording.[18] The talking machine was the perfect *fin de siècle* tool for rendering Indians intelligible by giving their noises form, thus making them classifiable and systematic.[19] The talking machine "cure" brought the savages without history into language and thus into history, and it was the white, female musicologist who engineered their passage through modernity's ear. Like audiologists for modernity's new prosthetic sense organ, these early female musicologists have helped tune our collective hearing and have trained us how to listen back to the racialized and gendered sounds of the twentieth century.[20]

Recording or Listening Back?

Search under the terms "ethnomusicology" or "Bureau of American Ethnology" on the popular online user-generated encyclopedia Wikipedia. com and you will encounter a photograph of Frances Densmore and Blackfoot Mountain Chief posing with a phonograph.[21] This photograph appears not only on the English-language site, but also on fourteen other language versions of Wikipedia.[22] Titled "Blackfoot Chief, Mountain Chief making phonographic record at Smithsonian, 2/9/1916" (hereafter referred to as "Mountain Chief Making"), this photograph was voted "featured picture" by the Wikipedia community for its capacity to serve as what they call a "visual equivalent" to the accompanying entry on ethnomusicology (see Figure 1.2).[23] The picture shows Frances Densmore seated, with her attention focused on her phonograph as her hand carefully adjusts the stylus. Seated to her left, with his attention directed at something beyond the picture's frame, is the presumed subject of the phonographic recording, Blackfoot Mountain Chief. Though chosen for its capacity to capture the essence of the field of ethnomusicology in one image, it is not immediately clear what this photograph depicts.

Figure 1.2. "Blackfoot Chief, Mountain Chief making phonographic record at Smithsonian, 2/9/1916."

The discussion on the Wikipedia entry "talk" page, where interested parties debate the entry's encyclopedic details, also reflects this ambiguity.[24] This debate hinges on the question of whether the photograph represents an actual recording event or the scene of listening back to a recorded event. Although the Library of Congress's title of the photograph

Figure 1.3. "Mountain Chief, Chief of Montana Blackfeet, in Native Dress With Bow, Arrows, and Lance, Listening to Song Being Played On Phonograph and Interpreting It in Sign Language to Frances Densmore, Ethnologist MAR 1916"

indicates that Blackfoot Mountain Chief is "making" a phonographic re-cord, what is actually pictured is a large playback horn (as opposed to the more narrow recording cone), and Densmore's hand seems to be placing the stylus onto the wax cylinder to play it back for Blackfoot Mountain Chief (Nin-Na-Stoko), who appears to be listening intently.[25] Not only is the photo's verisimilitude debated by interested parties on the photo's Wikipedia talk page, so is its similitude with another one that stages an almost identical scene. The photograph titled "Mountain Chief, Chief of Montana Blackfeet, in Native Dress With Bow, Arrows, and Lance, Listening to Song Being Played On Phonograph and Interpreting It in Sign Language to Frances Densmore, Ethnologist MAR 1916" (hereafter "Mountain Chief Listening") seems to want to invoke a similar scenario to that of "Mountain Chief Making" (Figure 1.3).

However, there is an important difference between the photos. Through Densmore's gaze, which the viewer is prompted to follow, we see the action of Mountain Chief's parted lips seemingly delivering "data" to the phonographic record. His raised right arm also connotes action, and if it is holding the lance that is obscured by the phonograph's horn (as described in the title) this further signifies that he is the subject of the photograph who wields the lance's authority. What is curious, however, is that "Mountain Chief Making" has gained such fame even though "Mountain Chief Listening" may be more semiotically representative of what the title of "Mountain Chief Making" purports to be taking place. What remains just as unclear is why the photographs were staged so similarly, yet taken one month apart. The Wikipedia "talk page" discussants consider the possibility that the photographs were staged only as an afterthought.[26] In fact, the reason given in support of the nomination of "Mountain Chief Making" to the Wikipedia "featured picture" list was: "Quite encyclopedic image of ethnographer Frances Densmore in the actual process of preserving Native American language and culture. The picture shows Densmore with Mountain Chief, a Blackfoot chief she was recording for the Bureau of American Ethnology."[27]

One reason why "Mountain Chief Making" is the more paradigmatic of the photos is because of its widespread reproduction in books and websites that feature ethnomusicological or Native American content. The photo's ubiquity signifies the systematic practice of comparative musicology and the paradigmatic representatives of these practices: a white female comparative musicologist becoming an agent in knowledge production and an Indian in full regalia being made absent to himself and made present for a deferred, future listener. This reveals that comparative musicology's epistemological role is both to record and archive sound for posterity's sake to later be heard by an imagined future listener, and to render a modern representation of Indianness for the Indian who must hear himself through modernity's ear.

Despite its titular claim to represent Mountain Chief's agency as the subject "making [a] phonographic record," I argue that "Mountain Chief Making" signifies the act of listening. What is pictured here is the act of listening to a version of Indianness, which Densmore and her device made phonographically subject. Densmore's role in making Blackfoot Mountain Chief the subject of the phonograph *is* the subject of the photograph. Before passing through the stylus of the gramophone and her ethnologist's ears, Indian sounds were perceived as formless, unsystematic noises, what Densmore's mentor Alice Fletcher referred to as "a screaming downward movement that was gashed and torn by the vehemently beaten drum."[28]

Fletcher learned to hear Omaha sounds as musical through the metaphoric deployment of the phonograph: "I therefore began to listen below this noise, much as one must listen to the phonograph, ignoring the sound of the machinery before the registered tones of the voice are caught."[29] And Densmore went so far as to admit in a letter to John M. Cooper dated August 4, 1940 that mastering the technology was in fact secondary to developing the ability to manage the Indians, writing:

> I do not know the Presto machine, which you are to use, but may have a chance to look it up in the meantime. The dealer will give you full instructions for using it, and the operating of the machine is of secondary importance. The psychology of managing the Indians so as to secure the best songs, sung in the desired manner, is the most important factor in the work, in my opinion. I will take pleasure in giving you the benefit of my experience in this regard. I had to formulate my own method, but I find that it gives equally good results in all tribes.

For Fletcher, Densmore, Wikipedia, and the audiences that have helped make "Mountain Chief Making" popular, the phonograph functions as an acoustic mirror reflecting the fantasy of a coherent version of a previously incoherent savage through the techniques and tools of ethnomusicology. And the female comparative musicologist is the doctor who, in the service of the nation, gives the savage the talking machine cure to treat the ailment of incivility with the power of discourse.

The Feminization of Listening and Social Mobility

William Howland Kenney has argued that the early culture industry targeted female listeners, stating, "On the one hand, the Victrola, Eldridge Johnson's domestic phonograph, like the piano before it, was intended to bring together women and music in the cause of civilization. . . . The phonograph reinforced the process of musical reception (listening) over musical production (playing an instrument) within the middle-class American home. . . . The phonograph trade certainly concurred in its own belief that, for several reasons, women were its best customers."[30] And Jonathan Sterne, who has also noted that the white woman emerged as the paradigmatic listener at the turn of the century, reiterates this.

The emergent media of the late nineteenth and early twentieth centuries grew alongside a whole class of women who were full participants in mass culture—and that participation was on an unprecedented scale. The listening white woman thus supplanted the image of the Victorian woman expressing herself and entertaining the family at the piano. This change was as much a result of real participation of women in emerging networks of sociability—including the networks of sound reproduction—as it was a result of the "image" of mass culture and new media as somehow feminized.[31]

The ascension of the white, female comparative musicologist in the public sphere as savior to "disappearing" Native American sounds, along with the attendant power this yielded for her, was transferred to the bourgeois woman who deployed the phonograph to perform her own domesticated version of modernity's ear.

According to historian Louise Michele Newman, white women were recruited during the late nineteenth and early twentieth centuries as uniquely capable of civilizing those African and Native Americans perceived as racially inferior. Social Darwinian theories at work during this time imbued white women with a social standing proximally near enough yet hierarchically above that of the Native and African Americans they were recruited to help civilize.[32] And due to their continued exclusion from suffrage and the barriers that marginalized them within scholarly and governmental institutions of authority, some white women gladly took up the call, seeing it as a path to improving their own marginal standing. To advance as white women required that they distinguish themselves from "inferior races" through the deployment of paternalistic social evolutionary discourses. Newman argues that the simultaneous development of the ideologies of social Darwinism and women's rights "accompanied and made possible white women's entry into the public sphere."[33] It was her race and her imagined predisposition to social reproduction through which

Social-Darwinian theories encouraged and enabled the development of ideologies concerning white middle-class women's emancipation that emphasized (white) women's specific role as the "conservators of race traits" and the "civilizers" of racial and class inferiors. The Anglo-Saxon

Protestant woman's self-proclaimed burden at the turn of the century was to help her nation in rescuing these so-called primitive and working-class peoples from stagnation and decay, to protect them from the violent abuses of the U.S. government (and primitive and working-class women from the supposed abuses of their men), and to assimilate evolutionary inferiors into a more advanced Christian civilization.[34]

Newman identifies suffragette and comparative musicologist Alice Fletcher as one of the women keen to be instrumentalized in the management of the Indian problem as a civilizing missionary. In fact, it was in relation to Indians that Fletcher had her first taste of power, writing, "Never, before I came out among the Indians, did I realize the power of woman's work, and how she is indeed the mother of the race."[35]

The white, female comparative musicologist experienced power through the mechanism with which she would record, translate, and sonically capture the Indian—namely, the phonograph. This prosthetic device functioned as a kind of phallic object arming her with a power she could not experience within the hallowed halls of academia. It made it possible for her to bring whole peoples into discourse, and hence history, by filtering them through modernity's ear. These recordings were conducted—much like studio, multitrack commercial recordings would later be—not live but in a context in which the musicologist prompted the performance and in which, due to technical or ambient interferences, she directed repeated takes. These earliest recordings were not of live speech or music but were staged performances by these white female comparative musicologists. As Jonathan Sterne has characterized this period, "Permanence in sound recording was much more than a mechanical fact; it was a thoroughly cultural and political program."[36] Considering the social class and position of racial dominance these women occupied in their time, we must recognize the catalytic effect of their presence within the social worlds they sought to document. Far from the realistic chronicles they were imagined to be, sounds recorded onto cylinders were the sonic aftereffects, echoic reverberations of, in part, female musicologists' struggles for political and intellectual recognition. I argue that these social tensions and power relations, not to mention the subjectivities of the comparative musicologists and performers, were also recorded onto the cylinders and remain audible as *aural traces*.

Aural Traces

The turntable of the talking machine is comparable to the
potter's wheel: a tone-mass [Ton-Masse] is formed upon
them both, and for each the material is preexisting. But the
finished tone/clay container that is produced in this manner
remains empty. It is only filled by the hearer.
—Theodor Adorno, "The Curves of the Needle"

The phonograph recording privileges the listening event, as Adorno
notes; the tone produced by the turntable awaits its hearer. Adorno's
tone-mass characterizes sound's materiality and temporality as featuring an absence or a place to be filled, a time that is waiting for a future
listener. Due to the gap between the recording event and the anticipated future context of the "hearer," the social life of the phonograph
has privileged listening back as a critical scene of meaning making and
enactment. As Jonathan Sterne has noted, "Audile technique emerged as
a distinctively modern set of practical orientations toward listening."[37]
In the act of recording, listening is imagined as the site where the com-
municative event is constituted; as first listeners, female musicologists
indexed futurity and stood in for the listeners to come.

In distinguishing writing from live speech, Jacques Derrida has identified a necessary absence similar to the one identified by Adorno—that
of the addressee or audience from the context in which the writing takes
place, or the absence of the author from the context in which the writing is
read, stating, "A written sign is proffered in the absence of the addressee."[38]
Through Adorno's and Derrida's reflections we learn that the absence of
the listener/addressee from the context of recording/writing necessitates a
secondary and future-tense location where meaning that is technically unknown, though anticipated by the collector/phonographer, is constituted.
By combining Adorno's aural materialism with Jacques Derrida's thesis on
the future tense of reception or listening, I argue for *aurality* as a trace maintained in the recording and as the context in which meaning and signification get constituted.[39] The "signature" and hence identity of the speaking
subject is determined in this secondary context of hearing, by the listener.

Within the recording context the recordist and her prosthetic ear/
hand—the phonograph that listens first—operate as a placeholder for

the future listener. This has the effect of producing a chain of surrogate listeners: the phonograph as prosthesis to the ethnomusicologist's ear, as surrogate to the listener's ear, is the site of *aurality* that I examine. The phonographer-as-listener imagines herself as a placeholder for the future listener that the recording anticipates. She may have had pragmatic empirical aims for phonographic fieldwork, but it would seem that a utopian longing for futurity inspired by her own precarious political position motivated her recording practice. It is her gendered ear that deploys the temporality of "listening back" as a deferred futurist modality of power. Within the field of comparative musicology, the recordist's role is to constitute and make legible a modern Native American subject. Aurality is the effect of a process by which the comparative musicologist's gendered ear is materialized for future listeners; in her effort to salvage what were thought to be "dying" native cultures, she recorded, instead, her own aurality.

Early ethnomusicologists inscribed their aurality on the recording in much the same way that a figure like Edward S. Curtis inscribed his perspective on the photographs of Native peoples for which he is known.[40] However, the invisibility of the recordist's inscription makes its ideological structuring harder to recognize. When one considers all the parameters left to the discretion of the recordist—the duration of the recording, the proximity of the recording medium to the performer(s), the featuring of particular individuals over groups or other individuals, and the omission of the recordist's presence—it becomes clear that the ethnomusicologist crafted Native American representations to her liking. And like Curtis, collectors were not the originators of these structural, ideological, and epistemological processes but were instead symptomatic of them.

As Curtis's photographs exemplify, ideology organizes meaning and perspective in still photography, television, and motion pictures. These ideologies structure the points of view through which spectators come to decipher the objects represented, producing epistemologies like "looking," "voyeurism," or "the gaze" that structure power through perception.[41] While it may be easier to literally see how a point of view structures affinities and identifications in visual media, we must carefully listen so as to be able to hear the aural positionality (*aurality)* in audio recordings. Only then can we locate the *aurality* at work in early sound recordings in order to read how they stage with whom the listener identifies and at whom his or her desires are projected, helping us to critically deconstruct the narrative logic within a recording. The comparative musicologist's aurality is evident as a trace that does not convey her interpretations of meaning or her intentions per se, but rather her *attention* to what *mattered* to her at the time. The recordings chronicle not the meaning that the comparative musicologist perceived but the *way* that she perceived it, conveying the phenomenology of her perception, with all its racialized and gendered intonations.

The female sound collector deployed as well as came to constitute a kind of epistemic ear with an omniscient role that imagined itself through, and hence indexed, a future listener. This has recursively produced a contemporary world music culture-industry truism—that a majority of listeners are white, middle-class women—thus reinscribing an omniscient perception onto the figure in whose place the collector stood to begin with. Whether in early BAE-sponsored expeditions or in more recent world music productions, the rendering of the aural other for consumption functions as a vehicle for the constitution of a normative, listening self. These renderings racially and sexually constitute the aural other as intelligible and available to the symbolic and imaginary orders. The white female comparative musicologist sent into "the field" to collect audio recordings of Native Americans is a predecessor to not only the ethnomusicologist or the world music producers working in the culture industry today, but also the idealized world music listener.

Having slipped under the perceptual radar, listening has had, borrowing from Carla Freccero, "a queer kind of history."[42] In a discussion of Derrida's notion of spectrality, with its attentiveness to "a non-living present in the living present,"[43] Freccero argues for a historicity that looks for the past in the present in the form of specters or ghosts. This queer kind of historical work calls on me to listen for the aural traces of how the multiple desires of white female comparative musicologists—for recognition, for power, and for the other in sound—resonate in the present in the world music culture industry. This temporality of "listening back" is akin to Gayatri Spivak's development upon LaCapra's definition of transference as historical transference: "The transference-situation in analysis is one where the tug-of-war of desire is at work on both sides—on the part of both the analysand and the analyst, with the emphasis inevitably on the analysand. Both come to occupy the subject position in the uneven progressive-regressive exchange. The task of the 'construction' of a 'history' devolves on both."[44]

Freud developed the psychoanalytic concept of transference to describe the displacement of affect from one idea to another or between patient and analyst in the context of analysis.[45] Building on LaCapra, Spivak deploys the idea of transference as a way to theorize the propulsion of historical process and the desires that motivate the constructions that get called colonial historiography. This rereading of transference as historical transference is productive for understanding the desires and affective transfers between not only the comparative musicologist and the future listener but also the relationship between Densmore and Blackfoot Mountain Chief. First, the Indian-as-afflicted-by-savagery is displaced through the comparative musicologist's "talking machine cure" to a biopoliticized modern subject.[46] Second, historical transference can structure the relationship between the comparative musicologist and the future listener. The musicologist records for the idealized "future-perfect" political time of the listener, with its utopian potential for suffrage and equality. Fetishizing the virgin savage's first encounter with modernity, the listener's colonial-nostalgic desire in turn imagines the context of original contact. The "progressive-regressive" exchange produces a temporality for world music in which the collector/musicologist/producer imagines herself within the deferred temporal site of listening, and the listener fetishizes the recording event. There is a temporality at work in the world music culture industry in which the desire for the future listener constituted at the recording event is met by a desire for the archived sounds and archivist at the listening event, only insomuch as each context imagines the other in modernity's ear as the *a priori* site of meaning. The aural traces of white womanhood I encountered in the field index this desire.

The Aura of Aurality: Confusing the Phonograph's Horn with the Ear

Reproduction can put the copy of the original into situations that would be out of reach for the original itself. Above all, it enables the original to meet the beholder halfway, be it in the form of a photograph or a phonograph record.
—Walter Benjamin, "The Work of Art in the Age of Mechanical Reproduction"

When Walter Benjamin theorized the aura, he imagined its diffusion through mass production as a process that liberates the "original" of its reified value.[47] That the "beholder" can meet the original in the form of a "photograph or phonograph record" represents for him precisely the potential that mechanical reproduction holds. No longer simply the domain of the bourgeois, the work of art is "liberated" from its time-space trappings because of its mass reproduction. By severing it from its cultural and historical context, from "its presence in time and space, its unique existence in the place where it happens to be,"[48] there is a transformation of performance event into commodity that not only splits the aura from the performance event but also its relationship to its own conditions of emergence and temporality. Benjamin's most widely cited essay resonates for so many in part because of its counterintuitive conclusion, which links the aura's liberation to mass reproduction.

The ambivalence that rings out from that essay's coda is representative of the best moments of Frankfurt school mass culture theorizing in its proscriptive refusal. In the spirit of that ambivalence, what if we consider aurality as the necessary context in which attention and value accumulate to sound? I argue that the aura that circulates after the original performance is severed from the "work of art" is the sound collector's aurality as trace. Like perspective, aurality describes not only the phonographer's situated perception or experience, what is imaged as unique and exceptional to the post-Enlightenment Western individual subject, but also an ideological structuration for perceptions shared by a group, culture, society, community, or collectivity. Indeed, as Erika Brady has written regarding the cylinder recordings of Native Americans that she duplicated onto magnetic tape for the Library of Congress Federal Cylinder Project, "The vividness of the voices [the cylinder recordings] preserved astonished me. The recordings had less surface noise than most and were exceptionally free from damage and distortion, but it was not so much what the cylinders lacked that struck me, it was what was *there*, surviving years of neglect—a kind of freshness of presence enabling the listener to imagine not only the singers but the setting, evoking the clarity of light and the quality of the air."[49] Brady senses "presence," "setting," and "air"—qualities not typically understood as audible. Brady identifies *with* the apparatus and *as* the future listener who is indexed, whom the recording anticipated all along. When the sounds reach her, she can easily lose herself in the fantasy they invoke, ignoring the apparatus and the recordist, and confusing the phonograph's horn for her own ear. As her experience testifies, these earliest recordings have captured much more than they perhaps bargained for, maintaining *traces* of the places, people, time, and sentiments surrounding them. Unlike the realist notions of "fidelity," "presence," or "essence," which assume a one-to-one relationship between a performance event and its capture on record, the theory of *aurality* understands *aural traces* as key components in the structuring logic of the recording. Contemporary audiences hear the recording through perceptions particular to the recordist who originally documented them in anticipation of the future listener's—in this case Brady's—encounter with them.

To illustrate how aurality works, I revisit "Mountain Chief Listening" (Figure 1.3). Consider the chair placed behind Mountain Chief, which I take to represent the place made in the recording event for the future listener. When the listener hears the recording, as Brady's testimonial exemplifies, she takes the seat that was there for her all along. I take up Anjali Arondekar's call "to consider, as it were, both the forensics and the metaphorics of the trace. That is, one must work with the empirical status of the materials, even as that very status is rendered fictive."[50] This trace works, as Spivak has stated, in a "progressive-regressive" exchange through time. Thus "Mountain Chief Listening" represents the anticipation of the future listener in the placement of the chair for the photograph just behind the subject of the recording. Perhaps another reason for the popularity of the other photograph, "Mountain Chief Making," is that the absence of the chair disavows the listener's presence better. This ambivalence allows the photograph to be taken up, as it ultimately is on the Wikipedia talk page and by the Smithsonian, as an archive of a recording event. Within the evolution of this culture industry there has been a displacement, such that the dominant image of what is willed as the event, as represented in "Mountain Chief Making," displaces a photograph like "Mountain Chief Listening," with its greater ambivalence regarding the importance of the future listening event. The absence of the chair covers over the futurist temporality of sound that is an inherent quality of its form.

What is disavowed and displaced onto "Mountain Chief Listening" as a more available reading is that it is not only an archive of a recording event but it is also an archive of a future listening event to the recordist's aurality. The seeming disavowal of listening as central to the recording process in "Mountain Chief Making" (as compared to the titular designation of listening in "Mountain Chief Listening") is nevertheless trumped by the trace of listening retained in the photo, as well as by the ambivalence that has resulted in the confusion between the two photographs by the Wikipedia discussants. Furthermore, the materiality of Blackfoot Mountain Chief's gaze, his demeanor, and the telltale sign of the phonograph's playback horn also gesture to this listener.

What is further disavowed by "Mountain Chief Making" as the dominant representation of not only this relationship but this period, and ethnomusicology in general, is the ambivalence contained in the transferential relationship between Densmore and Blackfoot Mountain Chief, as well as that between the future listener and the recording. There is an almost overdetermined identification with Densmore as the source of authority, given her command over the "talking machine" and the almost trancelike state Blackfoot Mountain Chief appears to be in as he listens back to his recorded voice.[51] "Mountain Chief Making" lacks the ambivalence contained in "Mountain Chief Listening," which one could read as representing transference—in the sense of Mountain Chief's willingness to be treated by the "talking machine cure"—and countertransference—in the sense that Densmore seems to be affectively at the mercy of the very utterance she is ostensibly there to tame.[52]

What is ultimately disavowed by the dominance of "Mountain Chief Making," however, is that subjectivation for both Densmore and Mountain Chief relies on the other's positioning vis-à-vis listening. If "Mountain Chief Making" chronicles Mountain Chief's passage through modernity's ear, his production as Indian for the archive, then "Mountain Chief Listening" chronicles Densmore's transformation from second class citizen to modernity's instrumentalist. It photographically represents how the sound collector, later music producer, and even the record label's aurality are phonographically maintained as an aura whose trace can be perceived in the recording. This trace produces a subject position to be occupied by a future listener, a "hearer" in Adorno's words. This is referred to in the music industry as a record producer or label's unique "sound" and is an audible signature across an oeuvre.

I draw the homophonic root "aura" contained in "aural" through the phenomenon of *aurality* to name the deferral of meaning anticipated by the recording event and indexed by the recordist as listening subject. Within the culture-industry context, this process is reified and capitalized upon to the extent that producers are imagined to be on par with musicians in imposing a creative imprint onto the final product. This imprint is what constitutes a coherent "sound" that can be heard across vastly different recordings and styles of music that link the music to an individual producer or record label. In the context of Kinship Records, for example, there is regular reference to the "Kinship Records sound" as a consistent and audible imprint. Described as audible across a diverse catalog of recordings that include styles as varied as Brazilian *bossa nova* and Asian Massive, this sound is the imprint of *aura* introduced through the *aurality* of the producers, a practice also exemplified by comparative musicologists at the turn of the century.

Aurality and the World Music Culture Industry

The twentieth century is a period characterized by the neoliberalization of sonic cultures. As I have already argued, this is evidenced by the fact that there were no methodological nor epistemological distinctions between BAE, academic, and commercial sound collectors. Each one mined cultures for a "value" to be extracted and distributed for profit in ways rarely benefiting the practitioners themselves. This culture industry has yielded capital and value within the marketplace, which has subsequently translated to value in and as American culture. The linking of scholarly and commercial sound collecting enables me to identify a process of market valuation for knowledge quite commonplace within contemporary scientific research. The science and industry coupling is so matter-of-fact that the notion "science and industry" implies a kind of tautology where either word would imply the other in its absence. And considering that Louise Newman declared Alice Fletcher the "foremost" female scientist of her time, one can imagine that a figure like Fletcher was necessarily also called upon as an entrepreneur, like her fictive colleague Lily Penleric.[53]

The figure of the "songcatcher" or "ballad collector" has become an archetype that takes many forms: comparative musicologist, folklorist, anthropologist, ethnomusicologist, audio engineer, soundscape recordist, hobby recordist, and even record collector or world music listener.

This archetype emerges through a lineage of listening that constructs pathways of connectivity through a "structure of feeling" or affective ties of affinity organized and standardized by the world music culture industry. The archetype's class and race matter as the historical form through which the aurality of the contemporary world music listener has been materialized.

In chapter 2, I develop upon this theory of aurality by using it to rethink one of the most common tropes deployed in critical discussions of world music: appropriation. I examine the advancement of aurality in the late twentieth century WMCI as a biopolitical optimization and the means to adaptability in a rapidly changing, multicultural world.

Listen, Inc.

Aural Modernity and Incorporation

The security door buzz dissipates. I ascend a long stairwell that leads to the lobby on the second floor of the old San Francisco Bay Guardian building on the outskirts of the Mission District. I move through a palette of color—goldenrod, olive green, sienna—earth tone-saturated posters, prints, and P.O.P. (point of purchase) paraphernalia that line the stairwell walls, boasting of the record label's roster of world music artists and albums. Twelve by twelve-inch reproductions of covers for albums released by the label over the course of the previous six years liven up an otherwise drab, turn-of-the-century industrial space. The theme is continued in the lobby, except for a distinct black and white photograph that catches my attention. This photograph, Art Kane's "Harlem, 1958," hangs in the center of the wall with pride, like a family portrait.

The jazz legends in the prominently featured and proudly framed black and white photograph bade me adieu each day when I left the building. Art Kane's famous star-studded photo featuring the era's jazz greats was the only nonproprietary image hanging in the office's general area. It appeared as if in a trophy case surrounded by images of Kinship albums. "Harlem, 1958" demanded each visitor's gaze, offering an object of contemplation prior to engaging in whatever business had brought the person to the company. As time passed, my interactions with this photograph became more and more meaningful. This iconographic representation of American jazz musicians—black and white, women and men, standing side by side—sat perched like a coveted photograph of a family reunion marking an ancestral heyday. Its prominent placement boasted an origin story marked by a proud community of white, black, and brown people standing shoulder to shoulder, representing the postwar ascendancy of bebop and the growing influence of jazz as a cultural form. This was the classical period in the music industry, one marked by heroic musicians, photographers, and an American musical renaissance. But hanging in Kinship's lobby, the photograph additionally represents the benevolence of a recording industry that breached the color line to produce the photograph, the genre, and the fantasy of jazz music's cultural unity.[1] The image tells the Kinship Records origin story through the prosperous but bygone era of the American music industry.[2] And in so doing, it hangs as a nostalgic reminder of an industry and business model that is no more: the business model of appropriation.[3] Its display indicates a self-conscious awareness of this period of appropriation and a distanciation from all that is problematic about it. Surrounded by images of albums produced through the self-described process of "intercultural collaboration," "Harlem, 1958" also stands as an anachronistic counterpoint to what Kinship imagines itself to be doing: contributing to a liberal political ethos of cross-cultural exchange and unity through music by explicitly disidentifying with appropriation.

In this chapter, I chronicle the shift in the WMCI's practices from those that promote pleasure through appropriation to pleasure through *incorporation*. As we have seen in chapter 1, early female comparative musicologists domesticated indigenous and African American sounds through their recordings for the Bureau of American Ethnology. They also played a role in bringing music into the modern home, where the phonograph was marketed to women as a replacement for the piano of the bourgeois Victorian parlor. Here I continue the discussion of the domestication of sound, but this time I focus on listening as a modality of domestication—or what I more specifically theorize as "aural incorporation." What happens when the industry—having long ago moved into our homes—moves into our bodies? I will argue in the following pages that the listener's body now figures centrally in the production and reception of musical commodities, functioning as one of the key sites of exploitation.

Appropriation has been used interchangeably with various concepts, including incorporation. In their comprehensive introduction to the edited volume *Western Music and Its Others*, Georgina Born and David Hesmondhalgh see these concepts as synonymous: "It is perhaps a truism to point out that those modernist and postmodernist composers who have drawn upon or made reference to other musics (non-Western, folk, or urban popular) are not producing that music but drawing upon it in order to enrich their own compositional frame. They are transforming that music through *incorporation* into their own aesthetic: appropriating and re-presenting it."[4] Born and Hesmondhalgh deploy both appropriation and incorporation to describe a form of musical referentiality against which a Western music can be defined. But what if incorporation functions beyond appropriation? And what if incorporation and appropriation have both been going on simultaneously?

Before moving forward, let me provide the reader with a few working definitions that will allow us to parse the specificities of these concepts. The Oxford English dictionary defines appropriation as "1. The making of a thing private property, whether another's or (as now commonly) one's own; taking as one's own or to one's own use; the thing so appropriated or taken possession of." In this definition, appropriation represents a kind of usurpation of objects belonging to others and is concerned exclusively with political economy. Incorporation, however, involves an important interstitial step in which an object becomes a part of the self by being taken into the body, concerning both political and libidinal economy. As Laplanche and Pontalis explain, Sigmund Freud's concept of incorporation actually has a broader definition: "It means to obtain pleasure by making an object penetrate oneself; it means to destroy this object; and it means, by keeping it within oneself, to appropriate the object's qualities. . . . Incorporation is confined neither to oral activity proper nor to the oral stage, though orality does furnish the prototype of incorporation. Other erotogenic zones and other functions may in fact serve as its basis (incorporation via the skin, respiration, sight, hearing)."[5] Appropriation is included as a subsumed function in their definition of incorporation. A more robust concept, incorporation concerns itself with the question of what drives the desire for appropriation. Building upon this, in the following pages I develop the idea of "aural incorporation" in order to highlight the important work the ear is made to do in the WMCI as the site for the incorporation of the other.

From Cultural Appropriation to Incorporation

Scholars working in the areas of ethnic studies, ethno/musicology, and postcolonial theory have explored the theme of cultural appropriation in ways far too vast to summarize here.[6] In the context of world music studies, appropriation would seem to form the very basis of the object of study.[7] Through critiques of the racist mimesis of minstrelsy and high-modernist sonic stereotyping of the "Orient," scholars and activists underscored the politics of profiteering and pleasure seeking at the other's expense. Throughout the nineties and early aughts, scholars and journalists famously took celebrities to task for either inequitably compensating the third world musical collaborators with whom they published albums (the most famous being, of course, Paul Simon) or for providing no compensation whatsoever to musicians whose sampled works made up a significant part of a published recording (as in the infamous case of Deep Forest).[8] These political economic debates are ethically important due to the obvious political and economic inequities between celebrities and their third world collaborators, but also because in the earlier period of the music industry dominated by five major record companies, big money was spent and made on making and selling records, money that rarely trickled down. Ironically, this proprietary debate has primarily been waged using the industry's logic, employing the very measures that the industry manages and utilizes to evaluate—and literally value—music: money and property. This debate, rooted in questions of intellectual property, can only concern itself with issues of ownership and entitlement. But "Harlem, 1958," hanging in the Kinship Records lobby, surrounded by color-saturated images of the company's own releases, represents how nimbly the industry has been able to respond to these debates. Promoting production techniques that emphasize collaboration and hybridization, Kinship distanced itself from the practice of appropriation by changing the way the music is made in the first place, and making this process a part of the product.[9]

This paradigm shift in the way appropriation and cultural propriety are understood has coincided with other historical and material transformations. What counts as property since these highly contentious debates dominated discussions of world music has changed.[10] The digitization of music has altered every stage in the commodity chain: artists are free to make any space into a recording studio with countless recording media utilized for storing music; they can function independently of record labels or opt for more formal relationships with record companies; and the record store, now considered an endangered species, is no longer the way most people access music because distribution methods have also radically diversified. This has resulted in a transformed relationship between artists and music production. Gone are the days when artists expected to "make it rich" in the music industry because, for starters, that monolithic entity called the music industry is generally understood as an antiquated concept. The industry is imagined to be at war with itself, in a litigious stranglehold and thought best to be avoided by many contemporary musicians.

Debates over cultural appropriation and intellectual property are in no way limited to the context of world music. By looking at other media, we can gain new insights on propriety and music. For example, Boatema Boateng has shown that the question of who retains the intellectual property of adinkra and kente textiles from Asante and Ghanaian cultural groups is internally quite hotly debated among textile makers. The nation-state, for its part, has its own conflicting stakes in the debate as well that diverge from claims made by African Americans who also imagine themselves to be the cultural inheritors of these artisanal products. Boateng reveals the complex and ambivalent nature of appropriation, asserting

> Questioning *all* ownership claims over cultural products like adinkra and kente undermines any naturalized notions of origin or ownership. Rather than being inherently Asante or Ghanaian, adinkra and kente are among a wide range of cultural products that have been *made* Asante or Ghanaian. The intellectual property protection of adinkra and kente designs must therefore be understood in the context of a series of cycles of appropriation that has been going on since, at least, the early eighteenth century when the Asante federation was established. In this process, cultural appropriation is an essential feature of nationalist projects—a feature that points both to the political nature of culture and to its instability as a marker of nationalist and other identities.[11]

Boateng's counterintuitive stance denies authority to legal and proprietary discourses to which interested parties have primarily appealed in questions of appropriation. Rather than being relativistic, Boateng considers the fundamentally ambivalent nature of proprietary questions when it comes to culture and, when moving beyond the law, the necessarily subjective and disputed nature of determining ownership.

Like Boateng, I consider the preoccupation with copyright and appropriation to take as a given that music is a form of property. But what if we do not limit ourselves to matters of property and money? What if we look to other materialities that determine musical value? While the emphasis on appropriation has tended to critique the breach of contract cultural producers have with their productions, my emphasis on incorporation privileges the biopolitical relationship between cultural productions and their users. And certainly, because cultural appropriation still takes place, we must remain vigilant about calling those practices out and seeking reparations. But appropriation, as I argue below, is not the only means of exploitation. If the listener's body is called upon by the WMCI as a site of production—decoupling the producer's privileged claims to his or her cultural productions—then the critique of appropriation fails us because the listener becomes in part a producer. Through an examination of the shifting of the business model from appropriating the other to incorporating the other, this chapter explores the changing politics of pleasure in the WMCI.

Take for example how the late 2000s once again saw the popularization of world music on the Billboard rock music charts in the form of white, primarily male musicians performing musical traditions from Africa. Beyond the obvious ways in which we can understand this practice as appropriative and endemic to rock music, I want to begin by briefly exploring why this practice took off around 2008, especially after *New Yorker* music critic Sasha Frere-Jones declared "miscegenated" music dead and gone from indie rock in 2007.[12] Shifting the analytical frame to aural incorporation is necessary, it seems to me, if we are to better understand not only the recent mass repopularization of African sonic signifiers in American indie rock but also the very drive that has sustained aural modernity throughout the twentieth century.

"Listen Inc.," read either as Listen Incorporated or listen incorporation, represents the way the WMCI business model has shifted from appropriating the other to incorporating the other. While in chapter 1 I explored how the white female comparative musicologist indexed her perception in the archive, here I explore how the WMCI fetishizes a reified understanding of feminine pleasure by conflating incorporation with invagination, or the anatomical symbolics of vaginality. In an attempt to chronicle the circulation of world music within a libidinal economy, I will illustrate through various examples how this practice of incorporation hinges on the construction of the self through the racialized, gendered other in sound, or what I call the aural other. The aural other is incorporated into the aural imaginary in a way that bolsters the listening self. The aural imaginary is the context in which listeners not only construct affective bonds with sounds and artists that are other to standard Western and American popular musical traditions but also incorporate these others in the production of the listening self. And while the context for my field-work has been the specific site of Kinship Records, this transformation is in no way limited to that company. World music has since entered the mainstream of popular music and has increasingly become a ubiquitous form. Tracing its movement into the more recently developed indie rock genre can help illustrate how incorporation functions.

Return of the (African) Repressed

I didn't become obsessed with music because I saw live shows that blew me away. I became obsessed with music because I was exploring my parents' record collection, and spending hours in friends' bedrooms listening to music. I like the imaginary space of the album. More than anything, I feel very at ease with the internet for music, because that's an imaginary space, not a physical space. . . . As we started to play, even the idea of forming a band then was like a lit-tle bit funny. Which is why we naturally gravitated toward the great African electric guitar tradition as opposed to the U.K./American guitar tradition, because it felt a lot fresher.
—Ezra Koenig

Ezra Koenig looked into the acoustic mirror of his parents' record col-lection and heard echoes of himself resonating through the dusty vinyl. Routing his musicality through the familial conduit of his father—"My dad is a massive music fan, so even just growing up in the house, he was buying new cool music, up through when I was born."[13]—Koenig articulates in one discursive fell swoop the foundations of his normative, oedipalized identity, of his proprietary relationship to musical kinship, and of the sonic as the means to his subjectivation. The Koenig parents' musical archive comes to constitute his subjectivity. This origin narrative is echoed and repeated throughout the world music culture industry (WMCI), as evident in tales like the one then Kinship vice president Jon Schwartz told me about his relationship to black music. It was from the intimacy he—a white Jewish Midwesterner growing up in the 1960s—felt with his black nanny, that he gained his oft-proclaimed "love of black people" and black music. Koenig's similarly cliché origin story (finding himself in his parents' vinyl collection) authenticates the artist's relationship to a racialized performance tradition (to which he is no heir apparent) because it sprang organically from the original family romance, while it also confirms the artist's uniquely individual style and identity.

But with the added displacement from mirror and seeing to acoustics and hearing, the mirror's function as archive is made apparent. Like the sudden visibility of masculinity when it adorns a nonwhite or female body, the archival nature of the mirror in its capacity to initiate subjectivity is only evident when its function is displaced from that normative site onto an acoustic one. What this origin narrative shows is that it *was* the era of appropriation that sutured blackness into white musical history; but now blackness returns as an embodied, performative knowledge, incorporated into contemporary white cultural production. Going on to cite some of the bands through which he first heard himself echoed, Koenig names Blondie and The Streets—two musical projects that in their own time (1980s and 2000s, respectively) overtly employed blackness as a musical "flourish"—and then he names groups like De La Soul, Dizzy Rascall, Tribe Called Quest, and Run DMC—hip hop performed by black artists. Koenig presents a fantasy in which he encounters both his other and then himself in black sound.

As the lead singer of Vampire Weekend—one of the most buzzed about indie rock bands of the late aughts—Koenig has been the music critics' favorite whipping boy, due perhaps to the coincidence between Vampire Weekend's ascendancy through an aesthetics of the 1 percent and the descent of the 99 percent.[14] On the other hand, with all three of their albums reaching gold status in the United States (selling at least 500,000 copies each), the band has been a doyen of the schizophrenic and financially insolvent American music industry.

The band's dizzyingly rapid ascendancy is credited to what *Chicago Reader* music journalist Jessica Hopper has described as the Afro pop "flourishes" sonically applied to many of their songs, received by the listening public as a surprising juxtaposition given their race (the band consists of three white guys and an Iranian American); Ivy League pedigree (all are alumni of Columbia University, as is widely publicized); and their preppy, 1980s, upper East Side aesthetic. I am much less interested in stoking the hot coals on which Vampire Weekend have been raked by music critics for enacting what *Washington Post* writer Chris Richards calls an "imitation of Paul Simon's 'Graceland'—penned by a crew of smug preppies with a presumably facile understanding of the African sounds they were stealing, no less."[15] I have elsewhere explored such superficial accusations of the misappropriation of blackness in sound (which assumes that there are good and bad forms of musical appropriation) waged by music critics.[16] Instead, I read a figure like Koenig and a band like Vampire Weekend as paradigmatic of a larger structuring fantasy in popular music, thinking through *Chicago Reader* journalist Hopper's observation that "the record works as an escapist fantasy for the recession—though exactly who will recognize themselves in that fantasy is debatable."[17] Actually the return of the (African) repressed at this particular historical moment, in the form of collective fantasy, is what intrigues me.

The repressed returned with a vengeance in 2008, manifesting itself in American indie rock, just after Sasha Frere-Jones had declared "miscegenated music" (a euphemism he uses to describe blackness in white music) dead in 2007.[18] *Seattle Weekly* journalist Ryan Foley summed it up thus:

> In many ways, 2008 was the year Afropop fully cracked the American music landscape. . . . But now artists are taking a different approach to capturing Africa's sonic exuberance and grit. Rather than simply weaving African styles into their music, they're fully refashioning genres with varying levels of attitude and aptitude. For all the success Vampire Weekend attained this year, many other artists weren't content with using the Afropop-cum-Western pop template. Instead, their tactics were wholly African: Turn every sound into a rhythmic element.[19]

The repressed has returned, according to Foley, and it is audible (not visible), rhythmic, and hence "wholly African," even though it returned in a form we had grown accustomed to since the popularity of blackface minstrelsy: in the form of a white man. While we have seen the return of this repressed over and over again—especially in popular music—we are surprised, shocked even, every time.

Employed by everyone from Paul Whiteman and Elvis to Mick Jagger and Paul McCartney, to Miley Cyrus and Robyn Thicke, this habit remains shocking, and profitable, because it enlists an uncanny reaction in the audience. In his 1919 essay, "The Uncanny," Freud applies his theory of repression to the slippery notion of "the uncanny." Though he struggles to describe this rather amorphous experience, he summarizes its effects as "[t]he most remarkable coincidences of desire and fulfillment, the most mysterious recurrence of similar experiences in a particular place or on a particular date, the most deceptive sights and suspicious noises."[20] The uncanny is exemplary of what he calls "repetition compulsion" or that psychic phenomenon of scenarios that repeat in different forms over the course of a life. Freud's notion of the uncanny can help situate the return of this repressed, especially as it takes shape in the form of white musicians laying claim to Africanness.

Freud parses out the circumstances that create two orders of the uncanny: 1) a class of the uncanny that "proceeds from forms of thought that have been surmounted"—which is his characterization of social, cultural, and temporal phenomena experienced at the large-scale level of a community, represented by the secular figure who encounters evidence of haunting or magic in ways that cannot be rationalized.[21] 2) A class of the uncanny that proceeds from repressed complexes. This takes place both at the scale of the personal (variant across people and their personal histories) as well as the sociocultural, in the means by which subjectivity is conditioned in relation to certain others. While both schema function within the systemic logic of psychoanalysis, they seem to originate for him in scenes of the castration complex that equate phallic power with whiteness. In the first instance, he characterizes the uncanny as that encounter, not unlike Dubois's double consciousness, where the ego surprisingly confronts its "double." This is a double that appears as a phylogenetic predecessor, "a harking-back to particular phases in the evolution of the self-regarding feeling, a regression to a time when the ego was not yet sharply differentiated from the external world and from other persons."[22] In a reference to his own *Civilization and Its Discontents* Freud refers here to the co-constitutive production of the civilized ego—formed as a result of acquiescing to law and responding by sublimating and repressing his desires—and "the primitive" who has no capacity or desire to do so. Thus the experience of the uncanny in this example is the shocking confrontation the ego has with a version of itself that is "primitive man." In the second instance we find Freud much more overtly engaging his more widely understood theory of the castration complex as that confrontation with the mother's or feminine lack. But as has been widely argued, this infantile fear translates in adulthood as again a fear of the loss of phallic power most potently contained in white, phallic power. We can therefore read the uncanny, in either case, as Kalpana Seshadri-Crooks has done, "as the uncanny object of race" writ large.[23]

Interestingly, Freud characterizes the function of the uncanny in literature (going even further, to describe the uncanny within the aesthetic) under the first class, describing how the uncanny can be elicited, as in when the writer moves in the world of common reality and then "oversteps the bounds of possibility" (which I would exemplify through magical realism). But what Freud did not, or possibly could not, consider under his historical circumstances was the critical way in which the uncanny can be deployed as a highly profitable tool by the culture industry. On the one hand, the African repressed represents in Freudian psychoanalysis the master signifier of primitivism, deploying the logic of the reckless sexual abandon Hegel ascribed to "the African"; civilization is the outcome of its repression. On the other hand, in the U.S. context, the African repressed represents slavery and its discontents. Therefore it is a familiar, disavowed core component of the modern, civilized self, what Freud, citing Otto Rank, calls double or doppelganger. When encountered as uncanny, this double is a shocking, primitive version of the self. So the indie rock incorporation of Afro pop trending in 2008 was merely a return of this African repressed through a performative uncanny that brought forth for fans the primitive other, what Lacan calls *objet petit a* or the little other.

The culmination of what Martin Jay has called the "scopic regime of modernity," which he charts in epistemologies and institutions as varied as science, perspective painting, and Cartesianism, has been the formation of psychoanalysis and the mapping of the unconscious mind. This ocularcentric order informed Lacan's mapping of the *imag*inary through which the subject comes to know himself and the symbolic through which this self becomes delimited.[24] Due to its development through the image-centered "mirror stage," the imaginary has primarily been taken up as a visual theory of subject formation in which the subject (mis)recognizes himself in the mirror and constructs a fictional sense of coherent identity around this image. Lacan's mirror stage is a representational framework illustrating the subject's coming into language, though we need not interpret it as literally pertaining only to visual images.

Revised upon and further developed by Kaja Silverman as "the acoustic mirror" stage, these critically important phases of psychic development constitute the "modern," subjected to the forces of markets and the sexual economies nation-building projects require.[25] These stages not only install the subject but they overdetermine the causal relationship between anatomical organs and the social roles they should perform, whether that be the determination of genitality in retroactively reiterating the institution of heteronormativity or the determination of the ears in the establishment of the acoustic mirror stage. The *aural imaginary* theorizes the imaginary order sonically, examining it as a means to decipher how fantasies about race and gender are structured within the symbolic. If, indeed, as Joan Copjec has stated, "psychoanalysis is the mother tongue of our modernity,"[26] what can it tell us about the sonic and the aural as regimes and registers of fantasy and subject formation? I attempt to historically situate the aural imaginary through what Lacan has referred to as the "partial drive" related to hearing: "the invocatory drive."

Aurality and the "Invocatory Drive"

The imaginary and symbolic systems prop up the phallogocentric order and work dialectically in the WMCI with the differentiation of the consumer through the formation of hardware marketed to bourgeois femininity (as discussed in chapter 1) and to establish specific markets through which this imaginary order is constantly screened and sounded anew. However, it is worth dwelling within the acoustic and aural components of this system, which have been in the background having benefited very little from critical reflection, despite the fact that they have been as foundational to Lacanian psychoanalytic philosophy as his more image-centered theories. For instance, Lacan asserts, "I must, very quickly, point out to you the difference between making oneself heard and making oneself seen. In the field of the unconscious the ears are the only orifice that cannot be closed. Whereas making oneself seen is indicated by an arrow that really comes back towards the subject, making oneself heard goes towards the other. The reason for this is a structural one—it was important that I should mention it in passing."[27] Here, Lacan echoes Adorno's comments on the phonograph's longing for the "hearer" I discuss in chapter 1, foreshadowing Derrida's "ear of the other" I discuss in chapter 4: whether in the form of the other, the hearer, or the listener, all are critically important in order to "make oneself heard."

Lacan's idea of the "invocatory drive" is one of the partial drives (which have no bearing on the reproductive aspects of sexuality, only on enjoyment, and are only "partial manifestations of desire").[28] For Lacan the drive circles around the *objet a*, or the little other that sets desire in motion. This *objet a* is different than the big Other, the ego's radical other, who can never be subsumed. Instead, the *objet a* is "the other which isn't another at all, since it is essentially coupled with the ego, in a relationship which is always reflexive, interchangeable."[29] While debates over appropriation have tended to imagine "the other" in the way that Lacan defines "the big Other," as in the ego's radical other, Lacan's discussion of the invocatory drive helps us to understand the schematics of aural incorporation in relation to "the uncanny."

We can on the one hand read Lacan's physiology of the ear in the above quote, as a way of defining the ear's exceptional function in psychoanalysis, but this would be quite uncharacteristic, since he otherwise denies biologism, and most certainly denies any genital essentialism in his theory. Instead of the ear's exceptionalism in psychoanalysis, his theory of the invocatory drive and the physiology of the ear diagnose, as in the case of Freudian psychoanalysis, the instrumentalization of organs and physiology within modernity. This reiterates the function that the ears have been reified to perform in the world music culture industry, supporting the idea that aurality constructs the identity of the consumer at Kinship Records. Consumers are subjects vis-à-vis aurality; they are listeners first. The listener's desire will hear what the listener desires, as in the following exchange. Here Kinship Records president Jon Cohen discusses one of his label's recent releases during a segment of his periodic appearance on a nationally syndicated radio show called *Voyager*, hosted by Nancy Dayne. Cohen has just played a thirty-second clip from a recent release by Zyzzy, the Amsterdam-based band fronted by Brazilian vocalist Raquelle Aveiro.

> NANCY DAYNE: Now correct me if I'm wrong, cause you know, I know nothing about these things. But you said "hip hop." I feel it. Of course, her, I hear the Brazilian but I feel African rhythms coming through too.
>
> JON COHEN: Yeah, absolutely. The rhythm on this particular song, which is called "Peregrino," which is Portuguese for "pilgrim," is from a style of music called Afro-beat, which was popularized by the great Nigerian artist Fela Kuti. And, yeah, this song is sort of an homage to him, and that rhythm you're hearing is definitely African, so, you don't know nothing, [Nancy], you're learning.

Dayne, performing foil to Cohen's world music expertise, is a kind of stand-in for what Kinship imagines as their ideal listener, a middle-aged white woman with a big appetite for world music. Dayne names the desire that she is listening for by interpreting what she hears as "African rhythms." What exactly is she hearing, though?

An invocatory phonic emphasis in the trope "African rhythm" overrides and supersedes the vast heterogeneity of musical sounds originating in Africa and attributed to sounds from the African diaspora. While rhythms tell entirely different semantic messages, allegories, and origin stories depending on the region, instrument, and tradition represented, the ubiquitous trope "African rhythm" collapses these histories and the heterogeneity of traditions, instruments, and forms on the continent to an empty signifier. Musicologist Kofi Agawu, bemused by the insistence upon "African rhythms" as the ubiquitous signifier of African sounds, writes, "Indeed, as soon as we recall that some styles in Senegal, Mali, The Gambia, Tanzania or Nigeria are strongly marked by Arabic or Islamic influence, and that . . . there are East and Southern African cultures dominated by xylophones and mbiras, as soon as we move outside the purview of the few symbolically powerful groups that have come to represent African musical rhythmic structure, claims for rhythm's predominance become a good deal more fragile."[30]

Cohen discusses this heterogeneity of African sound on another episode, but Dayne, his auditory foil, seems to be reluctant to let go of her wish to hear "African rhythms." Take this exchange, following a thirty-second clip of instrumental music with Kora and trombone.

> JON COHEN: So you can start to hear from the kora the sort of harp-like texture of the instrument but it also of course has a very African feel to it as well.
>
> NANCY DAYNE: Yeah, except, you know, I always think of all African music as being so beat-percussion driven. And this feels more a bluesy, jazzy melody is driving it.
>
> JC: Absolutely. I think if you remember when we did *Desert Blues* that's one of the things we talked about. People think of African music as this "get up and dance" sort of driving music, and in fact it does sort of have a very introspective side to it as well, and there is a connection with the blues and the blues is very connected to jazz and that's sort of the path that makes this collaboration make so much sense.

Here Dayne insists on associating African music with rhythm, despite having been introduced to the Malian blues tradition by Cohen on a prior episode of the radio show.

Employed by ethnomusicologists as well as record label executives, the term "African rhythms" exemplifies the invocatory phonic rather than semantic relationship world music listeners are structured to have with African and African diasporic musics. Nancy Dayne is certainly not alone in insisting that she hears "African rhythms." Agawu has exhaustively surveyed the ubiquity of this signifier from its emergence in the eleventh century to its contemporary popularity. He concludes, "That the distinctive quality of African music lies in its rhythmic structure is a notion so persistently thematized that it has by now assumed the status of a commonplace, a topos. And so it is with related ideas that African rhythms are complex, that Africans possess a unique rhythmic sensibility, and that this rhythmic disposition marks them as ultimately different from us."[31]

Certainly, this trope has been resignified and rejiggered to fit the epistemologies of the moment, but its endurance across a millennium presents us with a daunting analytical task. For our purposes, I want to think about this trope as it pertains to world music and fantasy. In particular, I want to respond to Agawu's conclusion "that this rhythmic disposition marks them as ultimately different from us." This difference is not simply kept at bay but becomes incorporated into the body through dance and listening. To give in to the empirical evidence to the contrary of "African rhythms" would be to, as Agawu has put it, "depriv[e] its practitioners of one of the most cherished sources of fantasy and imaginative play."[32] Agawu goes on to conclude, "African rhythm, in short, is an invention, a construction, a fiction, a myth, ultimately a lie."[33] But what sustains this lie? What has enabled the endurance of this lie that Agawu has convincingly traced to as far back as the eleventh century? And what pleasures does this lie sustain? Agawu's characterization of "African rhythms" as fantasy is the precise starting point for answering these questions, and it illustrates the projective nature of listening. "African rhythms" can be better described as a wish, and Kinship Records is in the business of wish fulfillment; it is a corporation built on incorporation.

Aural Fantasies

This CD should be listened to in the dark with or without the one you love (or love right now), sipping something cold and smooth with a bite. You are alone and lost at night in a foreign city, and you just want somewhere to sit down and have a drink. You stumble down a dark lane looking for someone, somewhere, and you spot light coming from a doorway. You walk in. You think it's just a bar, and you take the nearest table and order a drink and look around while you sip. Then the sound. Oh, the sound. It's pure, slow, hot love. You look at the people around you and see so many possibilities. You melt back into your seat, and make eye contact with the stranger at the next table. You realize you aren't lost; you're right where you want to be.
—Paphian

This testimonial, entitled "Turn off the lights," voluntarily left on Amazon.com as a review for the Kinship Records compilation *Torch Songs* (which I discuss in greater detail in chapter 5), exemplifies the role of fantasy that sound plays in the aural imaginary of American-produced world music. Paphian's description—"Then the sound. Oh, the sound. It's pure, slow, hot love"—is no mere daydream about the (mostly) female torch singers on the album, although these performers figure centrally within that fantasy. Instead, what Paphian describes is a fantasy in which sound, the listener's body, escape, and affect fold in on one another (invagination) in the construction of an imaginary site of contact with *other* bodies. Paphian's testimonial responds to the hailing by the sound production on the album's opening track, "Harvest Moon," by Cassandra Wilson.[34] It features a very closely mic'd vocal accompanied by chirping crickets, a sobbing cello, and acoustic guitar harmonics. The texture of sound, as I will attempt to show, is a very complex thing. It is of course beholden to the shape of sound waves, the acoustics of the built environment, and the technologies that propel sound waves through these spaces. But bracketing for the moment the fascinating effect these variables have on a listener's perception of sound, I want to focus instead on how the perception of listening is in no way limited to these acoustic properties. The aural imaginary and the symbolic order of fantasy precede the arrival of music to the reified organ of the ear. When considered in the context of listening to the song, Paphian's comments seem to be a logical response to the acoustic intimacy of the recording quality and Wilson's lilting, drowsy, almost whispered delivery of "Come a little bit closer, hear what I have to say." The testimonial harbors an intensity that responds to the call or hailing of intimacy in the recording itself.

Aural fantasies function at multiple levels, but the ear is central to their formation. While they do not literally take place within the ear, that body part is the structuring logic for how they function. Sound production techniques fantasize about aural fantasies and are optimized to produce them. Through refined recording and engineering techniques as well as sonic narrative production, the musical culture industry has made sure to carefully craft how feeling is structured in music. This was perhaps Adorno's greatest lament when he commented on the burgeoning music industry of his time. What he called the "regression in listening" was in part a lamentation on the capitulation of the listener to the emergent musical culture industry that made aesthetic promises to fulfill the affective needs that it helped produce in the first place. His eulogy marked the genesis of the industrialization of the aural imaginary.

The aural imaginary exists at the interface between the listener and the culture industry, a formation that emerges through capitalist and colonial relations. The ear is central to how the record company imagines the listener and the ear functions for the WMCI as a synecdoche for the whole of the listening body.[35] The precedence of the aural imaginary and aural fantasy is what perpetually reproduces the hallucination of "African rhythms," even when they are not present or their naming is illogical. Given the perceptual logic through which this political and libidinal economy has been formed, what are the psychical and structural limits of how we can perceive world music or the pleasures it is structured to enact? How have listeners' ears been historically trained? How do listeners *make sense of* music performed on unfamiliar instruments or sung in a language they do not speak? It is through the WMCI's brokering of fantasy that the encounter with the other of music (world music) and musical others (world musicians) takes place.

The Biopoliticization of Modes of Perception

As many scholars have helped to historicize, epistemologies that structure the order of things situate how the senses perceive the world out there.[36] The differentiation of the five senses—historically preceding but critically instrumentalized during the enlightenment—has resulted in a distribution of labor for each sense organ, which is imagined to serve a distinct perceptual purpose. Like the allegorical question presented to the wolf by Little Red Riding Hood, who responds, "The better to see you with, my dear. . . . The better to hear you with, my dear," there are of course pernicious political forces that have manifested this sensory differentiation; the wolf's eyes and ears are revealed to be desiring machines rather than mere sense organs, machines that have locked in on devouring Little Red. This allegory compels us to ask: What ideological ends has a differentiation of the senses served? What is the social and cultural history of this differentiation?

As Don Ihde has said of the auditory process, "The gradations of hearing shade off into a larger sense of one's body in listening. The ears may be focal 'organs' of hearing, but one listens with his whole body."[37] The WMCI denies the somatic hearing that Ihde describes, preferring to identify consumers as listeners and the ear as the context for signification—the better to be seen and heard with, my dear. Somatic hearing has been disciplined through processes of industrialization and colonization, slowly and carefully parsing the senses out into distinct modes in order to distinguish their use-value, maximizing the profit and biopolitical potential along each sensual path. This biopolitics of perception emphasizes the optimization and isolation of the senses with promises of dividends paid on both the libidinal as well as political economic registers. Technologies that have been developed in response to this have further isolated and focused our senses and modes of perception.[38] For example, Walter Benjamin observed that industrial capitalism of the late nineteenth century was distinguished by phantasmagoria different from that described by Marx, precisely because of ocularcentric qualities. Benjamin noted that it was the "commodity-on-display" that yielded a new form—"representational value"—that could be consumed visually.[39] His *Arcades Project* chronicles the Paris arcades as a space of architectural sociality in which Parisians could not only absorb the aura of commodities by walking through an enclosure designed expressly for their presentation, but also feast upon and consume their representation. The emergence of "representational value" marks a paradigm shift in which capital combines with sensuality to create a form of pleasure that focuses consumption through an isolated sense organ: the eye. This practice of visual consumption has developed into a core value in advanced capitalism, as evidenced by the enormous importance of visual economies like film, television, and print media.

According to Christian Metz, "The cinema was born in the midst of the capitalist epoch in a largely antagonistic and fragmented society, based on individualism and the restricted family (=father-mother-children), in an especially super-egotistic bourgeois society, especially concerned with 'elevation' (or facade), especially opaque to itself."[40] For him this psychic genesis and its fusion to cinema is definitive of a period—modernity—that represents the perfect storm of epistemic, psychic, technological, economic, social, and political events that would beget what he calls the "perceiving drive."[41] Alongside this arose the fetishization of particular forms, such as light (cinema and photography) and sound, as portals to particular and distinct imaginaries. As Jonathan Sterne has argued, intertwined with this has been the emergence of an "acoustic modernity" that paired brilliantly with visual modernity, making audible processes previously attributed only to visuality.[42] It is through cultural industrialization and concomitant technologies imbricated with perceptual and sensory differentiation that the imaginary process has been isolated to particular parts of the body. How does the feminization of listening I discuss in chapter 1 tie in with the differentiation of modes of perception? This, it seems to me, is key to the production of an aural modernity and hence the imposition of the laws of subject formation through which that modernity can be realized.

In her essay "Work, Immigration, Gender," Lisa Lowe skillfully argues against the long-held Marxist understanding that functions as the crux of his theory of alienation—that the laborer is undifferentiated and abstract within capitalism. Lowe instead argues that there is an emphasis on a "'racialized feminization of labor' in the global restructuring of capitalism."[43] She states that it is this "differentiation of labor" through which U.S. capital has accumulated and profited in the global restructuring of capital, writing, "One of the distinct features of the global restructuring of capital is its ability to profit not through homogenization, but through the differentiation of specific resources and markets that permits the exploitation of gendered and racialized labor within regional and national sites."[44] This insight builds on third world, black, and transnational feminist theories that have skeptically charted the appropriation of women's rights as a barometer for liberal humanism promoted by the UN Decade for Women and the CEDAW (Convention on the Elimination of All Forms of Discrimination against Women) treaty. This treaty imposes liberal feminism on developing nations as a condition for access to development monies through the IMF and World Bank. Informed by and productive of stereotypes about third world women as ideally suited conduits for development through microlending programs, the racialized feminization of capitalism following the UN Decade for Women and the differentiation of the laborer that ensued was a strategy of globalization and capital accumulation that has impacted not only through which bodies surplus is reaped but more symbolically how commodities arrive at bodies.

For our purposes, the differentiation of labor applies to the work that bodies do in an engagement with commodities, whether as producers or as consumers. The differentiation of the laborer at the level of consumption, I argue, has also been feminized. The differentiation of modes of perception and the privileging of the ear as the site of consumption reifies the ear in its capacity to, in Laplanche and Pontalis's terms, "obtain pleasure by making an object penetrate oneself; it means to destroy this object; and it means, by keeping it within oneself, to appropriate the object's qualities." This definition of incorporation reifies a feminized form of pleasure through the logic of what Derrida has called invagination (which I discuss in chapter 4). It employs social and sexual roles stereotyped as feminine; it is that feminized positionality from which incorporative pleasure in listening is thought to derive. In keeping with the feminization of labor, the WMCI has reified the listener's ear and imbued it with the stereotyped qualities of feminine pleasure assumed as the modality of pleasure for incorporation. The WMCI profits on feminized listening.

Feminized listening has been thought by some scholars to be a radical alternative to the phallogocentric structuring of listening. For instance, the "sonorous envelope," as theorized by Guy Rosolato and developed by Kaja Silverman in her thesis on the "acoustic mirror," is that presymbolic encounter with the world in the womb, one characterized exclusively as sonic, rather than scopic, tactile, olfactory, and so on.[45] Published in the mid-1980s, Silverman's meticulously argued thesis on the woman's voice in classical Hollywood cinema attempted to make a space for a different way of relating to the maternal voice, one more akin to Julia Kristeva's reclamation of the woman's maternal bond as nonphallic. For Rosolato, auditory pleasure is rooted in the maternal voice. For Silverman, this retroactively constructed cultural fantasy is a fantasy of origins, one that stands in stark contrast to the subject's post-traumatic, symbolic life and the presymbolic, infantile envelopment in sound, especially the predominating sound of the maternal voice.

In *Desire in Language* Kristeva maps a feminist retreat—what Silverman names the "choric fantasy"—that moves away from the superego and the symbolic. Whether waged by Kristeva as a proto-poststructuralist feminist intervention into a hostile and male-dominated psychoanalysis of the 1970s, or revitalized by Silverman to mount a feminist critique of film theory in the marginalized sphere of film sound in the mid-1980s, the WMCI has coopted the utopian potential of the "choric fantasy." In an effort to maximize the escapism promoted by the womblike, enveloping symbology of sound, and in concert with the more general domestication of sound by the musical culture industries over the course of the twentieth century, this two-pronged political economic and libidinal economic model has enabled the incorporation of feminist desires and listening practices into enactments of liberal pleasure.

As I have already discussed, industrialization and its concomitant technologies, working in lockstep with perceptual and sensory differentiation, isolated imaginary processes to particular organs. Thus, the resonation that takes place through listening has been cultivated as unique and is uniquely capable of affecting bodies and enabling processes that can bring bodies together through auditory fantasies that privilege listening or auralphilia. Culture industries and their technologies, including the music industry and the more specialized world music industry, developed both in response to the sensual differentiations that emerged through industrialization and modernization while also enabling these very processes. Listening with the ear developed as a critical focal point for an emerging commodity: recorded sound. Isolated, the ear functions as a contact zone between the private life of the individual listener and an imagined performer or performance whose sonic essence is captured, enhanced, and mixed down perfectly on a recorded medium (note how the earliest audio technologies mimicked the ear both mechanically and in their aesthetic design) to optimize fantasy, making the ear the destination for recorded sound. As Greg Downey has put it, "If music is constituted in the ear as much as on an instrument or in a throat, we may be able to locate processes that condition the ear, preparing it for its active role in music performance."[46] Today's music industry has seen a revival, perhaps because of the refocused attention on the ear through downloadable music designed for mobile MP3 players and private music consumption through headphones. The music industry's optimization of not only recording processes and distribution methods but also the consumer—resignified as listener—furthers this process of differentiation.

Listen Inc.

In the context of world music at Kinship Records, the ear is the site of agency for the determination of difference, and that agency endows the ear with a power to signify. Kinship attempts to systematize engagement with its products by placing an emphasis on the consumer as listener, and the ear is enlisted as the means for the cathexis of desire. The ear is central to the way the record company imagines the listener, while for listeners the ear is a synecdoche for the whole of the listening body. It is the orifice of sonic incorporation, a contact zone that brings the other into the body of the listener. It is not only in the site of composition and musical arrangement, which I concede has historically been central in constructing sonic otherness and normativity,[47] but with the advent and expansion of the world music culture industry, a complex social process has emerged in which the consumer is called upon to sonically construct the other in the aural imaginary through listening. The body is essentially remapped and the ear is interpellated as the main site for the production of the (aural) other and the (listening) self.

This is best exemplified by the ubiquitous interpellation of the listener by liner notes, music journalism, and publicity as well as within the sonic space of the song's production techniques. The listener is invited to validate the success of what is constructed as an "unlikely" musical collaboration by listening for what sounds good. As regular music contributor on the nationally syndicated travel show *Voyager!* Cohen notes that some cross-cultural musical collaborations are logical because they sound so good: "People who listen to this program may be starting to get the idea that I'm a real sucker for these sorts of unlikely-on-paper collaborations between cultures but, when they actually happen you say to yourself, 'Wow, why hasn't that happened before?' because on this particular record the sound is really, really beautiful and somehow it just sorta makes sense." Cohen, as cultural intermediary, is responsible for facilitating the unexpected cross-cultural musical collaborations that simply sound "beautiful," translating these sounds and their value to listeners. Not only are musical genres mixed, but cultures—sonically distinguished through "traditional" and "modern" signifiers—are blended in the gendered process of hybrid music production, which I explore as the subject of chapter 4.

Conclusion: The Business of Incorporation

The ear is a heuristic in my research because it is a symbolic contact zone where the listener interacts with the performer. The eardrum, or tympanic membrane, is also a symbolic surface that functions much like the screen does in cinema; the narrative logic of the listening subject's imaginary is projected onto this membrane. As Lacan has characterized it, "At the scopic level, we are no longer at the level of demand, but of desire, of the desire of the Other. It is the same at the level of the invocatory drive, which is the closest to the experience of the unconscious."[48] And as a structure closer to the unconscious, it is characterized by Kalpana Seshadri-Crooks as that which "is already racialized and inscribed within a racial symbolic by the signifier Whiteness, which largely functions to subsume and homogenize incommensurable difference."[49] Just as the penis is a reification of the symbolic phallus, so also is the ear both symbolic and reified. It is an invaginated organ, enabling incorporation yet maintaining phallic authority. But in addition to the drive being phallic and invaginated, it is also racialized. What I refer to as "Listen Inc.," interpreted as "listen incorporated" can be said to summarize the business model of the WMCI both as a corporation structured around listening as well as one structured through the desiring fantasies of the listener (who is also a fantasy for the record company). This business model capitalizes on the listener's desire to cathect the invocatory drive through listening as incorporation. The promotion of incorporation through listening happens at many levels in the WMCI, whether through listening or through the performative uncanny, which seemed to be trending in 2008 among bands like the aforementioned Vampire Weekend (who literally deploy the trope of incorporation in their name).[50]

This incorporation is also promoted by the very fact that most listeners have no context or linguistic proficiency in the music that the WMCI promotes. Therefore, the WMCI highlights descriptions of the musicality of language that emphasize the sonic and phonetic aspects of the music over the semantic and historical (which abound in reference to Brazilian Portuguese, in particular). In addition, the absurdly vast amount of cultural variation contained within the world music genre guarantees that a majority of listeners will neither comprehend the lyrics, which are often sung in a language other than English,[51] nor will they have been exposed previously to the particular musical tradition being represented.[52] How, then, do we explain the success and endurance of a genre consumed primarily by listeners who do not comprehend the music? In the case of Bianca Costa, a majority of the songs on her first few albums are sung in Portuguese yet her biggest markets are in Japan and the United States. Many listeners testify to having less of a connection with the semantic content of her lyrics than with the sound of her music. As "Michael from Brooklyn, NY" attests, "This is the most beautiful and intoxicating non-English speaking music I have ever heard. This is coming from a guy that hates subtitles in movies and heads for the first McDonald's when he is traveling abroad. I don't usually think writing biased reviews for Amazon is helpful to anyone but American audiences need to know about Bianca Costa! This was love at first sight (listen) for me and it will be for you too!"

The language barrier has necessitated a privileging of the role of cultural intermediaries like record companies, music journalists, and disc jockeys who function as cultural (as opposed to linguistic) translators. The record company plays a major pedagogical role in translating musical traditions and scales, framing the history of an artist's career relative to their local music scenes and even interpreting colonial histories that are imagined to have begotten the hybrid variation of a particular subgenre. Kinship has developed brand loyalty among a fan base that looks to the record label as a source of geopolitical and cultural knowledge. Rarely does the record label provide lyrical translations, foregrounding instead the invocatory phonic qualities of the vocals relative to the overall sound of the song, genre, or music from the region in general.[53] Cultural translation occurs through the production of fantastic narratives of the other, fantasies both representative and constitutive of the listener.

Preoccupations with the proprietary in studies of world music have ignored the libidinal economic order that both makes world music viable and in which this genre circulates. Appropriation can only happen after incorporation has taken place; the other's music becomes mine only after I have incorporated it into *my* history and identity. The African repressed as *the* uncanny is more akin to the *objet petit a* or "little other" and hence more incorporable than the radical Other who can never be incorporated into the self. In the following chapter I explore how the *objet* of the aural other is not merely incorporated into the self but also becomes an opportunity for the "loss" of the self, through the notion of "*signifiance*." I examine how the experience of *signifiance* is partially the outcome of recording and mixing techniques through a close reading of sound production practices at Kinship Records.

3

Losing the Listening Self in the Aural Other

Signifiance and World Music

Wedged in the middle of my mom's huge Count Basie and
Duke Ellington collections were a few unusual-looking discs.
One album cover said something about Pygmies, Africa,
drums—enough to capture any boy's imagination and make
it drift to the unknown, the far away, and the dangerous. I
slipped the disc out of its sleeve, put it gently on the old RCA
Victrola that had been stationed for years in our living room,
and retreated into the depths of the big green chair Grandfa-
ther usually occupied. As the sound of the recording floated
out into the air, I drifted to another place and time. The playful, high-pitched voices—so different from any sounds I'd
ever heard—made my living room walls disappear. The music began to open a strange new world. My mind went wild
with the possibilities. I was roaming through jungles with
the Pygmies, eating their fruits, singing their songs, sleeping
and foraging for food with them. I had access to their daily
lives, their experiences and their essence. What an amazing adventure for a city kid—a romp, a voyage to the other
side of the world. That recording lit my imagination with an
intensity that would ultimately guide my life. Every day I
rushed home, put on the sounds of the Pygmies, and melted
into their very being. I pressed my ear to the speaker grill so
no one else could hear my secret world. . . . The music made
me powerful, and even though the singing was in a language
I didn't understand, I was getting it. I was receiving its message, and it made me feel special.
—Mickey Hart, *Songcatchers*

In 2003, with the help of coauthor K. M. Kotsyal, Grateful Dead drummer and world music producer Mickey Hart published the book *Songcatchers: In Search of the World's Music.*[1] In this colorful and glossy National Geographic publication, full of archival photographs and features, Hart (Kotsyal) tells a dire tale about the adventures of numerous comparative musicologists and ethnomusicologists in their pioneering quest to salvage the world's disappearing musical knowledge through the practice of songcatching. Mickey Hart presents an origin story about his coming into consciousness as a songcatcher by illustrating how the alienation suffered by postwar moderns like himself, atomized as he was in his domestic shelter, could be ruptured by the sounds emanating from that old Victrola. The phonograph-cum-Victrola-cum-stereo cabinet disguised itself as just another piece of wooden living room furniture but functioned for the young Hart as the portal that transported him away from the doldrums of his postwar youth, far from "any bullies who might be waiting for [him] just outside [his] living room door.[2] Like the acoustic mirror I reference in chapter 2, which Vampire Weekend lead singer Ezra Koenig looked into to find himself, Mickey Hart describes finding himself in his mother's record collection only to get lost in an outcrop that leads to the "essence" of the pygmies, Africa, drums. And it is thanks to the songcatchers he memorializes that this experience can be shared by new generations.

Hart's description of "drift[ing] to the unknown, the far away, and the dangerous" is a common motif in descriptions of listening to world music. This phenomenological account of a first encounter with the other's music—this primal scene—echoes an interaction with the other in sound described famously by Roland Barthes in his deconstructive and psychoanalytic rendering of "the grain" he could hear in "the voice." I bring these disparate figures into a perhaps unlikely dialogue in order to cultivate a methodology for critically engaging music's impact on the modern's ear. I begin where Barthes begins, with the premise that "[t] here is an imaginary in music whose function is to reassure, to constitute the subject hearing it."[3] What is remaindered from this encounter with the grain of the other's voice—*signifiance*, or the loss of the listening self within the aural other—is what is now brokered by the WMCI.

Barthes's retooling of Julia Kristeva's original concept helps me elucidate a process that is central to the listening practices endorsed by the world music industry in its systematic promotion of pleasure through listening. Marketed primarily to the bourgeois woman, phonographs promoted a feminized listening. The contemporary world music industry reproduces this feminized listener through market and demographic research that constructs her as the "ideal listener." In chapter 2 I discussed how listening with the ear is a reified process understood to symbolically function like the reified vagina within a heteronormative logic: It is an organ to be penetrated by an active sonic force. The musical culture industry harnesses and capitalizes on the logic of this symbolization, which I name incorporation (borrowing from Freud). In this chapter I want to consider this process as Barthes has theorized it in order to read the feminization of Barthes's ear, while also critically deconstructing the ideological and epistemological implications undergirding this process and, especially, the "loss of the self" sought through this process of signifiance.

The Grain of the Voice

Barthes poetically characterizes the imaginary capacity of the "grain of the voice" in his discussion of the voice and music, describing it as both the text as well as the performer's body. He writes, "The 'grain' is the body in the voice as it sings, the hand as it writes, the limb as it performs."[4] The *signifiance* enabled by the "grain of the voice," as Barthes explains, results in the loss of the self, an inversion of the signified subject. This notion of *signifiance* is key to opening up an analysis of sound that does not reduce it to text (be that lyrical or musical) or meaning, enabling the analysis of what Barthes refers to as "the 'aesthetics' of musical pleasure."[5] For Mickey Hart, that aesthetics of musical pleasure is as much about his interactions with the material artefacts of musical playback (the album, the RCA Victrola, the speaker grill) as it is about the symbolic invocations of the aural imaginary ("roaming through jungles with the Pygmies, eating their fruits, singing their songs, sleeping and foraging for food with them"). With the help of Barthes I will additionally argue that it is through the "grain of the voice" that alterity is communicated and pleasure in listening takes place.[6] Barthes writes:

> If I perceive the "grain" in a piece of music and accord this "grain" a theoretical value (the emergence of the text in the work), I inevitably set up a

new scheme of evaluation which will certainly be individual—I am determined to listen to my relation with the body of the man or woman singing or playing and that this relation is erotic—but in no way "subjective"
(it is not the psychological subject in me who is listening; the climactic
pleasure hoped for is not going to reinforce—to express—that subject, but
on the contrary, to lose it). . . . I can hear with certainty—the certainty of
the body, of thrill.[7]

Barthes develops here a theory of listening that considers the relational
erotics of performer and listener. Although they never meet, these figures aurally engage in the temporal space of the listening event. The
way in which Barthes describes a "scheme of evaluation" that is determined relationally between the listener and the body of the "man or
woman singing or playing" is critical. It is the texture of the performer's
body, the imaginary flesh with which Barthes the listener has an erotic
relationship—not his literal body. The "grain of the voice" describes
something other than the physical body, it is a body rendered in the
imagination, stimulated by sound waves. The grain is a vehicle for fantasy that ignites the aural imaginary. Just as the grain on a piece of wood
veneer shows its fibrous makeup, the grain of the voice *represents* the
singing body and not the body itself, its imagined fleshiness. And just
as the grain on a piece of wood veneer texturally conveys its fibrous
makeup through touch, the grain of the voice conveys the embodiment
of the singing or performing body and presents the listener with the
opportunity for an affective engagement with an imagined performer. It
is an encounter with this imagined embodiment that is centrally important in the world/electronica culture industry. The relational erotics of
performer and listener are sonically constructed along racial (and/or
ethnic), geographic, and gendered lines, thereby hinging the "scheme
of evaluation" on certain presumptions made by the record company
about the ideal listener—the white woman I discuss in chapter 2—and
her others. It is her feminized listening that is structured into their staging of this encounter.

Kinship Records purveys a form of world music—referred to by the
company as "global pop" or "world/electronica," which systematically
follows a musical production formula that generates what the company
refers to as "genre-bending hybrids that include a variety of musical styles

as well as a mix of the ancient and the modern."[8] The systematic use of this formula has resulted in a consistent "sound" for the company on which consumers, journalists, and critics have come to depend. The Kinship brand is organized around a stylistic, sonic, and cultural theory of hybridity that generally congeals around the modern/traditional binary (which I discuss in chapter 4). While Kinship Records is the only U.S.-based world/electronica record company to actively and consistently use the term "hybrid" in its branding and marketing efforts, the concept of hybridity is at the heart of the genre. It is a style of music that mixes highly manipulated production and synthetic instrumentation (what Kinship refers to as "Western sounds") with classical vocals and instrumentation from India, Iran, Mali, Brazil, Turkey, and many other regions. World/electronica, as I imagine it, refers not only to a "sound" but also to a process of refinement in which sounds are manipulated and juxtaposed in ways that achieve specific commercial results. When examined under the lens of Barthes's relational erotics, world/electronica's sonic hybridity and its "aesthetics" of musical pleasure are revealed to be centrally organized around an aural other distinguished from the listening self.

Sonic *Signifiance* and Loss

In her discussion of *Writing Degree Zero*,[9] Julia Kristeva reflects on Roland Barthes's (re)interpretation of "the semantic density of language," on his designation of *écriture* as a "negativity" and, in a moment of self-referentiality, she declares through the concept of *signifiance* that for Barthes, writing displaces, condenses, repeats, and inverts the linear order of language, producing an "over meaning." Stating that writing uses the "fundamental laws of *signifiance*," Kristeva reads her own influence in Barthes's work.[10] As a testimony to their ongoing scholarly engagement, Barthes deploys Kristeva's definition of *signifiance* in "The Grain of the Voice," a piece published almost twenty years prior to Kristeva's chapter on *Writing Degree Zero*. Translator Stephen Heath draws the reader's attention to the etymological origins of the concept in Barthes's thinking, elaborating further on the specific usage of the term in his work, "As a theoretical concept initially proposed by Julia Kristeva . . . *Signifiance* is a *process* in the course of which the 'subject' of the text, escaping the logic of *ego-cogito* and engaging in other logics (of the signifier, of contradiction), struggles with meaning and is decon-structed ('lost'). Contrary to signification, *signifiance* cannot be reduced, therefore, to communication, representation, expression: it places the subject (of writer, reader) in the text not as a projection . . . but as a 'loss,' a 'disappearance.'"[11] Heath's characterization of *signifiance* as "contrary to signification" positions the terms as inverses: one signals meaning and the other is its "loss"; the two concepts mirror one another. Signifi-cation, representation, and meaning have traditionally been objects for semiological deconstruction; a concern with *signifiance* marks a depar-ture from this meaning-centered practice.

Moving away from a meaning-centered practice is necessary for Barthes, who determines that musical interpretation through language has tended to reduce music to the adjective, or what he more appro-priately refers to as the "epithet."[12] Unlike Kristeva, who theorizes signifiance through reading and writing, Barthes explores musical per-formance and listening as "another semiotic system"[13] that could elabo-rate the process of signifiance differently and perhaps better. Barthes turns away from the interpretive epithet by changing the object of analy-sis, or as he describes it, "It would be better to change the musical object itself, as it presents itself to discourse, better to alter its level of percep-tion or intellection, to displace the fringe of contact between music and language."[14] Going on to state, "It goes without saying, however, that the simple consideration of 'grain' in music could lead to a different history of music from the one we know now (which is purely pheno-textual),"[15] he pays particular attention to the *jouissance* enabled by singers and mu-sicians who articulate the "gestures" of their bodies within what Barthes (yet again borrowing from Kristeva) calls "geno-song."[16] Barthes reads musical performance and listening as practices that enable the inver-sion inherent in the process of *signifiance*, chronicling an experience endemic to Western modernity. Though he does not elaborate on it as such, I argue that Barthes's reflection illuminates the importance of the "loss" enabled by sonic *signifiance* within contemporary musical culture industries and within the aural imaginary.

I refer to the world music industry's harnessing of pleasure-through-listening as "sonic *signifiance*." Critical components of this industrialized form of pleasure in world music are race and gender, which, as I will attempt to show, exist as specters within the imaginary of listeners who are seeking the "loss of the self" in *signifiance*. While I fully acknowledge that listening practices are situated, unpredictable, and temporally uneven, I bracket this in order to reflect on music as a commodity and the practices employed by a culture industry that stands to profit from standardizing interactions with the commodity form. In addition to industrializing cultural forms, the culture industry must standardize affective engagements with these forms, working hard to ensure quality and pleasure for the musical consumer. In the context of world music, this pleasure is necessarily bound up with complex processes of racialization and gendering that are at times overt and at others subliminal. By examining the production and marketing practices at Kinship Records, I aim to show in this chapter how specters of racialized gender are sonically figured in the imagined relation between the "grain" (of the voice or of the performing body) and the listener.

Kristeva's original concept of *signifiance* follows logically from her oeuvre by mapping a feminine form of "desire in language" that is not rooted in the phallic order of, as Lacan has put it, "signifiers." Kristeva's *signifiance* represents a liberatory form of loss that can bring the feminine subject closer to what she terms "the semiotic" or what in Lacanian parlance we might call the *real*: that preoedipal, prephallic, pretraumatic site. Thus, *signifiance* marks for Kristeva a feminine *jouissance* that can find not only liberation in the space of lack but also a nonphallic form of pleasure. Barthes narrows in on the feminine *jouissance* that results from the "loss of the self" in music just as the music industry has narrowed in on the potential for pleasure in listening as a pleasure produced through the feminization of listening. There are critically important differences between the political motivations behind Kristeva and Barthes's coinage and the culture industry's deployment of this practice. For Kristeva, feminine *jouissance* had the potential to liberate the writing, listening subject from the phallic trappings of language; the industry's neoliberal aims have absorbed and diffused that revolutionary potential for the sake of profit. As I argue throughout this book, the WMCI has systematically coopted feminist political strategies into its logic of capital accumulation (a topic I explore in detail in chapter 5).

As he positions himself as a feminized listener, I read Barthes's deployment of Kristeva's concept of *signifiance* to interpret the effect of operatic baritone Charles Panzera's voice on his body and the capacity for Panzera's voice to affect Barthes's gender as a feminized listening.[17] At the same time that I read Barthes's embodied discovery and interpretation of a queer sonic encounter with Panzera as radical, I do so in order to chart its waning when coopted as the *modus operandi* of musical encounters between the normative world music listener and the other in sound. Barthes's *signifiance*—which was, in the time and place where it emerged, a gendered, sexual, and formal breach of the heteronormative order—is no longer disruptive in the context of the world music culture industry. As the method that guarantees pleasure in listening, *signifiance* is now the means to capital accumulation. As I discussed in chapter 2, this results from a process of musical incorporation in which the listener's body is remapped, with the ear becoming a reified organ in the tradition of the vagina (invagination); the feminized listener of modernity becoming the symbolic stand-in for a particularly incorporative modality of listening. Harnessed and industrialized as it is by the WMCI, it is no longer radical to claim this feminized form of listening, and we would be hard-pressed to refer to it even as queer, because it functions as a hegemonic form of listening within this culture industry. In this new context, *signifiance* is not radical but instead reifies feminized listening in its most phallic sense: as a pleasure that results from a fetishization of feminine lack, a pleasure that irrupts in the listener through loss.

In the phallogocentric order, loss is the space occupied by what Lacan refers to as "(not) woman," which Jacqueline Rose describes in the following way: "The woman, therefore, is not, because she is defined purely against the man (she is the negative of that definition—'man is not woman'), and because this very definition is designated fantasy.... As negative to the man, woman becomes a total object of fantasy (or an object of total fantasy), elevated to the place of the Other and made to stand for its truth."[18] Thus, the loss experienced by Mickey Hart and industrialized by the WMCI is enabled by the reification of the trope of feminine lack. When the reification of a heteronormative invagination of pleasure becomes a means of capital accumulation, it is most certainly no longer feminist, nor queer.

What was in its time perhaps Barthes's queer reading practice appears again, and this time he goes into more explicit detail about the incorporative fantasy of *signifiance*. "[Sarrasine] enters a theatre by chance, by chance he is seated near the stage; the sensual music, the beauty of the prima donna and her voice fill him with desire; because of his proximity to the stage, he hallucinates, imagines he is possessing La Zambinella; penetrated by the artist's voice, he achieves orgasm; after which, drained, sad, he leaves, sits down and muses: this was his first ejaculation. . . . The voice is described by its power of penetration, insinuation, flow; but here it is the man who is penetrated."[19]

Barthes fantasizes through *signifiance* and takes it a step further by literally interpreting the capacity of the voice to penetrate the ear and of the ear's capacities for incorporation. As quoted in Joke Dame's essay "Unveiled Voices," Barthes's interpretation in *S/Z* of the phallic voice of castrato Zambinella in Balzac's *Sarrasine*, "portrayed as active, virile, and phallic," is a reductive fantasy.[20] Dame sees this as being in contrast with Barthes's reading of Sarrasine, the male subject, who "has been placed in the female position: passive, overwhelmed, and overpowered." This stereotypical role reversal is troublesome for Dame, who accuses Barthes of denying the active role to the feminine and the passive role to the masculine. Contrary to this, however, I would argue that Barthes had it right all along, precisely because of the structural position of feminine lack and Kristeva's definition of *signifiance*, or loss, that Barthes deploys in his reading of the impact of the voice on the listener's body.

Lost in *Arabian Journeys*

Inspired by the events of September 11, 2001 the Kinship Records compilation album *Arabian Journeys* paradigmatically presents us with the opportunity for *signifiance*. Like many Kinship releases, it circulates with text that pedagogically curates the music, presenting the album and introducing each song.[21]

> *Arabian Journeys*, the latest adventure in world music from Kinship, documents the extraordinary power and far-reaching influence of music from the Near and Middle East and North Africa, the music of the Islamic Diaspora. A host of different ethnic groups inhabit the Arab world, whose shared musical culture is earmarked by several easily recognized characteristics. The flowing, highly ornamented melody lines based on skilled improvisation, the linking of smaller melodic kernels

to form a larger arrangement like the patterned tiles decorating the wall of a mosque, the use of sound to effect spiritual transport and an atmosphere of immanence. These are some of the distinguishing features of Arabian music, along with the distinctive sounds of instruments such as the oud (the Arab mandolin) and the spiky report of the taut-skinned darbuka drum.[22]

This text frames the geno-sonic elements that lay within the tracks using textural signifiers. And reading while listening, the music's highly manipulated beats and production elements become pronounced just as clearly as the instrumentation described in the text. According to Barthes, *signifiance* is not accomplished at every listen. Elements of both geno-song and pheno-song exist within this hybrid mix. He presents a performance taxonomy that distinguishes those through which he is able to achieve *signifiance* from those through which he is not. Borrowing yet again from Kristeva, Barthes offers the opposing terms "geno-song" and "pheno-song" to classify and distinguish performance types. While pheno-song refers to the technical and stylistic aspects of performance, geno-song, which he describes as "the voluptuousness" of the sound-signifiers of language,[23] is where Barthes locates the potential for *signifiance*.

Elements of both geno-song and pheno-song exist within this hybrid mix. "Western sounds" and production values qualify as the "phenosonic" components that structurally reorder the "raw" and "ancient" sounds of "tradition" and the musicians who produce them, which figure as the "geno-sonic" aspects of the song.[24] The imagined distinction between the two is critical for the feminine jouissance *signifiance* enables. The terms geno-sonic and pheno-sonic refer to sounds that can be read using Kristeva's geno-text/pheno-text and Barthes's geno-song/pheno-song logics.[25] Building on this, I recognize the presence of both geno-sonic and pheno-sonic elements in Kinship Records' releases. Where and how these map are the result of systematic production practices that the company uses to produce the cohesive label "sound." While each of the ten tracks represents an intercultural collaboration that yields the branded "hybrid form" that Kinship consistently produces, the text only describes the sounds of the "Islamic Diaspora." This text frames the listening experience, working to create cohesion between songs written and performed by unrelated people.

In addition to the general introduction to the compilation, each track listing includes a few sentences that work to contextualize and mediate the listening event. Track nine, entitled "S'ma"—a collaboration between Acid King and Masr Music—paradigmatically represents the hybrid world/electronica formula and conveys this to the listener with the following text,

> "S'ma" conjures a shortwave broadcast from Zanzibar, as heard against a sunset soundscape of crickets and distant howling dogs. The track is typical of the inspired collaboration between Norwegian musicians Eirik Grotle and Anders Granly and the elegant intonations of the great tarab orchestra Masr Music (whose melodies often derive from Cairo film scores). Hovering above the proceedings are smouldering female vocals and the unlikely but winning admixture of tarab strings and spooky electronics. As the insects drone and the backing singers wail into the distance, one thing is certain: to experience "S'ma" is to know that you've visited a truly exotic destination, not found on any map.[26]

While still working to translate the song, what this text attempts to put into language is the experience of *signifiance* that awaits the listener, emphasizing the geno-sonic components for which she should listen. By emphasizing the spaces opened through the soundscape, this text does more than translate meaning; it points to the potential for loss of the self in sound that can only be found by listening. Per Mickey Hart's method of phenomenological description, routed through Barthes's semiological deconstruction, here is a description of what I hear in this song:

> Song fades in, beginning with the caws of tropical birds and crickets, katydids and cicadas humming, buzzing, and chirping, creating a choral forest. Dogs howl and bark across the stereo spread and slowly, a vocally driven song sung in Arabic fades in, though it does not necessarily sound like it belongs to this song, sounding extra-diegetic while in the same soundscape (as if one is slowly approaching, like a voyeur, listening to a shortwave radio playing in the first house on the edge of a little town). A Dopplerized car coasts by from right to left channel, acting as a sound bridge to the synthetic kick-drum that leads into the high fidelity main section of the track; vocals, choral forest, and howls slowly die away (the

radio is turned off or volume reduced; perhaps the listener is walking away from the house on the edge of town). When the kick drum doubles up, the vocals have faded and a highly distorted bass line begins. The bird caws are looped and synthesized, reverberating into a delay at the end of every fourth measure. Then the vocals begin again (this time without the short-wave fuzz effect) offering themselves as belonging to the song. The "grain of the voice" in these vocals is highly pronounced with the help of technologies like condenser microphones and high-end studio reverb units. A pre-programmed (canned "Middle Eastern" sounding) string section begins, delays are applied to the vocals, and saturation filters added to the percussion, which further move the listener away from the edges of town that marked the beginning of the track to the postmodern, post-9/11 ambience of a technologized, trip-hop groove joined by what sounds like a darbuka being thumped and overlaid with the mantric re-frain "S'ma." Then, with forty seconds remaining, all the production falls away and the listener is returned to the edges of the small town, made a stranger again, voyeuristically listening to the shortwave broadcast of a female vocalist whose melancholic Arabic singing seems to color a world the listener no longer occupies.

The order and technical detail of synthetic drums and high-tech studio production—what we might interpret as the pheno-sonic elements—offer rhythmic consistency and introduce what the producers and record label would understand as a sonic modernity to the track. On the other hand, it is the "smouldering female vocals" (for which no singer is given credit) that function as the geno-sonic elements, figuring as the body in the song. There are additional sonic textures—cricket chirps, bird caws, a car passing by, dog barks and howls, crackling speakers—that contribute to the geno-sonic space, providing the song with multiple layers of sonic grain that collect and accumulate to create the potential for *signifiance*. These layers create an elsewhere ("a truly exotic destination, not found on any map") occupied by others who collectively figure a fantasy world in which a listener can lose herself. Situated within the acoustics of pre-modernity, as signified by the ambient sounds of a small, faraway town populated with crickets, dogs, birds, and noisy old cars, the vocals are initially situated as part of the environment, part of the soundscape of exploration, one grain among many that together place the song in "a truly exotic destination, not found on any map." These multiple layers of sonic grain contribute to the creation of a cultural acoustic soundscape, an ambience constructed equally by the sounds of human, insect, animal, and mechanical bodies. When the pheno-sonic components of Grotle and Granly's production work enter the song, they strip away all the layers of sonic grain except for the vocals, slowly enhancing them in terms of volume and fidelity—thus beginning the process of hybridization between the pheno-sonic and geno-sonic components and opening the window to *signifiance*. If the geno-sonic saturation produced by the multiple layers of sonic grain at the beginning of the song function to position me as an explorer voyeuristically listening in on a scene of which I am not a part, the dialectic of hybridization that the introduction of Grotle and Granly's production techniques enable draws me closer and eventually into the mix, enabling the loss associated with *signifiance*.

The listener indeed gets lost, and the orchestration of the sounds in the song encourages this. World/electronica music producers readily employ technologies that model spaces and various instrument types (vintage, new, broken, analogue, cracked, and so on), manipulating sound so as to evoke spatiotemporal senses of other-worldliness. Though he did not comment on the technologies of sound production, Barthes's notion of *signifiance* aptly represents the spaces opened up by these techniques and machines. Sound production technologies are used to pronounce and suppress presences and absences of all sorts of bodies and grains with the objective of manipulating the listener's relation with these bodies and with *signifiance*. These technologies have the capacity to amplify and mute the "grain of the voice," enabling producers to apply them as sonic textures the way a painter might apply paint. Stripping away the multiple layers of sonic grain in order to pronounce and resituate the vocals works to fix them within the geno-sonic realm. Sound production technologies bolster a power structure that has the capacity to "engrain" certain sounds within the geno-sonic space of the song.[27] What I hear at the beginning of "S'ma" (while acoustically positioned as a voyeur) does not have the same sonic impact as what gradually becomes blended with the pheno-sonic elements Granly and Grotle introduce. It is through the dialectic of hybridization that the "smoldering female vocals" become "engrained" or fixed within the space of geno-sonic spectrality. To be engrained is to be fixed within an aural materiality, which sets up a power dynamic between the listener and the spectral voice that is enacted within the temporal space of the listening event. The dialectic between the pheno-sonic and geno-sonic is animated within the aural imaginary, and it is through this process that sounds become engrained. The anonymous female vocalist's spectrality creates the conditions of possibility for *signifiance*.[28] It is in the dialectical dance between pheno- and geno-sonic elements that this manipulation works to construct a space for the loss of the self in sound. The listener's pleasure is made possible when voices and sounds are engrained in the geno-sonic space of the song.

Because the first *Arabian Journeys* was such a huge success for the label, Kinship released an *Arabian Journeys II* in 2003. Cohen describes the new recording and the inspiration behind it in a dialogue with *Voyager* host Nancy Dayne .

NANCY DAYNE (ND): trancelike . . . that's a good phrase.

JON COHEN (JC): A lot of this music is sort of built around repetitive patterns that just sort of build, and build and build and build and that gives you that trancelike quality.

ND: I'm just curious with, you know, the other global frictions between the Middle East and most of the rest of the world these days, how's that affecting the music and these types of collaborations?

JC: Well that's why I thought it would be interesting to sort of reexamine this series because when we put out the first [*Arabian Journeys*] after September 11th, we had a lot of people telling us, "Oh, you're crazy . . . don't put that out . . . it's gonna do terribly." The fact of the matter is, people's curiosity about the culture, the Arabic culture, has actually been piqued quite a bit in the wake of what happened on September 11th and of course, world events since. And when it comes to musicians collaborating, you know, the politics just don't come into play. When musicians sit down and the music works, they just sort of rise above all that. And obviously, that's a very, very wonderful example for us all.

ND: It's inspiring, isn't it?

During one of his regular appearances as the world music guru on the nationally syndicated travel-themed show *Voyager*, Cohen plays a song by Turkish electronic musician DJ Allen that features the ney, a flute prominently played in Iranian and Turkish music, often in a vocal melodic style. The ney's breathy, melancholic sound, as Lalita Sinha has stated, can be mistaken for a voice, "at certain notes it is difficult to identify the difference between the flute sound and the human voice."[29] Performed, the ney has phonetic qualities of intonation similar to spoken language and could easily be heard by the nonfluent ear as vocally sung language. As Cohen mentions, the label, thought to be radical for releasing the first *Arabian Journeys* compilation immediately after 9/11, understands music to "rise above" politics. The trope of world music as a universal language is overtly deployed here. What is understated in Cohen's commentary, which was said to me as an aside by prominent Middle Eastern DJ Shadi Assouline, is the fact that music from the so-called "Islamic Diaspora" never sold as well as it did after 9/11. Perhaps Cohen's metaphor of rising above politics could be interpreted differently: the desire for incorporation was heightened by politics.

Geno-Sonic Spectrality

The curatorial text provided for "S'ma" guides the listener through an interpretation of the "smoldering . . . vocals" as connected to a body that seems unproblematically female. This example makes the connection between *signifiance* and gender seem obvious and self-evident. However, it is important to bear in mind that the anonymous vocalist is never mentioned in the album credits and the role performed by the vocals, including the radio effect applied at the beginning and the more intimate mic'ng and vocal placement within the mix that occurs toward the middle of the track, is a careful manipulation of presences and absences that plays with materiality and spatiality. Analyzing the voice in this context means contending with what Avery Gordon has called "ghostly matters." As Gordon explains, "Being haunted draws us affectively, sometimes against our will and always a bit magically, into the structure of feeling of a reality we come to experience, not as cold knowledge, but as transformative recognition. . . . In haunting, organized forces and systemic structures that appear removed from us make their impact felt in everyday life in a way that confounds our analytic separations and confounds the social separations themselves."[30]

There is no "real" material woman associated with the vocals performed in "S'ma"; gender and ethnicity—like place ("Zanzibar"; "a truly exotic destination not found on any map"), temporality (as signified by the shortwave radio effect), and religion (Islamic Diaspora)—are sonically and texturally/textually signified. Racialized gender in world/electronica music need not indexically stand in for a "real" woman for the pleasure of *signifiance* to take place. Just as Gordon has stated for the importance of haunting, the magic of *signifiance* allows listeners of world/electronica music to *feel* something from which they are otherwise removed. Similarly, the perception of the grain of the voice as the body in the voice, as described by Barthes, is not a literal or material cognition of a "real" body, but rather a figural one. How bodies get figured within listeners' imaginations and whether or not the bodies' grains are felt is linked to how geno-sonic specters are elicited and how they are put into dialectical relation with the pheno-sonic components of a song.

The grain of the "smoldering female vocals" is overtly offered to the listener as the "body in the voice" and the anonymity of the voice furthers the potential for *signifiance*. The dialectic performed between Grotle and Granly's sound production and the "smoldering female vocals" positions the voice as the vector for *signifiance*. Although it is not a material body, the "body in the voice" gets figured through racialized and ethnic imaginaries mediated by the curatorial framing devices, sound production technologies, and the dialectical opposition with unmarked pheno-sonic signifiers. The inversion of the listening subject through *signifiance* into loss and absence is predicated upon the imagined racialized body that is necessarily gendered. Additionally, it is not just bodies but spaces and temporalities that are racialized and gendered in the listener's imaginary ("heard against a sunset soundscape of crickets and distant howling dogs").

Kinship Records has harnessed the displacement, condensation, repetition, and inversion deemed by Kristeva to be inherent in the process of *signifiance* by systematically employing production techniques that create a cohesive sound and produce racialized-gendered sonic bodies in which consumers seek pleasure-through-listening.[31] Though Barthes celebrates *signifiance* as a means through which listeners are relieved of the burden of subjectivity by inversion into a space of subjective loss, in the WMCI this transformation takes place at the expense of the racialized-gendered voice whose subjectivity must be denied and whose voice must be engrained in the geno-sonic space of the song. When deployed by the culture industry, *signifiance* maintains a racialized and gendered division of labor that relegates even imaginary or spectral bodies to a geno-sonic space for consuming pleasure.

In 1977 Barthes foretold a future moment when the pleasure of a musical text would be of greater importance to interpreters of culture than a textual analysis of that musical form. Barthes anticipated a moment in which pleasure, materiality, and subjectivity invert, folding in and out of states, writing and erasing, creating creases and crevices—all resulting in palimpsestic re-and-un-codings. The aesthetics of musical pleasure Barthes summoned in the 1970s has come to manifest itself in capitalism as a strategy employed by a record company whose aim is increased sales. While this seems like a less-than-noble objective through which to free the subject, the result enables interesting, problematic, and complex manifestations of *signifiance*.

In the world/electronica culture industry, *signifiance* functions in a libidinal economy where pleasure-through-listening and the "loss of the self" in sound is predicated on a dialectic in which a racialized-gendered geno-sonic voice is curated by pheno-textual and pheno-sonic production practices. This libidinal economy functions through a division of labor that limits the subjective capacity of the racialized-gendered voices to a space of spectrality, and this spectrality figures the conditions of possibility for the liberation of the listener through sonic *signifiance*. This division of labor does not necessarily structure the work that artists and performers can literally do; instead, it organizes the work performed in the listener's imaginary.

In chapter 4 I explicitly engage the laboring that racialized and gendered sounds are put to within the aural imaginary through a deconstruction of the trope of hybridity so ubiquitous not only within the WMCI broadly but at Kinship Records in particular. I examine hybridity in sound as a means to the hybridization of the listener who seeks greater adaptability in a rapidly changing, multicultural world. I also uncover the anxiety induced by hybridity's other—miscegenation—as those unpleasurable sounds the musical hybridists at Kinship Records are always hedging against through careful production practices.

4

Racial Noise, Hybridity, and Miscegenation in World Music

Variety is the spice of life. We all know that. But today, there
is a new explosion of excitement as the combining of music
from all cultures and languages accelerates. This book documents and bears witness to the emergence of a new sensibility. It is like the dance of chromosomes as they divide and
recombine, creating new hybrid life forms . . . In many ways,
World Music is the music that best reflects the world as it exists today, perched on the edge of the next millennium.
—David Byrne

Whether in its capacity to enact a "new sensibility," or in its ability to
reproduce "new hybrid life forms," world music is understood by many
of its producers, brokers, and consumers as productive. In his foreword
to world music radio DJ Tom Schnabel's collection of interviews with
some of the most celebrated world musicians of the 1980s, David Byrne
rehearses the multicultural benefits of listening to world music, yes, but
also highlights another value to world music listenership: evolution.
Going on to further develop his genetic metaphor, Byrne continues,

> Every culture, including ours, filters what it receives through its own sen-
> sibility, and eventually reshapes its musical environment to meet its own
> ends. Rhumbas played by Africans become something else. Indian modal
> systems interpreted by Afro-American jazz musicians are no longer rec-
> ognizably Indian. New forms and hybrids are created, the best retaining
> some cultural identity while bringing forth something unique. The world
> is richer for it, the gift has been passed on—in somewhat mutated form.[1]

Following Byrne's pithy foreword, Schnabel echoes these sentiments
in his description of the counterintuitive logic he brought to the creation
of his radio show *Morning Becomes Eclectic*, reflecting on the resistance

he received from industry insiders, stating, "Radio experts told us from the beginning that such a mixed format would never work. My experience has been quite the contrary."[2] Opposition came from a radio orthodoxy who at the time endorsed programming conventions that hemmed radio formats into not only styles but shows that catered to narrow demographic groups organized into crude categories of race, class, age, and gender. Schnabel's mixed format program was, according to him, the first of its kind and instantly proved a success. Schnabel's discussion of the radio orthodoxy's prohibitions on the mixing of formats, read in the context of U.S. history, can be understood through the historical precedents that have prohibited mixture: Jim Crow segregation laws, antimiscegenation laws, and the customary practices that continue to make interracial and intercultural unions taboo. By breaching these prohibitions, Schnabel and Byrne present an organization for sound and radio listenership informed by the historical precedents of integrationist practices and laws but also, as made evident by Byrne's reliance on genetic metaphors, by a logic rooted in an evolutionary biology that promotes adaptability through genetic variety. In what follows I explore the discursive linkages uniting music, genetics, and adaptability in order to further map the resignification of the ear as an erotic orifice, one that has perhaps a greater capacity to adapt the listener to a rapidly changing anthropocene in which change has outpaced biological evolutionary time.

In the present chapter I read the feminization of listening discussed in chapter 1 and the reified vagina/ear of chapters 2 and 3 for the reproductive function these processes anticipate. In these previous chapters I discussed how the vagina trope in Western epistemology reifies that anatomical organ through an imposition of a teleological reproductive function, imagined to achieve its greatest potential as a birth canal serving the ideological function of social and economic reproduction. This chapter explores the symbolic outcome of the incorporation of the aural other and the material productivity of pleasure-in-listening. I examine "modernity's ear" as an invaginated organ that has been biopolitically resignified as a site of social reproduction particularly well-suited to reproduce that most valorized modern ontological state: hybridity. And just as in the case of the vagina's reified reproductive function, things do not always go as planned. Like the newborn who phenotypically reveals a breach in the social order of things, aural incorporation threatens with the unintended outcome of miscegenation and thus carries that prohibitive anxiety within it. What I will show below is that the tension between hybridity—understood as an optimization of life—and miscegenation—understood as a diminishing of life—is as prevalent a discourse with the mixing of sound as it is with the mixing of genetics, overdetermined as they both are by race. Pleasure-in-listening to hybrid world music is offered as a means of hybridizing the listener, a form of artificial selection which enables greater adaptability in a rapidly changing, multicultural world.

Hybridity is the ubiquitous trope used to describe a process of materialization in world/electronica accomplished through the mixing of what are perceived to be unlike sonic, cultural, and gendered/racial elements. This process of materialization offers the aural other to consumers and constitutes the listening self in the process. Pleasure hinges on this coconstitutive materialization, but the instability of this process has various unintended consequences: the threat of unsuccessful mixture risks as well the unpleasure of *aural miscegenation*. What I interpret as musical hybridity's shadowy other, where unfamiliar noises blend with familiar sounds to produce a new form, aural miscegenation is hauntingly present in the political economic quest for hybrid music. Hybridity is the object onto which the taboo and presumed unproductive ancestral American fantasy of miscegenation is displaced. It is informed by a mashup of evolutionary discourses—the Frankentheory resulting from what Peter Bowler has called "the modern Darwin industry" (which I will elaborate upon below)—foregrounding the teleological aim of improvement and encouraging a desire for musical hybridity as that which helps adapt the listener to her constantly changing multicultural surroundings.[3] I scrutinize hybridity as a master trope that promotes adaptability through interracial cross-fertilization. In what follows, I not only discuss the centrality of the notion of hybridity to Kinship Records and the world/electronica genre more generally but I consider it alongside the term *miscegenation*, which carries with it the sexuality sterilized from hybridity.[4]

"Something Strangely Familiar"

So these four musicians are sitting backstage, each preparing for a solo performance in a Norwegian music festival, and each one trying to warm up before going onstage. Two are Norwegian, two are West African and they're all in one room. At some point, they begin to notice that their apparently unrelated traditions are actually sounding quite beautiful together. They hear something strangely familiar in the music of an unfamiliar tradition[,] something that suggests that even countries which are thousands of miles apart can be musical neighbors. The result of that chance meeting in 1996 is a remarkable recording called *From South to North*. A quietly surprising collection of folk songs and lullabies, this recording blends two traditions that probably shouldn't sound so great together—except that they do.

This unlikely quartet is able to start a song in one language and end up in another, leaving you to wonder when—or even if—the song moved from one country to the other. On Selsbak's recording, old Norse epics and lullabies blend imperceptibly with age-old songs from the rich Wolof and Manding traditions of West Africa. The delicate rhythms of Senghor's kora seem as at home backing up a herding song from Norway as they are in the traditional works. And two unusual mouth percussion instruments lend an indefinable, almost otherworldly sound: The munnharpe is the Norwegian form of the familiar jaw harp (also known as jew's harp or mouth harp); the African do-do is a mouth bow. It looks a bit like the result of an archery bow mating with a meat thermometer. (Kids, don't try this at home.) The point is, it's a fairly unusual instrument, traditionally used in the Ivory Coast to contact the spirit world, and while it has a very different sound, it complements the Norwegian mouth harp quite nicely. The voice of course is an international instrument, and since all four members of the ensemble sing, that is a thread woven throughout the recording. What you won't hear are the drum machines and digital sequencers that are part of so many cross-cultural or World Music recordings. From South to North makes its point simply, but beautifully. It doesn't command you to dance, but it certainly invites you to at times. You might say it speaks softly, but carries a big stick.[5]

A collaboration between Norwegian vocalists/mouth harp players Agnes Selsbak and Bjørn Borgos, Côte d'Ivoirian vocalist/djembe player Ousmane Keita, and Senegalese vocalist/kora player Saer Senghor, the biographical text framing *From South to North* narrates a form of musical hybridity that produces pleasure in the ear by virtue of the perfect pairing of seemingly opposed component parts. The narrative tack Kinship takes in this biography celebrates "good" hybrid blending, which the ear hears as morphologically similar sounds. Kinship enlists the listener's ear as the site in which difference is heard and the union between different cultural sounds is consummated (the process of incorporation I discuss in chapters 2 and 3). It tells a story in which sonic similarity (between what should be dissonant sounds and incompatible musical traditions) sparks a musical connection between Scandinavian and West African musicians.

The biographical text for *From South to North* points out what a fit ear should hear: the similarity in the sounds and musical traditions that the different pairs bring to the studio. Through musical hybridization what are assumed to be radically disparate cultures are united. Accordingly, the Norse lullabies blend "imperceptibly" with the Wolof and Manding songs performed by Senghor and Keita; the rhetoric hails the consumer's ear to experience these sounds in order to enjoy the magic of this unbelievable union. But in addition, the agency bestowed upon the ear endows it with a power to mean. The listener constructs the subjectivity of the sounds that enter it utilizing a cultural logic of intelligibility. This is a process of subjectivation in which sounds are gendered and racialized, the means through which sound, and in particular its reception—aurality—figures as a site in the production of difference. It is the ear that is given the agency in this story; the rhetoric in the liner notes beckons the reader to experience this sonic compatibility by listening for him or herself. Difference is understated and subdued; the insistence on similarity in sound only gestures to it. The narrative thrust is constructed around similarity; difference is the subtext here. Absolute, almost binary difference is what the narrator presumes as a given between the West Africans and the Scandinavians.

Used in reference to world music, hybridity at once reifies and reconfigures the sexualized weight of its epistemological roots. Musical hybridity makes sense to us, seems natural even, because it employs the logic of heterosexual procreation "blending imperceptibly," as the *From North to South* biography insists, to form something new. But what of those instances when we can perceive the different component parts constituting the genetic blends begotten by heterosexuality? The biography ushers the listener away from this other, more anxious outcome that results from a breach in the social order of things. By putting pressure on the sexual etymology of hybridity and by contrasting it with its shadowy inverse, miscegenation, I explore the symbolism of hybridity so prevalent at Kinship Records in which disparate sounds are blended, mixed, and united to form a hybrid creation. It is a logic that works under the guise of the theory of natural selection by promoting the idea that the hybrid form bears the best attributes of the various units that combine to form the new whole. In an effort to create a new and better totality, musical hybridity depends on an evolutionary trope in which the "modern" blends with the "traditional." The resulting sounds, songs, and albums are perceived as the evolutionary progeny, an improvement upon the individual parts from which they were conceived. But, by not only mixing sound but also bodies materialized through sound, hybrid music makes evolutionary promises that are actually in the tradition of a form of artificial selection made accessible to consumers through the marketplace. Though this bodily mixing takes place in the aural imaginary, it is anxious about its material prehistory (inflected as that is by the coercive miscegenation that constituted chattel slavery as a mode of economic re/production). While musical hybridity is lauded for its capacity to better adapt the listener to her rapidly transforming environment, to better propel her toward what Nyong'o has called that "horizon" point of racial hybridity which is, according to him, the ever-persistent "American national fantasy," it is tainted with a burden of history that perpetually haunts it.

Hybridity and miscegenation are relationally produced; they are the proverbial opposing sides of a coin. While hybridity yields celebrated offspring, miscegenation designates abject unification, producing anxiety and fear. There is a fine line that separates the pleasure of hybridity from the anxiety marked by aural miscegenation; hybridity is a socially acceptable outcome onto which the desires and fantasies of miscegenation have been displaced. With roots in antebellum politics and law, miscegenation has a charged American history, one that does not connote hybridity's proper adaptability with its biopolitically productive deflection of miscegenation—the phylogenetically inherited form of desire. The world music industry, as exemplified by Kinship Records, purveys a dual fantasy of hybridity/miscegenation, and the consumer participates in this fantasy through listening practices that are culturally bound to sexuality and desire for the other.

A genealogy for the discourse of hybridity can be traced through a radically transformed and rejiggered dream of hybridization from that envisioned in Darwin's theory of natural selection. Darwin privileged genetic inheritance as the means to species evolution, writing famously:

> Any change in the numerical proportions of some of the inhabitants, independently of the change of climate itself, would most seriously affect many of the others. If the country were open on its borders, new forms would certainly immigrate, and this also would seriously disturb the relations of some of the former inhabitants. . . . In such cases, every slight modification, which in the course of ages chanced to arise, and which in any way favoured the individuals of any of the species, better adapting them to their altered conditions, would tend to be preserved; and natural selection would thus have free scope for the work of improvement.[6]

While this emphasis on genetic inheritance may have at one point promoted what Simon Porzac has called Darwin's emphasis on "nature's queer heterosexuality," this conclusion is in stark contrast to what we popularly associate with natural selection, which Porzac goes on to explain, "appears as constant, regular, and progressive."[7] The Darwinism we're much more familiar with is that promoted by Richard Hofstadter, who according to Bowler is partially responsible for "the linking of biological and social progressionism . . . through *social Darwinism*" and its economics of laissez-faire individualism.[8] According to him, it was Hofstadter who initially highlighted Herbert Spencer's coinage, and Darwin's later adoption of the terminology "survival of the fittest," as a synonym for natural selection. While admitting that Darwin did accept Spencer's phrase, Bowler attempts to debunk the linking of natural selection with what he terms the "apologists of capitalism."[9]

Five years after the publication of *Origin of the Species*, in the Civil War's culminating year, came the (at the time) anonymously and deceptively published pamphlet *Miscegenation* (which was later attributed to David Goodman Croly). Adding to the distortion that culminated in the "non-Darwinian revolution," was this parodic manifesto which preyed on the racist anxieties boiling over on the subject of evolution and its implications for racial mixture. Signifying on commonly held white fears of the potential outcomes of abolition, Croly coined the term miscegenation, defining it as the blending of the various races of men and circulated the publication as an Abolitionist polemic in the hope of inciting a backlash against Abraham Lincoln. Croly writes:

> If any fact is well established in history, it is that the miscegenetic or mixed races are much superior, mentally, physically, and morally, to those pure or unmixed. Wherever on the earth's surface we find a community which has intermarried for generations, we also find evidences of decay both in the physical and mental powers. On the other hand, wherever, through conquest, colonization, or commerce, different nationalities are blended, a superior human product invariably results.[10]

Whether intentionally or not, Croly satirizes the logic of natural selection by imagining a postbellum America in which the racial differences that so rigidly distinguished free from unfree would result in what many whites inherently feared: miscegenation.[11]

Whether in biology, politics, or populist rhetoric, Darwinism came to signify both harmony and competition, employed as a "theory" to uphold seemingly any idea. According to economist Thomas C. Leonard, the haphazard application of the moniker "Darwinism" to radically opposing systems and ideologies was practiced in the establishment of the discipline of American economics as well. However, instead of interpreting early economic theories as Darwinist or even as social Darwinism, Leonard argues, we must understand this incipient economism through the pseudoscientific system of racial biology promoted by Darwin's cousin Francis Galton: eugenics. And, just as Shakespearean (or perhaps even Freudian) in its formation around a family drama, it was none other than David Goodman Croly's only son Herbert Croly who introduced eugenics theory into American economics theory.[12] It was the young Croly's particular emphasis on artificial rather than natural selection that resonated at that time. As Leonard writes:

> In his influential *The Promise of American Life*, Herbert Croly of the *New Republic* put his case for a vigorous national government in eugenic language, arguing that artificial selection, by which he meant state-guided reform, was superior to natural selection (read: laissez-faire). The state, said Croly (1909, 191), had a responsibility to "interfere on behalf of the

really fittest. . . . Darwinism calls fit those who have most successfully reproduced, an *ex post* judgment. Eugenicists, on the other hand, tended to regard fitness as a moral or racial attribute, something judged *ex ante*. The social control of human breeding, after all, could not succeed without a prior judgment as to who (that is, which groups) was biologically superior. . . . Where Darwinism saw fitness as the outcome of a selection process, eugenics made fitness the basis for initiating a selection process.[13]

With the burden of his patronym came the young Croly's responsibility to promote a postbellum antimiscegenation doctrine framed in economic theory, just as his father had done in the antebellum period through hoax (and with hindsight we can see that they both performed hocus pocus but simply chose different venues for this).

* * *

Darwin asserts that neither climate nor other physical conditions determine species diversity; rather, diversity is attributable to inherited qualities of difference. It is this most powerful, residual effect of Darwin's theories that has translated in a cosmopolitical and neoliberal context in the world music culture industry's promotion of adaptability through listening. Given the wider historical context of colonialism, industrialization, and capitalist expansion, the discourse of "survival of the fittest" has functioned as an ethos that metaphorically represents cultural progress within capitalism through the prism of species adaptability through biological reproduction.[14] The heterosexual imperative metaphorically masked through *laissez faire* economics, remains as a trace in the culture industry's deployment of adaptability through hybridity.[15] It is a history that informs the reproductivity of the hybrid process both in enabling the listener to become hybridized and by enabling the song to be a site in which component parts become hybridized in the mix. But the emphasis on "artificial selection," whether in the context of biological or economic eugenics, is in my estimation the critically important modern concept that has carried over into the logic informing the benefits of listening to hybrid world music. While the theory of "natural selection" underwent countless mutations in its trapeze act across two centuries, shedding perhaps some of its most radical potential along the way, it has endured as a motivating impetus behind the production and consumption of world music.

World music represents an aesthetic and technological enactment of domestication and husbandry—through the symbolics of both artificial and natural selection—applied to sound and the imaginary. The titillating and taboo fantasy of miscegenation—present, if even only as phylogenetic holdover—is sublimated through world music into the wish for hybridity, consumed in an effort to accomplish not only a pleasure rooted in desire for the other but ultimately in a narcissistic wish for fitness and adaptability of the self. Hybridity presents a rational destination for this drive, an opportunity for cathecting a desire that is considered abject and bad. Through hybridity, a non-Darwinian evolutionary model gets mobilized in the sublimation of this troublesome yearning.[16]

Kinship Records can be understood as a cultural production center that capitalizes on this yearning by enabling the listener to focus the drive on pleasure through listening. The world music consumer is sold on this form of listening as a productive exercise, an engagement with the other that is safe, hygienic, private, and within the comfort of one's own personal space. *New Yorker* music writer Sasha Frere-Jones's lament—that indie rock music has "lost its soul" because it lacks the signifiers of black sound that were once prevalent in rock music—is in fact a lament for the failure of indie rock's white men to properly desire the sounds of black men.[17] Just as miscegenation was identified as the desired object of rock music, there is a similar incitement for hybridity as the desired object of world music. Rock-n-roll's increasing obfuscation of black masculinity and men over the course of the twentieth century and the displacement of black performing men by white men performing blackness is matched in world music through what I argue below is the further manifestation of the feminization of listening, as not only a white feminization but also one that denies any space (symbolic or material) to black masculinity. In world music the ear is the privileged corporeal site for this hybrid evolutionary engagement with the other and figures as the invaginated sexual organ where this relationship is consummated.

Aural Incorporation and Invagination

In his essay "The Law of Genre," Derrida deconstructs genre/gender as inherent to taxonomic ordering, whether it be an ordering of a biological nature or an ordering of a literary type.[18] From this premise, Derrida develops what he calls "the law of the law of genre," which is the paradox at the heart of the law that simultaneously prohibits mixture while also depending on it for a generic distinction to be maintained (illustrated by the "hymen" or wedding ring of the matrimonial bond). Thus, the "law of the law of genre" is in fact a law of contamination and mixing, which (and this is the most critical aspect of this formulation for the purposes of this chapter) Derrida presents through the notion of "invagination," employing a feminized anatomical metaphor to represent this law:

> The law of the law of genre . . . is precisely a principle of contamination, a law of impurity, a parasitical economy. In the code of set theories, if I may use it at least figuratively, I would speak of a sort of participation without belonging—a taking part in without being part of, without having membership in a set. With the inevitable dividing of the trait that marks membership, the boundary of the set comes to form, by invagination, an internal pocket larger than the whole; and the outcome of this division and of this abounding remains as singular as it is limitless.[19]

Playing on this feminized anatomical representational schema for "the law of the law of genre," Derrida emphasizes the process of "the fold," which he argues is an essential component in the construction of boundaries and borderlands. Hence, the pure, structural taxonomic order that informed the non-Darwinian revolutionary logic of adaptability and blending through natural selection is for Derrida rooted in a structural order always already contaminated. Natural selection is thus a symbolic reordering rather than a biological one. And we must pay heed to Derrida's word choice here as no mere accident or pseudofeminist aping but one that keenly picks up on the feminization of the process he describes. It is precisely this feminization that genders modernity's ear.

In a lecture delivered at the University of Montreal and later published and translated as *The Ear of the Other* Derrida relates the ear through the same metaphor of the fold, emphasizing the ear's universality across bodies, "You must pay heed to the fact that the *omphalos* that Nietzsche compels you to envision resembles both an ear and a mouth. It has the invaginated folds and the involuted orificiality of both."[20] Noting the homophonic similarity between *auto* and *oto*, he contends that hearing is the key process in autobiographical discourse and the site at which the signature is made.[21] Just as the recipient of a check must endorse it with a signature in order to redeem its value, he explains, it is through the addressee's ears that meaning is made; it is, as Derrida asserts, "the ear of the other that signs."[22] It is this "ear-organ" that perceives difference and mutually constitutes the self in relation to this difference. Through a vaginal metaphor Derrida theorizes the function of the ear as that organ which receives the speaking subject's own utterances as speech, pointing out, "The ear is not only an auditory organ; it is also a visible organ of the body."[23] The play on the homophone *oto*—meaning to hear—used in place of the *auto*—meaning self—transforms autobiography to *oto*-biography, thus establishing the significance of "the ear of the other" in the constitution of the speaker's/writer's subjectivity as well as the listener's.[24] Derrida recognizes the speaker, performer, singer, and writer's subjectivity as an action performed through hearing. Signature takes place when the *ear of the other* perceives the address; this functions to constitute the addressor.[25] This is the critical function of modernity's ear: The listener determines the subjectivity of the sounds heard, including race and gender. But additionally, as I have already illustrated, there is an erotic aspect to this aurality. If we consider that the listening subject is driven by a desire for pleasure-in-listening, then in fact both the listener and performer are constituted as sexual subjects through listening. *Oto*-erotic attempts to account for this.

The "*oto*-erotic" combines Derrida's *oto*-biography with Freud's "autoerotism." For Freud, the autoerotic moment in psychosocial development introduces fantasy. Laplanche and Pontalis define Freud's concept of autoerotism as "that moment—recurring constantly rather than fixed at a certain point in development—when sexuality draws away from its natural object, finds itself delivered over to phantasy and in this very process is constituted *qua* sexuality."[26] Transposing the logic of autoerotism onto a concept that centers the ear dislodges sexuality from its reified association with genitality while also destabilizing the stereotypic association between visuality and subject formation, thus revealing modernity's ear to be an invaginated organ with the power to transform the listening subject. *Oto*-erotic pleasure is both derived from the copresence of a foregrounded hybridity and its shadow, miscegenation. It is precisely in the realm of fantasy where we shift (perhaps imperceptibly) from the literal function of genetic mixing to the symbolics of musical hybridization occurring in the aural imaginary. While dislodging sexuality from genitality, holding onto the notion of the ear as an "invaginated" organ makes clear how it has contributed to and been produced through the epistemology that structures the feminization of listening.

Oto-Erotic Sex Reassignment

Kinship is cognizant of the ear's power to sign. Much of the text that frames the music enlists the active listening capacity of the consumer's ear as the site of signification for not only racial difference but also gendered difference. The gendering and sexualizing of Brazilian Kinship artist Djavan da Silva is a case in point. The biography that frames his album prepares the listener to *hear* da Silva's gender as racialized feminine. Consider the following biographical text written for da Silva's album *Essential*:

> Djavan's softly sensual vocals are often reminiscent of Caetano Veloso, and his guitar playing hints at jazz and chamber music, but with a lyrical elegance that is pure Brazil. The first three tracks, all Djavan originals, are as compelling an introduction as any singer has had since Cesaria Evora made her international debut. "Resposta" is just Djavan, his silken vocals and fingerpicked guitar creating a lovely, intimate song that shows just how accurate his instincts are: the noted arranger leaves this one alone but he pulls out the stops on the next track. "da Felicidade" begins with echoes of Brazil's samba percussion; then the drummer settles into a steady, gentle groove, over which float Djavan's vocals and guitar. The song evokes soft winds and languorous tropical nights. Not surprisingly, *Essential* is deeply rooted in bossa nova. Djavan also uses jazz to good effect on *Essential*. His take on the standard "We Called It A Day" draws on the sounds of late 1950s "cool" jazz, with what is essentially a lounge-jazz piano trio accompanying Djavan's guitar and English vocals. And the sultry "Febre," with its restrained trumpet and piano intro, is a slow jazz ballad. Djavan's "Teu Sorriso" is a beautifully composed and produced song that begins and ends with the Brazilian berimbau, an African-derived instrument. Djavan adds drums and his guitar, uses some unexpected harmonic twists and subtle tape effects, and sets it all to a gently rocking

rhythm. The whole arrangement shows impeccable taste, a keen sense of what's going on elsewhere in the musical world, and a quintessentially Brazilian approach.[27]

The text describes da Silva as "soft," "sensual," "elegant," and "quintessentially Brazilian," evoking that nostalgic moment in popular sixties-era jazz when a tame Brazil was presented to Western audiences by A&M mogul Herb Alpert; when the United States heard as soundtrack to South American neoliberalism a nonthreatening, feminized Brazilian *bossa nova*.[28] The framing of this album feminizes da Silva by purging the racial noise of black masculinity and emphasizing instead (just as in the listening salon dialogue I discuss below) Brazilian music as the paradigmatic hybridized form.

In response to a question posed about the gender of the autobiographical "I," Derrida describes the ear's key role in subjective signification:[29] "The sex of the addresser awaits its determination by or from the other." He writes, "It is the other who will perhaps decide who I am—man or woman. Nor is this decided once and for all. It may go one way one time and another way another time."[30] It is the listening subject who determines the gender of the speaker, writer, or performer. This gendering is linked to an economy of pleasure that enables the listener to play with the sounds in the music in an *oto-erotic* performance that cathects pleasure in the ear. Through this process we can better understand the desire of the listening subject than we can the intentions of the performer, as it is within this listening subject that signification happens. The ear is an orifice, an opening that is common to all bodies, regardless of sex. When put to work in the world music industry, this orifice functions as a sex organ and operates under gendered rules of hearing. Furthermore, Derrida's gesture helps to reframe listening as a performative act; like speech acts that enact what they describe, listening functions performatively to enact into incorporeal materialism what it imagines aurally.[31]

Noise/Sound/Music

You may think you're afraid of African music. . . . It may sound weird to you if all you listen to is John Cougar Mellencamp and U-2. But you may be surprised when you actu-

ally hear it that it shares a lot of things with the music that
you already like. And if you come to it with somewhat of an
open mind, you're probably going to be moved by it.[32]
—Jon Cohen, president, Kinship Records

Music has long been a tool in the Western civilizational project and
musical notation and recording have been employed to classify and hierarchically order subjects and the sonic world at large.[33] This science of
music has historically been bound to a legacy of the rational use of sounds
and the reduction of these sounds to harmonics and scale. According to
Jacques Attali, this legacy has confused music with pure syntax.[34] But,
Attali urges us, music is not mere syntax or simply science; it is "science,
message, and time—music is all of that simultaneously."[35] Furthermore,
music is rooted in a "comprehensive conception of knowledge about the
body, in a pursuit of exorcism through noise and dance."[36] As Jon Cohen
notes in the epigraph above, Kinship Records is in the business of transforming that which "sound[s] weird"—thus read as noise—into music
that consumers can be "moved by." If, for Attali, noise is the *a priori* state
of sonic vibrations and sound represents the cultural codes imposed
upon noise, noise is the site of nature or what we have otherwise learned
through enlightenment philosophy to read as the realm of primitivity.
Thus, we can read Attali's theory of noise as in fact a theory of race, which
I will amend as *racial noise*.[37] A theory of racial noise allows us to better discern how the prohibition of or desire for the mixing of sound is
only logical based on an epistemology of racial mixing. What happens
to racial noise and disorder in the process of sonic blending? Does aural
intelligibility also denote racial and gendered intelligibility? If, as Attali
argues, sounds and their arrangements fashion society and its notions of
power, can we read power through the racial economy of sound?

Music, sound, and noise are categories that the listener distinguishes
through her ability to interpret aural stimuli as bounded to a structure
determined to be "musical." Alice Fletcher famously commented on the
unbearable noises she heard coming from Native Americans until she
herself performed the work of translating them through *modernity's ear*,
by recording them, transcribing them, and thus transforming noise into
music.[38] In *Noise*, Attali elaborates on the distinctions between noise
and sound, and their capacities to enunciate power, writing:

More than colors and forms, it is sounds and their arrangements that fashion societies. With noise is born disorder and its opposite: the world. With music is born power and its opposite: subversion. In noise can be read the codes of life, the relations among men. Clamor, Melody, Dissonance, Harmony; when it is fashioned by a man with specific tools, when it invades man's time, when it becomes sound, noise is the source of purpose and power, of the dream—Music.[39]

For Attali, the arrangement of noise into an ordered taxonomy of sounds—as either melodic, phonetic, dissonant, harmonic, or clamorous—is simultaneously the arrangement of a society and its organization of power. These are culturally determined distinctions, bound to other kinds of intelligibilities.

As the prediscursive, prelinguistic realm, noise was for Attali the way to sonically imagine a nonideological political liberation in 1977 France.[40] Building on Attali, I contend that the distinction between noise, sound, and music requires the imposition of discourse as well as the construction of cultural intelligibilities (much like the process I describe in chapter 1 as "phonographic subjectivation"). Hybrid world music incorporates sounds that are initially read as racial noise followed by a translational and transitional shift to an intelligible zone of music (through framing devices like packaging or by mixing them with more legible, Western sounds). Titillation and pleasure results from flirtation with the danger zone of racial noise. The designation of sonic information as sound rather than noise requires a symbolic resignification either through interpretation or hybridization and the listener must be familiarized with the aesthetic and cultural systems that order those sounds into music. The world music culture industry understands sonic information discursively constructed as racial noise to be aurally experienced as discomfort and unpleasure. The sonic hybridity employed by Kinship Records attempts to weave together noise, sound, and music to achieve a sonic experience that oscillates between the familiar and the unfamiliar, the hybrid and miscegenation, the here and the there. In some cases, as in the following transcript of a dialogue at a world music listening salon in which I participated in 2010, the pleasure-in-listening hinges on the understanding of the literal hybridity of the musical producers.

DAVID PHILIPS (HOST): . . . These Brazilianists, they tried to make a racial democracy. They just said, sleep with everybody. The native Brazilians, the Africans, the Whites, everybody slept with everybody. So you see there's amazing mixtures there. There still is a class society there but it's very different than Peru or Ecuador or Chile. Very, very different. Much more mixed. And Baden Powell is that way. . . . The music, I mean, I say that it's lyrical but it's also incredibly sophisticated. Really sophisticated. Just complex. Just this amazing amalgam of classical, of the best jazz, the best everything. It's got it all.

In his introduction to the music of Baden Powell, Philips makes literal the simile I draw between sonic and racial mixing. Brazil's cultural exceptionalism (opposed here to Peru, Ecuador, and Chile) is the result of a miscegenation (perhaps by virtue of Brazil's dominance in the slave trade) that makes Brazilian world music possible. This is a music that unites "the best of everything" since Brazilian racial mixing, as the following continuation of the dialogue suggests, mixes the best of everything too:

DAVID PHILIPS: Here is a song, this is from an album that won a Grammy. Happy to see it even though Caetano Veloso has an ego the size of a battleship.
[laughter from group]
P: He makes really, really great music. And the thing that I like about this song is you sort of hear the fusion of the European, almost the classical sensibility, with the African drumming. It's got both the kind of refinement and complexity of classical with the power, the sort of primal libido power of the African drums.
[WOMAN'S VOICE]: How old is he now?
P: Caetano?
[SAME WOMAN]: Mmm hmm.
P: Caetano was pushing 70. Although he's this gorgeous mixture of Portuguese, African, and native Brazilian. Unlike the other countries in South America, Brazil, in spite of being a racial democracy, it's still a very class-oriented society. But everybody slept with everybody so you can get kids with like Afro-type hair and . . .
[WOMAN'S VOICE]: . . . And green eyes.
P: And green eyes and these incredible mixtures.

[SAME WOMAN]: And café au lait skin. [audibly gulps and laughs]
P: And café au lait skin. You see some beautiful, beautiful children.
  Beautiful people. Oh my god.

Brazilian musical exceptionalism, as exemplified by Caetano Veloso, is only possible because of the decidedly good form of mixing that has resulted in "Beautiful people. Oh my god," who also make beautiful music. But in a comment made by one salon participant, there also emerges a self-consciousness about the abject, the ugly produced as the constitutive outside this emphasis on the beautiful:

[MAN'S VOICE]:But the light-skinned ones are still the high caste ones.
P: [Hesitantly] Yeah, yeah. The darker the skin, the worse off you are.
[SAME MAN]: That's true around the world.[41]

As this dialogue makes blatantly clear, there is a sexual logic to sonic mixing and hybrid music production anxious about how best to achieve "the best of everything" blend that yields hybridity. This is an anxiousness regarding the darker, lower-caste outcomes, the excesses of racial noise in miscegenated music.

As I discuss in chapter 1, the world music culture industry has from its incipient, comparative musicology beginnings been concerned with transforming noise to sound and then to music. Here we can see how this transformation takes place through the ubiquitous concept of hybridity, and the sexual history from which it was born. Hybrid music, presented here as that musical amalgamation that contains "the best of everything," is also conflated with the bodies born from a history of colonialism, slavery, and miscegenation. This conflation between hybridized bodies and hybridized music is not unique to the dialogue at the listening salon but is instead a paradigmatic logic inherent to the WMCI. So while musical hybridity is a symbolic form of artificial selection that enables the listener to cultivate a more adaptive self, as evidenced here, it is structured through a quasi theory of natural selection routed through a titillating anxiety about miscegenation.

Cesar Braga-Pinto has written about Brazilian vocalist Caetano Veloso, to whom da Silva is often compared, stating: "For Caetano, identity, like pleasure, is never *self-identical*, but is an interminable relationship

with the other's desire."[42] Although Braga-Pinto's analysis is focused on
Veloso's performance personae, his emphasis on "the other's desire" is
nevertheless apropos in the U.S. context, where Veloso has had great
success and is probably one of the most popular Brazilian musicians.
Veloso's identity play and gender ambiguity that emerge from what
Braga-Pinto refers to as a "tradition of transgendered voices in Brazilian popular music," is not as agentially open-ended among U.S. listeners as in the cases that he examines, however.[43] Veloso's popularity in
the United States is framed through the logic referenced in the listening
salon dialogue, hinged as it is there on the conflation between his body,
his virtuosity, and his voice as exemplary of "the very best of everything"
that results from the right hybrid outcomes. This forecloses the kind of
play and agency Braga-Pinto claims for Veloso as a figure in Brazil. For,
as he concludes of Veloso's personae, "The performance of a displaced
sexual identity may enable new interpretations or the reappropriation of
hegemonic identity categories. . . . The 'translatability' of gender performances may thus become the site of political struggle." It is precisely this
"translatability" that is at issue in the world music economy.[44]

To what degree the sonic gender play of a figure like Veloso or da
Silva has enabled an overt politicization of gender in sound in the United
States is unclear. Nevertheless, as the biography to da Silva's album *Essential* (quoted above) illustrates, Kinship has preemptively assigned a
feminized gender to da Silva's voice, which imposes an overdetermined
structure of relation between the listener and da Silva. This structuring
forecloses the multitude of gender interpretations perhaps available to
Veloso's Brazilian audiences given his long career there, with its palimpsestic layering of gender performances and within his musical oeuvre.
Instead, Kinship's framing of da Silva polices his gender, forcing him into
a feminized role that is the most hegemonic position for such a figure in
this genre. This policing is in keeping not only with the historical practice
of miscegenation as economic mode of production that excludes black
men from the equation but also with the association of racial noise with
black masculinity. The only way that American audiences could pleasur-
ably listen to Veloso or da Silva, the label's economic logic assumes, was
in this emasculated, feminized, and hence deracinated, form.

World music promotes hybridity in the context of the sonic mix but
hybridity is also the ontological condition for sale. The company name

signals this, promoting kin connections between cultures across difference. But what does it mean to claim kinship through hybridity, and how does the figure of the musical *other* function in particular ways to form incestuous yearnings within these family ties? In order to answer these questions, I explore the *other* as gendered female in the fantasy of hybridity, examining how this fantasy replicates a heteronormativity that unites seemingly disparate sonic signifiers in a symbolic conceptual union. As I discussed in chapter 2, the WMCI resignifies the ear as invaginated organ for the purposes of incorporating the aural other. Hybridization-through-listening is one of the aims of this incorporation. The culture industry exploits the ear-as-invaginated-organ through production practices that bring the aural other into the listening self for greater adaptability in a rapidly changing world.

Birthing Hybridity: The Gendered Division of Labor

With an Englishman's underbite, Ibiza-all-night-clubbing sunglasses shading his eyes, and head propped on a sporty black warm-up jacket zipped tightly around his neck, Robert Royhill's profile adorns the cover of his 2003 release *In-Between*. His likeness has been graphically manipulated using digital imaging effect processors that create the impression of acidic, digital decay around the right hand side of the photograph, giving it a pixilated look. Place this package within the context of the first track and one is left with the sense of a striking contrast.

A melancholy cello sobs as a berimbau taps in syncopated time with hand claps. Faint critter sounds can be heard in the background. Hand percussion rises on the right side of the stereo spread, while a loon hoot trembles on the left. Two minutes into the song Khoi San singer !Ngibu makes himself known and wails words that have been phased in order to fit the tempo through Royhill's production work. !Ngibu sings slightly ahead of the rhythm, resulting in the sense that his song contains a message more pertinent than the music. Epic synthesizer swells follow suit, echoing !Ngibu's looping vocal lines. Then a drum kit joins the sonic cast of characters, followed by a faint flute-like setting on the synthesizer, which eventually rises above !Ngibu in volume. Then slowly the instruments fall away just as they came in. The song ends with a soliloquy by !Ngibu accompanied only by the hand claps and berimbau.

While the music plays, I read the following biographical text that curates my listening experience to track one:

> The vocals on the track "Looking Back" are sung by !Ngibu, an 80 year old (he thinks!) Bushman from the Kalahari, Namibia. The Bushmen or 'Khoi-San' are, like most ancient tribal peoples, under severe threat of extinction due to removal of land and hunting rights, racial prejudice, and what we in the modern world might call progress. I was fortunate enough to be one of a number of musicians/producers invited to write a track using and interpreting the Bushmen's songs as source material for an album aimed at raising money and awareness of the Bushmen's plight, entitled "SanEscapes." It was a great privilege and a very moving experience to actually meet !Ngibu and other members of his family when they came to London in May 2002 to perform what are not only centuries old songs, but also their living history. Ironically, in order to survive and retain their 20,000 year old culture, the Bushmen have been forced to join the modern world to draw attention to their plight. On "Looking Back" I have tried to express this by gradually bringing more modern instruments and Western rhythms into the track as it builds—perhaps it should have been called "Looking Forward!" We should all look forward and hope that the Khoi-San of the Kalahari, who are an integral part of the origins of our own human ancestry, survive. If we lose the Khoi-San, we will surely be losing a large part of ourselves. For more information about the Bushmen and how to help them please contact WIMSA at www.san.org.za.[45]

In-Between, as framed by packaging and artwork that employ standard visual signifiers from the dance/DJ/electronica genre (commonly featuring a photograph of the DJ/producer as the focal point in the cover art), presents itself as electronic music. But the sounds of the first track leave the listener wondering if s/he is indeed listening to music produced by the man represented on the cover. This tension is quelled as the listener eases into the second track, a cover of Peter Gabriel's "Games without Frontiers," which is drenched in synthetic production and digitized sonic accessories. And while the song contains obviously non-Western sounds like the tabla drums, the density of digital manipulation overwhelms those elements. *In-Between* paradigmatically represents the hybrid formula described above, especially as it exploits the other's voice and temporality as feminized. Royhill—represented through technovisual album art, sole-producer credit, and, along with Kinship, copyright partner—is the undeniable signifier of modernity performing a salvage recording for the new millennium. !Ngibu, the vocalist on the first track, who is presented as the native other at risk of extinction, is the authentic force of "history" that brings value to the song. The text describes the ironic "plight" of the Bushmen as both produced and potentially spared by modernization. Royhill, figured as the benevolent first world artist who has mobilized his power to bring attention to this "cultural extinction," self-reflexively positions himself as the modern producer who propels the song, "Looking Back," forward, passing !Ngibu's voice through modernity's ear by way of recording and his sound production work (much like the work of early comparative musicologists I discussed in chapter 1).

This song, and its representation through textual framing, is emblematic of the hybrid process in which feminized sound (indigenous, at risk of extinction, geriatric, timeless, situated within the bleak and dusty acoustics of the "bush") is the source of authenticity and the site of germination for the seed of modernity (provided by Royhill's production work). In Royhill's own language, his technological production enables "Looking Back" to look forward as the song stages hybrid conception. Royhill's purportedly altruistic act involves implanting the seed of modernity within !Ngibu's voice, in an effort to help the Bushmen "survive" in a process of artificial selection. The ears of the listener determine the success of this union. The intercultural tryst is a success if it brings pleasure and if it is intelligible as a hybrid union.

Within the logic of modernity, the modern, with its authority and hegemonic power, is gendered masculine. Modernity is signified through masculine tropes of technology and technical mastery subtly introduced as sonic foundations, while tradition is signified through feminine tropes placed in the sonic foreground to arouse a sense of the authenticity communicated by timeless tradition. Feminized signifiers like the voice and the masculine "production values" come together in music as meaningful through the mobilization of the trope of heterosexual conception—a symbolic grafting of the logic of reproduction and the invagination of the ear. Decoupled from a material body that can provide visible evidence for sex/gender, world music's sounds and voices are gendered within the listener's ear.

There is a gendered division of labor that structures the *oto*-eroticism of hybridity in world music. The nonthreatening, feminized sounds of the other are only incorporable into the hybrid formula when they are no longer read as racial noise. So figures like da Silva or !Ngibu, neutered of the virile racialized masculinity that could pose an offensive threat to the listener, are heard as producing a feminized sound that is put to women's work. These feminized sounds perform gendered labor in the listener's ear—the invaginated site of reproductivity—entering and producing pleasure in the ear of the hearing subject that leads to the oto-erotics of this encounter. Through labor, these feminized sounds give birth to hybrid sonorous offspring. It is the feminized voice combined with the masculine "modern production values" that conceive of new *hybrid* sounds. This gendered division is further manifested through the trope of labor as childbirth in that hybridity is born from the presence of a feminized sound impregnated by the more subliminal, male-gendered production values that fall to the background. The feminized sound bears the obvious mark of alterity, while the masculine "production values" are less audibly marked in the mix. The feminized sound does not have to be generated from a female body, but in the context of the hybrid union it is necessarily gendered female vis-à-vis its relational position to the aural signifiers of modernity. Aural mixing becomes legible as hybridity through this particular formula; deviation from this rule signals the abject zones of miscegenation, unintelligibility, unpleasure, and the designation of racial noise.[46]

Hybridity tames the unpredictability out of racialized noise, purging the excesses of sonic racialized masculinity. As a more pleasurable, marketable form for racial noise, hybridity is available for incorporation by and hence contributes to the hybridization of the listener. And certainly, there are examples within the Kinship catalog in which hybridity is eschewed for an exclusively traditional or modern designation. In these cases, this gendered division of labor is not applicable; authenticity is established in other ways. But in order to be recognized as a legitimate child of this intercultural sonic union, a song's maternity must be read as other and its paternity read as modern. It is specifically albums that claim to mix (seemingly) disparate concepts (West African + Scandinavian; Traditional + Modern; East + West) that this tension comes into play ("South-South" hybrid unions in contemporary popular American world music are rare). A song's masculine, technological production becomes the privileged signifier of modernity and the feminized, racialized other functions as the signifier of authenticity. This formula reveals that Kinship Records and, I would argue, the world music genre in general, operate under a musical kinship model that privileges patrilineal descent as a means of access to various kinds of mobility (market, stylistic, social, artistic) and relies on matrilineal descent as the link to authenticity and the social cachet of alterity, revealing that musical hybridity has been musical miscegenation all along. All in all, while this might seem at first to queer normative systems of social and symbolic reproductivity, I argue that it in fact reifies hegemonic heteronormativity by emphasizing the reproduction of the listening self against the third world, aural other, a formula that we have grown accustomed to since the invention of the phonograph.

Conclusion

The designation of the ear as the organ that signs the other's difference refigures human anatomy and endows the ear with the power to *produce* subjects. In addition to its determination as a site for the production of pleasure, the ear can be imagined as a kind of sex organ. If it is imbued with that status, then the ear is also an organ of *reproduction*: invaginated, the ear becomes a symbolically *reproductive* site for hybridization. Although sounds penetrate the orifice of the ear in much the same way penises have been mythologized as objects that penetrate passive receptacles, the ear as a hearing organ is not a passive vessel; listening is how signification happens, thereby endowing the ear with the capacity to be penetrated with agency. The ear is the agent of meaning in this formulation, where the seed of hybridity is sown. Although it is an orifice, it is an orifice with the power to mean, which deeply complicates a simple reading of the ear as a passive receptacle. In a biopolitical optimization that imagines that, in Darwin's words, hybridization can "better [adapt] them to their altered conditions . . . for the work of improvement," hybridization through listening is a path to greater adaptability in a multicultural world.

The world/electronica genre brands itself through musical hybridization and an ethos of intercultural collaboration. This has been the industry's neoliberal response to critiques of world music posed throughout the 1980s and 1990s, when world music was seen primarily to appropriate and exploit third- and fourth-world musicians and musics. If in this earlier period the industry disavowed the power differential between the first-world star and the indigenous artists hired as session musicians (whether or not they were integral to the production, as composers of the music), this difference is now embraced. The WMCI's promotion of intercultural collaboration overtly names cultural differences between collaborators as inherent to the sonic beauty that results from their work. Furthermore, the popular musical circuits of the black Atlantic have produced global stars who are no longer imagined to make traditional musics but instead make hybridized African diasporic forms. As Timothy Taylor has put it, "World musicians may not be expected to be authentic anymore in the sense of being untouched by the sounds of the West; now it is their very hybridity that allows them to be constructed as authentic."[47]

Hybridity is a process that Kinship Records sells. This process, in part, happens in the listener's ear and figures as a transformative engagement with the other's sounds, culture, and voice, making the other knowable to the listener in a safe and controlled manner. Hybridity, the musical model and biological trope on which Kinship Records has proliferated, is premised upon the intelligibility of imported sounds and a heterosexual union between Western/Modern sounds and Non-Western/Traditional music that mobilizes a sexualized fantasy that desires hybridity and fetishizes miscegenation. Aural pleasure is what's for sale and the consumer is promised an experience of pleasure that flirts with the other. Bringing the other into the listener to enact the *oto*-erotic performatively constitutes them both.

Music and sound figure as destinations for desire. This process works to materialize difference through the production and consumption of sound and music. This represents a site for the production of alterity that is distinct from the scopophilic regime of the fetish, which has historically and analytically functioned as a focal point in the materialization of difference through the privileging of *visible evidence*. Many scholars have identified this epistemology of vision as the means through which difference has historically been constructed as corporeal, biological, and ontological. Contrastively at Kinship Records, music and sound work to figure difference as a designation determined in the *ear of the other* and mobilize difference within an aural economy. Judith Butler has argued that "sex" is a designation carefully produced by regulatory regimes that "work in a performative fashion" to materialize bodies, and in particular their sex.[48] As the case of Kinship Records exemplifies, it is the performative and phenomenological process of musical hybridization that materializes bodies in world music. The "ear of the other" that hears alterity is the sex organ that *signs* the other into intelligibility. In chapter 5 I conclude by an extended reflection on the idea of the fetish as it pertains to commodity fetishism as well as the psychoanalytic fetish object in order to determine whether or not it continues to motivate desire. I inquire into the material productivity of the *oto*-erotic by exploring the performativity of fantasy in the WMCI.

The World Music Culture of Incorporation

"Paul"

"Ummm . . . uhhhhh. . . ." I project myself into the future by ten years, trying to imagine the regret I will experience when looking back on this day, on this album cover. Something in my gut tells me "Don't do it"; my mouth reluctantly says, "OK." This is the first project on which Paul has been granted full control as "Creative Director." He has been the in-house graphic designer at Kinship Records for over six years working under the thumb of micromanager and label CEO Jamie Alexander. He hopes to be spared in this project the tug-of-war that ensues between them around the artwork and layout of every other CD. Going to Jamie with the news that he chose a flaky model who fell through at the last minute would totally undermine Paul's authority and surely make this the last time Jamie concedes creative control. Whether or not he likes or trusts me, Paul thinks fast and approaches me as the only woman in the office who fits the general description of what he's in search of for this album cover: light brown, big hair, racially ambiguous.

"Sure," I say as he whisks me away to the conference room-cum-photography studio. Paul has rented a vintage 1940s ribbon microphone and studio lighting for far more money than he intends to pay me (is he going to pay me? I wonder to myself . . .). With the simple placement of the signature microphone and the right lighting, he has transformed the fluorescent-lighted white box into a stage where the likes of Billie, Ella, or Patsy may have performed. I am wearing casual work attire, hardly a "look" that complements the glamour the microphone evokes. I reveal my self-consciousness to Paul, who says, "Don't worry; I'll Photoshop your shirt out of the picture." I awkwardly proceed to the microphone half conscious of the fact that I am being photographed.

The shoot goes on for about an hour, rather short for an image that will grace an album cover forever. But Paul's digital camera allows him to review all the images and reproduce shots if he feels I'm not projecting the exact "look" that he wants. How does he want me to look, I ask him? "I'm going for that sexy, sultry, exotic thing and you're perfect." The tables have turned. I, the ethnographer, am the object.[1] This chapter focuses on the formation of the libidinal economy and its attendant sensual and somatic taxonomies in order to map this key formation marrying the twentieth-century ascendancy of the world music culture industry with modernity.[2]

While exiled in Los Angeles in 1944, Horkheimer and Adorno claimed, "The whole world is passed through the filter of the culture industry."[3] This declaration foreshadowed that a scholar of the culture industry would herself be made to pass through its filter, if she were to be granted any access to it whatsoever. When I initially embarked on an ethnographic study of the world music culture industry, I did not imagine that by its culmination my own image would constitute one of the representations I was to study. In an uncanny and unintended repetition of "Blackfoot Listening," an image of half my face with photoshopped nose ring, lips parted, appearing to sing into a ribbon microphone covers the 2003 Kinship Records album *Torch Songs*. On the one hand, the anthropological protocol of reciprocity would necessitate this as my burden of ethical responsibility; giving over my likeness and everything it signifies to the record company for profit, a *quid pro quo* for its willingness to have me around, for giving me access to what has grown into the content of this book. On the other hand, one could read this as exemplary of the inertia of the culture industry, of my having to succumb to being "passed through the filter of the culture industry" by simply standing too close to it, exemplifying my own passage through modernity's ear.[4]

I have argued throughout *Modernity's Ear* that the world music culture industry encompasses not only cultural producers, brokers, record companies, and media distributors but has indeed always included figures like me, scholars of music interpellated as cultural producers, brokers, record company employees, or just simply entrepreneurs of music. Adorno and Horkheimer diagnosed it as such in 1944. In chapter 1 I focused on the female comparative musicologists or "songcatchers" who, after being elbowed out of the academy by misogynist male colleagues, literally capitalized on the "feminization of listening" that was taking place as the phonograph slowly replaced the piano in the bourgeois home and recordings were marketed to the woman of the house, under-stood as catering to her tastes. In some ways, this is what Horkheimer and Adorno's "culture industry" attempts to theorize: the "dumbing down" of music for the feminized masses.

Theodor Adorno and Max Horkheimer coined the term "culture in-dustry" to describe a logic organized around the consumption of cul-tural objects. In his introduction to the Adorno anthology *The Culture Industry*, editor J. M. Bernstein defines this term in the following way: "The culture industry, which involves the production of works for re-production and mass consumption, thereby organizing 'free' time, the remnant domain of freedom under capital in accordance with the same principles of exchange and equivalence that reign in the sphere of pro-duction outside leisure, presents culture as the realization of the right of all to the gratification of desire."[5] The industrial metaphor was apt, given the war economy context of its coinage, one that called upon all citizen subjects to support the effort through labor, consumption, conservation, and domestic (re)production. It signifies a Fordist model of standard-ized mass production. This is decidedly less applicable today, especially for world music production that prospers through the differentiation of the laborer and the listener. Furthermore, sound production is an entirely different matter now than during World War II, with hardware in decline and the digital on the rise. While I have utilized Adorno's concept to represent the context for my research, calling it the world music culture industry in the previous chapters, I want to shift now to an elaboration on that concept, one that can more adequately represent the contemporary circumstances for world music production and con-sumption, defining it instead as the world music culture of incorpora-tion (WMCI).

Sound's materiality is in waveform. Sound takes material form in vibrations of air that move through space and time, reverberating off of and resonating in various other materials, including the bodies that hear it. Sound's ephemerality was always slipping through the fingers of capitalism, until the invention of the phonograph. This device de-termined the course of the music industry and sound's materiality as concretized through proprietary hardware: the wax cylinder, the acetate disc, the shellac LP, the vinyl LP, the reel-to-reel, the 8-track, the cas-sette, the compact disc. These media formats represent the technological advances of their period and reify through commodity fetishism the tactile and embodied relationship listeners have with sound as dictated by these formats and the hardware needed for playback. As we have moved through the twentieth into the twenty-first century, the ephemerality of sound's form has slowly been "liberated" from the medium, leaving us at the current stage of the MP3 and musical streaming formats that require very little by way of hardware.[6]

Sound's form is a hermeneutical tool; a wavy and reverberant materiality, it reflects, is productive of, and also engenders through resonance. I examine the pleasure-in-listening generated in the world music listening event as yielding a form of materialization of the performing cultured/ raced/ gendered/ sexualized/ geographically located body on the one hand, in chapters 1, 2, and 4, as a process of signification of the aural other and on the other hand, a process of *signifiance*, or loss of the self through fantasy in chapter 3. In every case throughout this book, I examine listening as a performative act that sets into motion a symbolic productivity through which pleasure-in-listening is sought in the aural imaginary. The other is made present in the listener's aural imaginary through a fantasy structure in which its raced/sexed body is coconstituted against that of the listening body. The pleasure-in-listening results from this coconstituted formation of the listening body structured against a fantasy performing one. The performative act of the listening event yields a virtual encounter between the listener and the imagined aural other.

This leads me to ultimately ask, is resonance the libidinization of waveform?[7] Bodies become resonant because of the performative productivity of both listening and fantasy. While I have argued in *Modernity's Ear* for aurality as a theory of the performativity of listening I conclude here by combining that idea with a discussion of the performativity of fantasy and the material productivity of the aural imaginary. My thinking emerges organically from the tradition that forms the prehistory to this project: Horkheimer and Adorno's theories of the culture industry. This idea challenged a fundamental dualism—the binary opposition between scientific "truth" and art as "illusion" characteristic of bourgeois thought since the seventeenth century.[8] What makes the culture of incorporation different from the culture industry as Horkheimer and Adorno theorized it? The acceleration of dialectical materialism has resulted in the virtual somatization of race, gender, and sexuality through incorporation.[9] There has been an ironic absorption of feminist political desire into the mechanics of this industry that has coincided with its deindustrialization. And as important as female anatomy has been to the feminist political imaginary and to feminist theory, so has the symbolics of female anatomy been to the culture of incorporation. Furthermore, there has been a shift of burden of labor onto and into the listener, thus complicating the schema of the commodity chain that imagined aesthetic objects being produced in discrete locations and then distributed in this form to different locations. Instead, as I have shown throughout *Modernity's Ear*, the listener's ear, her aurality is a critical site of production for the WMCI.

Aural incorporation is a performative process that materializes a palpable, somatic pleasure in a listening body. It is aural in my case study because of the emphasis placed by the record company on the listening subject and the agency bestowed upon the ear. And this aurality works through the logic of invagination, thus reifying the ear, much as the vagina is reified.[10] Throughout this book I have both held on to the long view of the process of cultural industrialization, a process that has transformed not only our sensibilities but also our bodies and embodiments, while also holding on to the aesthetic as a critically important aspect of materialism. And not only has the aesthetic been a critical site for the political but it was always with the ambivalent understanding that the aesthetic was not only commodified but fetishized. Susan Buck-Morss writes that for Benjamin, the reproduction of a work of art "emancipates the work of art from its parasitical dependency on ritual. . . . Instead of ritual, it begins to be based on another practice: politics."[11] According to Buck-Morss, Benjamin argued that the liquidation of art was prophetic, and "programmatic of the future, in that its collectivist production process transcended the division of labor between artist and technician, brainworker and handworker."[12] And in this prophetic declaration Benjamin anticipated the transformation of the business model that I chronicle in *Modernity's Ear*: the listener's ear has become the site for the production of the commodity—pleasure—thus transcending the limited definition of productivity taking place in a site of production that precedes and is discrete from the site of reception. This prophecy is further reiterated in Benjamin's claim: "During long periods of history, the mode of human sense perception changes with humanity's entire mode of existence. The manner in which human sense perception is organized, the medium in which it is accomplished, is determined not only by nature but by historical circumstances as well."[13]

The historical circumstances to which Benjamin gestures represent a shift in consciousness. One of the most striking aspects of this shift is the move away from a human sociality based solely on human sensual interaction with other humans within nature to one in which human sociality is mediated by things. Reification, or *thingification* has been critiqued in Marxism through the determination that true sociality is only authentically possible when social interactions are arrived at between people within the human relationship to nature. When mediated by things, human sociality becomes eclipsed by a sociality between objects. But expressive commodities occupy a strange liminal zone between things and people. Expressive culture is a mode of sociality in which human subjects interact with things that are not dislocated from the bodies that made them but are always imagined as traces, remnants, and direct residues of bodies.

Marx's notions of abstraction and the commodity fetish hinge upon the erasure of the undifferentiated human producer of a commodity and the fetishization of the inanimate, nonhuman object this laborer has produced. But according to Lisa Lowe, the differentiated laborer's raced and gendered specificity makes all the difference in neoliberalism.[14] And as I argued in chapter 4, the differentiation of the laborer is marketed by the WMCI for optimized adaptability in a multicultural, neoliberal world and is offered through incorporation as a means to differentiating the listener. Like a shadow, a footprint, sweat, or excrement, an echo, or a communicable disease, expressive culture represents a thing that is the byproduct of bodies, always gesturing back to bodily producers. As Benjamin has stated, "The fetish character of commodities is not a fact of consciousness, but dialectic in the eminent sense that it produces consciousness."[15] Along with Adorno ("On the Fetish Character of Music"), Benjamin's insistence upon the fetish character of aesthetic forms and his simultaneous rejection of the thesis of false consciousness forces me to contend with fantasy as a site of historical materialist productivity. Walter Benjamin claimed that the elimination of the "aura" of a work of art through mechanical reproduction had a positive effect;[16] this was a

turning point in Marxist engagements with the enchantments of capital and political economy.[17] Thus, Benjamin is credited with liberating
aesthetic objects from their reified states. Benjamin goes on to write on
perception: "The fifth century, with its great shifts of population, saw
the birth of the late Roman art industry and the Vienna Genesis, and
there developed not only an art different from that of antiquity but also a
new kind of perception."[18] Benjamin's claim that perception is culturally
and historically mediated implies that sensuality is also culturally and
historically mediated and is not a static experience, but a dynamic, ever-
changing process of bodily experience. World music as a sonic form of
alterity is perceived and consumed by the world music fan as a deeply
sensual experience, allowing me to consider both world music and its
listener as the barometer for a paradigm shift in perception.

Sensuality meets thingification in a deeply satisfying and lucrative
union in the WMCI. The world music culture of incorporation is a libidinal economy for it both relies on and is productive of a sensual need
that is satisfiable only through the sensual consumption of expressive
culture. Walter Benjamin's *aura* is particularly apt when exploring the
imaginary power of the *aural* in music. While the context for the development of Benjamin's aura concept was theorizing its emancipation
through reproduction (of works of art, photography, and phonograph
records), there is an uncanny play on words that leads me to want to
derive a new context for the application of his aura—that which is perceived with the ear (aural) and that which pertains to aura (aural). In
response to the critique of modernity's ocularcentrism, Jonathan Sterne
has coined the term "ensoniment" to name the sonic processes through
which modernity has come into being.[19] Ensoniment names the formations which have "rendered the world audible in new ways and valorized
new constructs of hearing and listening."[20] I deploy his notion in order
to explore the material effects of this ensoniment and the dialectical
means by which listening subjects come into being through this process. What I call "the dialectic of ensoniment" has resulted in a mass
cultural formation—the world music culture industry—that, building
upon Benjamin, recovers sensual pleasure by displacing aura from its
previous place as a mystical component of the work of art onto aura as
the *aurality* of the listener. In chapter 1 I read this specifically as the trace
of the sound collector's aurality that circulates with the recording. But

as I have argued throughout *Modernity's Ear*, the white woman's aura as trace, evident through her mystical aurality, is inscribed onto the recording even before the recording is made. It is audible and made material through various performative processes that necessitate the listener's ear as the site of reception for her aurality. The theories of "tone-masse," "grain," and "the ear of the other" that I explore in detail throughout the book all signal the constitution of subjectivity at the site of the ear/hearing/listening. The mystical aura is revived in the WMCI as *the aural*.

Aurality: Hooked on Phonics

Popular American musics hail listeners in part through hooky lyricism that is easy to sing along to and remember—but not world music, says DJ David Philips. World music contains component parts that are semantically unintelligible in the context of more familiar-sounding rhythms, song structures, or scales. It is not unusual for world music fans to listen to lyrics sung in an unfamiliar language and to songs that feature unfamiliar-sounding musical instruments. As Philips has said of his own experience of listening to world music, "Everybody has their own way of listening to music. I listen to the music first and want to be taken by the music, almost like held captive. But I don't listen to the lyrics, I listen more to the sound of the words. And then on the second time maybe I'll look and I'll go for the lyrics but I'm listening to different things. I don't care what language it's in. It doesn't matter. I'm listening to something in its entirety. People get hung up on words."[21] Here, Philips reveals that he is not only willing to tolerate incomprehension but that this unintelligibility enables a process paramount to semantics: to be taken and held captive by music. And contrary to his disclaimer that everyone has their own way of listening, I would argue that Philips's motivations for listening are in no way exceptional. The vast variety of languages and styles represented in the world music genre ensures that every world music listener will at some point prioritize the sound over meaning, semiology over semantics. But where is he being taken? By what is he held captive?

David Philips's form of listening is endemic to the political economics that structure listening in the world music culture industry—what I term aurality. For Philips, listening to world music is a performative act structured as an event where meanings about performers, regions, genres, and musical instruments are set into motion in fantasy and the aural imaginary. This event can be mediated at different scales, from the individualized psychic level to the culture industry level. These scales work in tandem, palimpsestically and dynamically. While still attentive to the inner workings of the aural imaginary, I shift my focus to the productive aspects of fantasy operating within this imaginary by expanding my idea of incorporation through Foucault's "incorporeal materialism" to investigate the performative act of listening and the site of reception as critical to not only meaning making but to the incorporealization of performers, cultures, and sounds within the fantasy of the listening event. What is productive about the performativity of fantasy is sonic racialized gender. I argue that *sonic racialized gender*—produced in the listening event—is the magical, mystical aura returned to the work of art in the form of aurality. Pleasure-in-listening results from the listener's capacity to materialize an imagined sense of this racialized gender.

In "The Discourse on Language," elaborating on how an event can be imagined as discursive, Foucault writes, "Of course, an event is neither substance, nor accident, nor quality nor process; events are not corporeal. And yet, an event is certainly not immaterial; it takes effect, becomes effect, always on the level of materiality. . . . Let us say that the philosophy of event should advance in the direction, at first sight paradoxical, of an incorporeal materialism."[22] Here, Foucault outlines the process by which events materialize, offering "incorporeal materialism" as a discursive formation with material implications. If we consider the listening event and we take seriously the encounter between the listener and the imagined performer, or the imagined site of performance, then this event has incorporeal materialist repercussions in listening as performative.

When we encounter other bodies in fantasy as aesthetic hallucinations, this can (and almost always does) transfer as bodily sensation producing a fantasy encounter that translates on to the body as intensity, and this intensity is felt.[23] This is best illustrated by the example I used in chapter 2, which I will repeat here:

This CD should be listened to in the dark with or without the one you love (or love right now), sipping something cold and smooth with a bite.

You are alone and lost at night in a foreign city, and you just want somewhere to sit down and have a drink. You stumble down a dark lane looking for someone, somewhere, and you spot light coming from a doorway.
You walk in. You think it's just a bar, and you take the nearest table and
order a drink and look around while you sip. Then the sound. Oh, the
sound. It's pure, slow, hot love. You look at the people around you and see
so many possibilities. You melt back into your seat, and make eye contact
with the stranger at the next table. You realize you aren't lost; you're right
where you want to be.–Paphian

This testimonial was written in response to *Torch Songs* (the CD on
which my face was used as cover art) and narrates the intensity experienced when music is the ideal context for an aesthetic encounter
that materializes an other in the aural imaginary. This encounter has
material consequences by producing pleasure-in-listening through
materializing in fantasy the very bodies imagined to be making the
music in the first place. As I discussed in chapter 2, it is through aural
incorporation that the culture industry encourages listeners to encounter the other in sound. It is through incorporeal materialism that this
resonates as intensity in the listener's body and translates as pleasure.
Is this just a classic case of racial, commodity, or sexual fetishism or is
something else going on here?

Fetishisms

Karl Marx identifies a central problem with the commodity form:
Commodity forms eclipse their producers within the imagination
of consumers, and objects take on the attributes of people, creating a
sociality of things. Marx's notion of *commodity fetishism* is the founda-
tion on which theories of libidinal and political economy develop. Both
Marx and Freud employ the term *fetishism* as central to their philoso-
phies, and although many have interpreted these scholars as theorizing
very different things, we can identify the trace of "primitivism" for the
term's origins in both their uses. *Fetish* has a complex etymology, but
in every regard, from the Latin *facticius* to the Portuguese *feitiço*, it has
signified the alien practices of the other. The term sprang up in various
disciplinary and geographical contexts in the mid-nineteenth century,

coinciding with colonialism and industrial capitalism. British ethnologist E. B. Tylor introduced it into his cultural analysis on magic and art in the latter part of the nineteenth century, thereby rooting one of fetishism's historical prongs firmly into cultural anthropology. This sublime and elusive concept, though slightly varied in meaning at different historical moments and contextual applications, has always been used to refer to the slippery intersection of desire, culture, pleasure, and race. It is the corporeal, sensual, irrational, and emotional experience of culture within capitalism, the very antithesis of rationality and calculated self-control. In contemporary usage, fetishism means different things to different scholars. In its nineteenth century deployment, it represented a zone of false consciousness and demarcated its opposite: an authentic zone where labor was not abstracted. In its mid-twentieth century usage by Horkheimer and Adorno, fetishism still retains a trace of false consciousness but there is no indication that there remains any zone outside fetishism. Similarly for Freud, fetishism is the inevitable relationship to the phallus that all moderns have. But does the term still apply in the context of contemporary world music?

When he first incorporated the term "fetishism" into his writings, Marx defined it as "the religion of sensuous desire."[24] Marx's emphasis on sensuousness is especially important for our purposes.[25] This deeply colonialist philosophical turn determined that the origins of religion were based in "primitive causal reason," a logic born not of reason but from "desire and credulity."[26] To borrow this line of reasoning and to call all religion primitive, credulous, and sensuous, and its practitioners savage, was Marx's heretic brand of religious critique. Fetishism was for Marx the means of tying together the seemingly disparate worlds of capitalist, Christian reason with primitivism, nature, and mythology. According to William Pietz, this dualism grew out of the Enlightenment discourse of "sensuous desire," which was fraught with a contradiction between the terms "desire" and "sensuous":

> Not only is "desire" the term for the purpose-forming subjectivity that
> characterizes the ethical world of humanity, but "sensuousness" indicates
> that immediate experience of lived reality which is the primordial mode
> of experience (the object of aesthetic feeling) out of which we subse-
> quently distinguish the two epistemic orders: physical nature (the object

of empirical understanding) and moral action (the object of transcendental reason). "Sensuous desire" is thus the direct "aesthetic" expression-apprehension of purposes and intentions within the subjectively objective world of immediate experience.[27]

"Sensuous desire" and the "fetish" are concepts that get mobilized by post-Kantian philosophers as representations of paradoxical phenomena that link civil societies with fetishist ("primitive") cultures. In particular, Marx seizes on the Hegelian notion of "civil society" as a "system of needs" in which "people's ability to produce the object of someone else's desire becomes the means for satisfying their own desires."[28] Theodor Adorno's theory of *musical fetishism* represents the application of Marxist theories of fetishism within the context of music. Adorno identifies the emergence of a popular music, what he terms "light music," which he sees as produced in opposition to "serious" music. He recognizes this development as a result of the marketing of music, the dependency on radio, and the association of music with advertising. This has led to what Adorno terms a *musical fetishism* of the voice, the instrument, the musician, and the work. His discussion of fetishism is haunted by an ambivalent tension around a concept that he appears to want to recover: sensual pleasure. Adorno presents musical fetishism as a development in opposition to sensuality and sensual pleasure. Consider the following contrast he makes between the two concepts:

> If the moments of sensual pleasure in the idea, the voice, the instrument are made into fetishes and torn away from any functions which could give them meaning, they meet a response equally isolated, equally far from the meaning of the whole, and equally determined by success in the blind and irrational emotions which form the relationship to music into which those with no relationship enter.[29]

"On the Fetish Character of Music and the Regression in Listening" marks Adorno's lament of the impact of modernity and capitalism on a pleasure he held very close to his heart. With this in mind, Adorno's scathing critique of popular music takes on a new light. "On the Fetish Character" can be read as a swan song written to chronicle what Adorno saw as the death of musical experience as he knew it. This paradigmatically modernist ode to his love affair with music reads to me like a lament of a certain authenticity of musical experience that in itself functions like a fetish object. Adorno himself appears to fetishize a bygone era of live musical encounter that has been murdered by the capitalist mode of production during a time of global expansion for the music industry, during a time when the phonograph could be found in bourgeois homes in every corner of the world.[30]

Furthermore, Adorno notes that within capitalism the listener becomes a consumer. I take this to mean that the sensual subject whose experience of music is characterized by an *active* listening has now been transformed into a *passive*, and hence *feminized*, consuming subject. And Marx notes that through reification, the social relations of people are overdetermined by the social relations between the products of their labor and also that human sociality is displaced onto objects that take on a sensual character. Marx bemoans the fact that sensuality, the experience that he early on claimed makes us human, has been dislocated from humanity and transferred onto things.[31] Both Marx and Adorno lament that rather than participating in the world through sensual sociality, within modern capitalism human relations are mediated by an engagement with objects. Not only has sociality been degraded, but what has been lost is a uniquely human sociality that both Marx and Adorno identify as being rooted in sensuality. But what Marx called a "system of needs" can also be understood as a libidinal economy,[32] which begs a consideration of Freud's theory of fetishism. A fundamental investment in sensuality unites the work of Adorno, Marx, and Sigmund Freud. All three scholars are concerned with sensuality and the human condition. It was the phenomenological quality of fetishism, and the libidinal economy, or the "system of needs," that first inspired Marx to seek out an analysis of capital. I argue that these theories, which functioned as stepping stones toward Marx's later critiques for which he is most remembered, are rich sources of potential for the analysis of sonic materialities and the culture industry.

Sigmund Freud describes fetishism as "a substitute for the woman's (mother's) phallus which the little boy once believed in and does not wish to forego—we know why."[33] Freud devises his theory of the fetish through the analysis of other, nonfetish-related neuroses within his male patients. These patients provide the source material for Freud's determination that fetishism in his male patients is the outcome of anxiety around woman's lack. Since the publication of this essay, Freud's notion of fetishism has been taken up by many scholars who have elaborated upon the meaning of the fetish as a desire that forms out of the anxiety of symbolic as well as material lack. When Freud states that the mother's phallus is something that the "little boy once believed in and does not wish to forego," he is referring to a nostalgic pleasure brought back to life by the fetish object. According to Freud, the little boy cannot bear the thought of woman's lack, for it signifies that she has been castrated and this elicits within the little boy anxiety around the possibility of his own castration. In fact, Freud refers to the deeply symbolic nature of castration anxiety in men when he writes, "In later life grown men may experience a similar panic, perhaps when the cry goes up that throne and altar are in danger, and similar illogical consequences will also follow them."[34] Here we find Freud referring to castration anxiety as linked in no simple way to fear of literal castration, but also entwined in this is the fear of symbolic castration involving the loss of power, revealing Freud's insights on the relationship between sex and power. If we follow Freud's line of reasoning further, we can see the connections between this fear of castration and the development of the fetish object. Freud argues that what ensues for the young boy who has determined that the mother has been castrated is denial. Rather than recognizing the mother's sex as different, Freud argues, the fetishist invests a great deal of energy in upholding a sense of denial, and this energy gets invested in a penis substitute, which becomes the fetish object:

> In the world of psychical reality, the woman still has a penis in spite of all, but this penis is no longer the same as it once was. Something else has taken its place, has been appointed its successor, so to speak, and now absorbs all the interest, which formerly belonged to the penis. . . . One can now see what the fetish achieves and how it is enabled to persist. It remains a token of triumph over the threat of castration and a safeguard against it; it also saves the fetishist.[35]

The fetish is produced as a defense against the threat of loss. It is a stand-in for some imagined lack that is unbearable for the fetishist. Studies of world music tend to wield fetishism as a kind of accusation made of fans, musicians, and labels who seek the "exotic" in world music and the fetishization of lack in the third-world musical other. For example,

Timothy Taylor writes, "I am . . . interested in showing how the discourses of hybridity fetishize hybridity, and indeed fetishize otherness, sometimes at the expense of the Other."[36] So in every case, whether Marxian or Freudian, the fetish is structured around a melancholic attachment to loss.

But if we consider the history of fetishism as having always been a history of our anxieties and fantasies about the sexualized savage, it is as well a history of us. We can then interpret it through Jean-Francois Lyotard's notion of a "libidinal economy," as a history of flows of desire.[37] Libidinal economy—a collation of Marxian notions of sensuality, Frankfurt School notions of desire in the marketplace, and Freudian notions of substitutive anxiety—represents for me a genealogy of sensuousness as that form of value that all forms of fetishism theorize.[38] The case of the world music culture industry illustrates that the economy of flows and the production of desire are not randomly directed but are organized by a logic that ascribes value to bodies based on the varying degrees to which they are able to produce affects and intensities for consumption. This relativity is hinged upon each body's proximity to various forms of alterity, which is exploited as surplus value by the world music culture industry.

Post-Fetishism

If the fetish object was imagined by both Freud and Marx as that which remained separate from the subject, whether it be the subject who produced the object of desire through labor or the subject who produced the object of desire through lack, disavowal, or displacement, no longer kept at a distance, no longer a form of false consciousness, we have now entered a period in which the fetish object is incorporated into the subject. I call this post-fetishism. Just as in all the other "posts," this does not demarcate the finite conclusion of fetishism and the beginning of an entirely new stage. Fetishism is not only critical to the historical becoming of this current, biopoliticized stage; it also structures the desire, which is very critically structured—as it always has been—around the racialized and gendered other. Whereas it was once understood as a form of false consciousness, it is now the *modus operandi* of the WMCI. Post-fetishism retains the desire for the bedazzling magic of the other that fetishism always contained, but requires only an engagement with traces of this Other to be satisfied, and these traces, as I discussed in chapter 4, can appear in miscegenated form through performers or hybrid musical traditions. Furthermore, what makes post-fetishism different from Marx's commodity fetishism is that the laborer's alterity is what enables pleasure-in-listening, but this labor is enacted in fantasy and does not necessarily relate to the performer's actual labor. So while it is on the one hand an abstraction of already abstracted labor, the pleasure emerges from a fantasy relation with what that original labor is imagined to be.

And if as the saying goes, "You are what you eat," and, if I convincingly argued in chapter 2 that world music is no longer simply a system of cultural appropriation but a system of cultural incorporation, then, as DJ David Philips said to me, "We are made of music."[39] Once taboo, fetishism now occupies the status quo for cultural production and consumption. As Emily Apter has put it, "[W]ithin contemporary discourse a kind of fetishism of fetishism is in the air."[40] Having lost its critical edge, we must consider what it means to be in a period of post-fetishism for the postculture industries, which I have renamed cultures of incorporation. In its neoliberal instrumentalization, the fetish object no longer represents the untranslatable Other; it is instead the incorporable other. The fetish still contains magic, but that magic can be extracted and incorporated and made the subject's own. Libidinal economy is an economic system in which the fetish object is taken seriously for the first time, no longer reduced to a secondary status of false consciousness. The world music culture industry is propelled by a desire that is born from a yearning for the consumption of alterity and is cathected by the sound of music obtained in the marketplace. World music enlists the desiring machine within the modern subject's body and stimulates this body to pleasure, utilizing sounds and images of alterity. It is the authenticity of the other, the aura of the aural, which resuscitates the listener back into being a body with organs again.

As I discuss throughout *Modernity's Ear*, the political economic transformations to the world music culture industry have coincided with an increasing post-industrialization of music, what I call in this concluding chapter the "world music culture of incorporation." This redefined WMCI emphasizes fantasy, the imaginary, and the virtual more than ever. The sound bridge connecting it with the world music culture industry of yore is still composed of the same physical properties; it is the structure of relations that is changing. That restructuring places greater emphasis on the site of reception, inviting the listener to be key to production. Hence, my face was good enough for the *Torch Songs* album cover because, with the help of Photoshop, the fantasy relation listeners are meant to have would emerge in their aural imaginary. I may have jump-started the signifying chain with various phenotypic features, but the real magic, the aura of their pleasure, takes place in the listener's aurality.

Epilogue

Modernity's Radical Ear and the Sonic Infidelity of
Zora Neale Hurston's Recordings

Is there a pleasure-in-listening that exists beyond the reach of market logics? Is there, instead, potential in the practice of an infidelity to original sound source, one that challenges the technological impetus of fidelity in twentieth-century sound recording with its aspirations for and hence manufacturing of realism and authenticity? Is there a genealogy of recording that reimagines the liveness, rawness, and visceral nature of the performance event through a reenactment and staging that preempts the desire to incorporate the other with a diffuse re-presentation of performance traditions, resisting normativity in listening, denying phononormativity?

I have examined in the previous chapters how the listener is produced through the techniques of world music production in a process much like the way film and photographic spectators have been produced by the techniques of visual production. My discussion of the aural imaginary in chapter 2, the white feminization of listening mobilized by twentieth-century American musical culture industries explored in chapters 1 through 5, and the instrumentalization of sound's formal qualities in the dissolution of the modern self as a means of pleasure explored in chapter 3 pave the way for the radical political possibilities for listening I pursue here. In order to get to what I describe in this chapter as radical listening relations, in the previous chapters I have had to work through the perversity of pleasure in the WMCI and the obscene register of listening relations that constitute its aural imaginary. Now I follow a trajectory that has emerged alongside the WMCI but has structured itself around listening differently. Thus far, my primary objective has been to explore how a perceptual apparatus that hegemonically renders an *aural other* in the constitution of a normative listening self—by passing phonographic subjects through the filter of "modernity's ear"—is proliferated in modernity. In this contrapuntal epilogue, however, I trace a genealogy for a form of pleasure-in-listening that is structured differently, that is not oriented around consumption but radical in the way it imagines listening relations. In what follows, I explore a counterformation contemporaneous with the musical culture industry's practices: a tradition of radical listening relations that produce imaginaries and ontologies that open outwardly away from the self/other dyad endemic to hegemonic notions of modernity, yet one that is nevertheless produced within and through modernity. To do so, I examine the field recordings Zora Neale Hurston made between 1933 and 1939 as a member of an expedition led by Alan Lomax and Mary Barnicle as well as in her role as fieldworker for the WPA. I explore the radical political possibilities for this listening other through a reading of Hurston's refusal of fidelity—what I call her sonic infidelity—as a method that charts another political economy of pleasure in listening that is not incorporative but radical in the way it imagines listening relations. I trace this tradition of radical listening relations through her critical folklore, ethnomusicology, and ethnographic methodologies as a way of offering an alternative genealogy for listening within modernity that is not overdetermined in the relationality between the listener and her aural others.

Folk. Lore.

Regardless of the medium, Hurston's method, combined with her craft, was always couched in the same "feather-bed resistance" used by interlocutors in her ethnography *Mules and Men* published in 1935—that rhetorical strategy that rejected the white man's prying, his gaze, and his ordering of things. As she has written,

> And the Negro, in spite of his open-faced laughter, his seeming acquiescence, is particularly evasive. . . . The Negro offers a feather bed resistance, that is, we let the probe enter, but it never comes out. It gets smothered under a lot of laughter and pleasantries. The theory behind our tactics: "The white man is always trying to know into somebody else's business. All right, I'll set something outside the door of my mind for him to play with and handle. He can read my writing but he sho' can't read my mind.

I'll put this play toy in his hand, and he will seize it and go away. Then I'll say my say and sing my song."[1]

While Franz Boas claimed that she could uniquely access "the true inner life" of the negro, Hurston in fact outlines in the idea of "feather bed resistance" the inaccessibility of this authentic "truth"; what becomes chronicled instead is the decoy "set . . . outside the door" for him to play with. Hurston's notation of this cultural practice in *Mules and Men*, considered to be the most "ethnographic" of her works, represents an overt denial of this mythological notion of "truth" in the very nonfictional context in which a reader would expect to find it most obviously laid out for him/her. This denial of the ostensible authenticity to which she was imagined by her mentor to have the greatest access is what I call her ethnographic refusal.[2] Instead of the "truth," Hurston goes in search of lies, making literal the suffix in folk*lore*. This is exemplified in another passage from *Mules and Men*:

> "Hello, heart-string," Mayor Hiram Lester yelled as he hurried up the street. "We heard all about you up North. You back home for good, I hope."
>
> "Nope, Ah come to collect some old stories and tales and Ah know y'all know a plenty of 'em and that's why Ah headed straight for home."
>
> "What you mean, Zora, them big old lies we tell when we're jus' sittin' around here on the store porch doin' nothin'?" asked B. Moseley.
>
> "Yeah, those same ones about Ole Massa, and colored folks in heaven, and—oh, y'all know the kind I mean."
>
> "Aw shucks," exclaimed George Thomas doubtfully. "Zora, don't you come here and tell de biggest lie first thing."[3]

Biographer Robert Hemenway has described Hurston's relationship to the disciplines of anthropology and folklore as "ambivalent." According to him this is reflected in Hurston's letters to Franz Boas, benefactor Osgood Mason, and even Langston Hughes during her periods of fieldwork in Florida.[4] Each recipient calls forth a different interpretive voice from Hurston, who displays frustration in letters to Boas regarding her fieldwork findings and elation regarding her new discoveries in letters to Hughes.[5] According to Hemenway, "Hurston's ambivalence about folklore study grew from her dual identity between

1925 and 1927 as a serious academic and active creative artist. Before going to the field in 1927, she had relatively little difficulty in maintaining both identities. . . . The type of reportorial precision required of the scientific folklorist bored Hurston; she was used to assimilating the aura of a place and letting that stimulus provoke her imagination."[6] What Hemenway describes as Hurston's bored response to the tedium of empirical detail I instead interpret as her deliberate refusal of empiricism. Hurston's ambivalence toward the disciplines of folklore and anthropology results in her extraordinary interpretive and formal innovations during this period. Hurston's interest in the *lore* in folklore translates most obviously into her fiction, as Hemenway has argued, while Gina Dent has described Hurston's ambivalence toward ethnography, especially after *Tell My Horse*, by noting: "It was inevitable that she moved closer to fiction and gave up writing ethnography, the kind of artifact-making operation that would freeze black culture in time."[7] This ambivalence translates in Hurston's breach of various methodological laws, including in her fraught production of field recordings.

As an anthropologist of African American folklore, Hurston interrogated the epistemological production of the category "Negro Folk." She rarely offered realist descriptions culled literally from her fieldwork, taking pains as well to avoid the noble savage and primitive archetypes de rigueur in the anthropology of her day. More so, her work chronicles the formation of new materialities and alternative formations within African American culture. Though on the surface it appears to be transparently about "folk," when one looks and listens more closely it is "lore" that matters to Hurston—those dreams, fictions, and fantasies that emerged postemancipation. Angela Davis has argued that music became an especially provocative and expressive vehicle for articulating the revolutions taking place in interpersonal relations among African Americans who were agents in their personal relations for the first time. As Davis has written, "The blues [. . .] the predominant postslavery African-American musical form, articulated a new valuation of individual emotional needs and desires."[8]

Hurston theorizes in the piece "Folklore and Music," how sound has the potential to materialize and function as a tool for its community of users:

Way back there when Hell wasn't no bigger than Maitland, man found out something about the laws of sound. He had found out something before he even stood erect to think. He found out that sounds could be assembled and manipulated and that such a collection of sound forms could become as definite and concrete as a war-axe or a food-tool.[9]

Prying apart the standard protocols for the study of "Negro music"—up until that point an exclusive enterprise of white scholars, record company representatives and hobbyists producing "authentic" field recordings of "folk"—Hurston reads the lore in the blues and children's songs as sites of cultural generation. Rather than representation, Hurston reads sound as a site of productivity with the potential for new outcomes that go above and beyond the circumstances of their initial production. Importantly, as Hurston writes, the discovery of sound's use-value happens prior to the imposition of reason. My consideration of Hurston's recordings begins from this place of theorizing sound's material productivity.

Hurston, like all students of Franz Boas, was trained to "record, record, record."[10] The important distinction in her work, however, is that, in the case of the WPA recordings she made with Herbert Halpert in 1939, she chose to forgo the then customary practice of staged field recordings of locals and instead made studio recordings of herself performing songs and discussing rituals. Also, in the case of the Alan Lomax and Mary Barnicle Florida and Georgia field recording expeditions she joined in 1935, Hurston seems to have been unable to restrain herself from interrupting, interjecting, and directing the songs being performed by local African Americans. What influenced her decision to forgo the then *de rigueur* Boasian method of recording ethnographic "subjects" in place of a refracted representation of musical and ritual performance through herself? Did Hurston actively set out to refuse ethnographic and phonographic interpellation, denying the future listener the pleasure of hearing Eatonville's residents translated as phonographic subjects? Or were her choices mere responses to the logistical limitations of field recording, mere accidental "outtakes" that were never edited out?

Then director of the Florida WPA's Folklore Project Stetson Kennedy sums it up when he says, "None of us had ever gone hunting for folksongs before, but we were soon able to recognize one the moment we heard it, and to realize that it was truly a bit of cultural treasure that we were discovering and preserving for future generations to enjoy."[11] He makes abundantly clear that the WPA's goal in the 1930s was to preserve sound for future listeners. As I argued in chapter 1, this is the *modus operandi* for the nascent musical culture industries, including comparative musicology, ethnomusicology, and the commercial music industries. It is this futurist desire for archiving and preservation that defines this period's modernity. The capacity to identify and fix a representation of a performance tradition deemed to be on the verge of extinction due to the vast and rapid work of modernization is the performative work of making and distinguishing moderns from nonmoderns. The archives for which recordists produced during this time (WPA, BAE, the Lomax archives, and others) interpellated recordists into feeding a desire for representations of nonmoderns. But the archive of recordings associated with Hurston's expeditions sound markedly different from those of her contemporaries. Whether or not she deliberately chose to resist the archive's desire, the result of her choices has been a refusal.

In a context dominated by the methods I outline in the previous five chapters, where I chart the seemingly overdetermined and insatiable desire to translate the other through representational technologies and Western epistemologies, Hurston in fact intervened by using her own body, voice, and innovations in a performance methodology I will elaborate on below as "phonographic refusal." Hurston deployed her own body as a kind of shield that blocked and refused the future's desire for "authentic" representations of "Negro folklore." By denying the archive fidelous representations of African Americans on record, providing instead performances of herself, Hurston refused to allow the future listener, the archive, and culture industry their fantasy folkloric object. At a time when convention called for recordings that strove for the highest fidelity to the source, Hurston responded with a kind of sonic infidelity; she refused the authenticity sought by the archive and its representatives in Barnicle, Lomax, or the WPA, and she eschewed field recording techniques developed for optimum resource extraction. By doing so, she found different value in recording technologies and in the production of the archive. In her hands, and under her direction, these technologies enable a different listening relation than what I have outlined throughout *Modernity's Ear*, yet one just as emergent in and through modernity.

For instance, in her rendition of "dat ole black gal," Hurston's banter with recordist Halpert is retained on record, where it would otherwise

be standard practice to edit the banter out. Halpert asks her to contextualize her performance in a way that has a pedagogical feel to it but is distinguished from other WPA recordings that present "actual folk," placed
in space and time in their "native settings"; this process does not honor
the myth of fidelity and the obfuscation of the machinery and epistemology of mediation. While other WPA recordings pass those perceived
as "folk" or the disappearing native through "modernity's ear" in order
to produce them as phonographic subjects for the archive, Hurston's recordings resist this conventional practice through her own embodied
performance of a repertoire of work songs, children's songs, and spiritu-
als. This is her "phonographic refusal."

Representational Refusals

Audra Simpson takes up the question of refusal as a methodology of
survival practiced among the Mohawk of Kahnawake as an anthropologist working in her own place and time among people who actively
claim her as a member of their community; she is in search of a method
in which "sovereignty matters."[12] This question is of course inflected
in every way that mattering materializes and she identifies refusal as
a manifestation of that mattering.[13] This notion of refusal is not only
developed as a means of theorizing the situated knowledge of her interlocutors, but is furthermore the method by which Simpson refuses to
communicate particular forms of knowledge about Kahnawake to the
discipline of anthropology in what she calls "a calculus ethnography of
what you need to know and what I refuse to write in."[14]

Simpson's description of Kahnawake and hence her ethnographic refusal can be imagined as perhaps the flipside of the coin to Hurston's
"feather bed resistance," representing different rhetorical stances vis-à-vis
the negotiation of power, especially when Simpson describes the function of the refusal employed by her interlocutors at Kahnawake as "I am
me, I am what you think I am and I am who this person to the right of
me thinks I am and you are all full of shit and then maybe I will tell you
to your face."[15] While Hurston charts a more seductive and playful form
of resistance involving a decoy as toy for the white man to "play with,"
a description presumably more palatable to a white readership in the
1930s, Simpson charts a decidedly more obstinate tone characteristic of

late twentieth/early twenty-first century Kahnawake styles of resistance. For Simpson, ethnographic refusal is a refusal of not only the prying ethnographic gaze, but a refusal of discursive forms, a refusal of even going to that discursive place that overdetermines who's who and what's what. It is a refusal to exceed that "ethnographic limit," that point at which "the representation would bite all of us and compromise the *representational* territory that we have gained for ourselves in the past 100 years."[16]

Although emerging from entirely different historical, cultural, and political circumstances, the epistemological interventions offered by Simpson and Hurston seem harmonious to me. They both chronicle that point at which the producer of knowledge confronts boundaries of knowledge production and makes authoritative choices that align with her community's wishes to refuse access.[17] To genealogically link Simpson's ethnographic refusal to the work of Zora Neale Hurston allows me to chart the presence of an alternative ethnographic stance, of relating otherwise to knowledge production, emergent at two very different historical moments yet responsive to similar epistemological and ethnographic circumstances. By building on this and connecting it with the argument I make regarding phonography in chapter 1, I argue that Hurston's audio recordings, her sonic infidelity, represent a form of phonographic refusal that offers a different genealogy for recorded sound than that organized around the WMCI.

My concept for describing Hurston's method of refusal can be applied to her entire oeuvre regardless of the genre of output (whether a novel, play, dance, folklore, film, photography, sketching, ethnography, or ethnomusicology). Thus, she was an anthropologist of "Negro folklore" despite the fact that she only produced two ethnographies (*Tell My Horse* and *Mules and Men*).[18] As I argued in chapter 1, sound and listening became entryways to modernity for white women in both the public and domestic sphere by making phonograph recordings for various archival collections, some of which made their way into homes through commercial marketing and distribution. This interpellated women as modern subjects who passed through *modernity's ear* positioned as listening subjects contrapuntally structured against aural others. White women were invited into modernity through their aurality, which relationally positioned them as consumers of the aural other, whether as producers or as listeners. Upwardly mobile female comparative musicologists and early ethnomusicologists sidestepped their professional struggles with misogyny and achieved acclaim in the work of recording and preservation. Like the fictional Lily Penleric of *Songcatcher* discussed at length in chapter 1, these early female musicologists remained shut out of the academy until their recordings gained traction within the popular marketplace or in the future site of archival encounter. But though her experience can be seen as parallel—also shut out of the academy and recruited as an archivist for the federal government—Hurston seems to reject the recording fever endemic to her times (as exemplified in the archives produced by Moses Ash and his Folkways Records, the Lomaxes, Seegers, WPA, Smithsonian, and so on), preferring the poetic presentation of lore and employing performance as a tactic of managing what Simpson calls that "ethnographic limit." One of the tactics Hurston employed was a refusal of standards of fidelity.

Like cinema, recorded audio is an assemblage of seamless cuts of unrelated parts (through multi-track recording, post-production or repeated takes) composed to achieve the greatest possibility for suture, requiring a commitment on the part of the recordists and the recording subject to honor the staging and anticipation of this postproduction moment of continuity production, and field recordings require this while still out in the field. Fidelity—literally the recording of sound with the least amount of sonic or mediatory distortion possible—in the context of field recordings requires that all parties acquiesce to the power of the archive and the power of sonic continuity by remaining silent while a recording is under way and by allowing the performers to do their imagined "thing." It structures all parties present as secondary to and deferential toward the recording and the future listening event. The performance event, which has been staged for the recording event, is to be sacralized for historical posterity and most certainly not interrupted. This deference toward recording is exemplified in the photographs of Frances Densmore and Blackfoot Mountain Chief I discuss in chapter 1, which stage the recording of what are presumed to be dying cultural sounds. As I argue, it is a deference that temporally defers meaning making and subject formation to the future site of listening. This deferral of meaning to the archive and the future listener makes it impossible for those present to listen in real time, requiring them instead to listen as proxies of a future listener, to satisfy the desire of the archive.

The twentieth-century evolution of music disciplines in the contexts of the American academy and the global music industry represent a science and industry dialectic that has collectively realized the Boasian project to "record, record, record," archive, and listen. The competition between scientists of music and the musical industrialists has had as its aim fidelity: a mythical goal of sonic realism that imagines recording as the capturing of completely unmediated and raw sound.[19] The project of sonic fidelity makes invisible the hand of the recordist and the recording equipment except insofar as an invisible stylistic signature might be left, audible only to the discerning ear. From the phonograph to the reel-to-reel, from the long-playing record to the cassette, from the compact disc to the MP3, there has been a drive toward greater fidelity in recording and playback media designed to optimize listening pleasure and the perception of sonic authenticity.[20]

Defined by Merriam Webster as "the quality of being faithful to your husband, wife, or sexual partner; the quality of being faithful or loyal to a country, organization, etc.; the degree to which something matches or copies something else," fidelity describes a faithfulness to a structuring logic, whether tied up in the heterosexual imperative, nationalism, or mimesis. The twentieth-century drive for innovation in sound has consistently been at the core a race for fidelity in both sound recording and reproduction. As Jonathan Sterne has put it: "Within a philosophy of mediation, sound fidelity offers a kind of gold standard: it is the measure of sound-reproduction technologies' product against a fictitious external reality . . . but, ideally, it is supposed to be a 'vanishing' mediator—rendering the relation as transparent, as if it were not there."[21] Recorded sound has been optimized to achieve the greatest fidelity to sound source, and listeners have been structured into the ideological production of fidelity by being endpoints in the delivery of fidelous sounds. Listeners are the destination for fidelous sounds and are called upon to determine the accuracy and authenticity with which recorded sound delivers on the promises of fidelity. Fidelity-as-fantasy-of-authenticity beckons its listener. Pleasure-in-listening has been learned through a cathexis of this desire for fidelity. As I have argued throughout *Modernity's Ear*, this pleasure-in-listening re-creates in the sonic realm the social inequities of the material world, structuring racialized sounds as serving the satisfaction of a deracinated listener.

Rejecting conventional thinking on musical *originals* and *copies* that have motivated the mainstream drive for fidelity in recording, Jonathan Sterne has argued that "[t]he original is itself an artifact of the process of reproduction."[22] Theorizing originals versus copies in the context of studio recording, Sterne makes the case that "the very construct of aura is, by and large, retroactive, something that is an artifact of reproducibility, rather than a side effect or an inherent quality of self-presence. Aura is the object of a nostalgia that accompanies reproduction."[23] But are his claims equally applicable to field recordings that are, by their very nature, hinged to the production of a folk authenticity provincially tied to place? Building on Sterne's discussion of fidelity vis-à-vis studio recording, I take up the object of field recording as a form that begot world music. Given that both the "field" and the "studio" are constructed, hypermediated sites that manufacture rather than document sounds, there is a relevance to that constructed difference I want to dwell within. Sterne primarily focuses his discussion of sound around three schematized forms: recording, telephony, and radio. By recording, he seems primarily to refer to studio recordings, despite the fact that the earliest known American-made sound recordings (after Edison's experiments) were made in the field of the Passamquody tribe members in 1890 by Jesse Walter Fewkes, future director of the Bureau of American Ethnology. But field recordings are distinguished from studio recordings because of the presumed correlation between place and sound.[24] Therefore, the field is literally imagined as the source for authentic sounds; on the other hand, the studio is the more controlled setting where these sounds become manipulated or manufactured.

Like the reified organs (ear, vagina) I discuss throughout *Modernity's Ear*, there is a reification of place that the field recording depends upon for the construction of authenticity. The original/copy debate is generally applied to the distinction between the original, live, *staged* performance and its copy on record. Field recordings begin with the notion of an authenticity in sound as tied to a fixed *place* naturally populated by a discrete notion of *a people*. There is no room for the constructed notion of staging and performance in this reified definition. But when we consider Zora Neale Hurston's recordings there is a clear consciousness about this *staging* and the performative component to the authentic production of "folk," a critical engagement with the reified connection drawn between *the folk* and their emplacement in the South. The notion of fidelity amplifies this reification of emplacement by imagining an ideal sound that simply reproduces and re-presents what is there. Hurston revealed her awareness of this problematic production of "folk" by refusing this commitment to fidelity and instead performing a sonic *infidelity*.

A Sonic Infidel

There is a long-standing debate in sound recording and scholarship pertaining to the relationship between an *original* sound source or performance and its reproduction. This debate is undeniably connected to those on writing and iterability that transformed our understanding of language and structure in the late twentieth century. As Alexander Weheliye has written, "The phonograph appears to unearth the iterability of speech by abstracting oral communication (or human sounds in general) from its scene of (re)creation beyond the death of the addressee."[25] Yet Weheliye point outs that this apparent abstraction does not in fact reify any *original* sound but instead, on the contrary, "the apparatus and the cultural practices (re)shape and (re)frame the musical object."[26] Thus, he argues that we should abandon the binary of original and copy and "think of repetition not as rearticulating the same but as activating difference," going on to state, "not repetition with a difference so much as the repetition of difference, wherein the original/copy distinction vanishes and only the singular and *sui generis* becomings of the source remain in the clearing."[27] If we take heed of Weheliye and James Snead's claims pertaining to the nonrepresentational qualities of repetition in black cultural production, then we can begin to better understand Hurston's recordings.[28] According to Snead, "In black culture, repetition means that the thing circulates (exactly in the manner of any flow, including capital flows) there in equilibrium. In European culture, repetition must be seen to be not just circulation and flow but accumulation and growth. In black culture, the thing (the ritual, the dance, the beat) is 'there for you to pick it up when you come back to get it.'"[29]

Through the notion of "black culture," contrasted with what he refers to as "European culture," Snead theorizes the cycles of repetition through which black cultural productions are reproduced, providing as well a theory of temporality that is not future-oriented so much as cyclical. Hurston too partakes in this theory of black cultural flow and exchange but additionally, Hurston's phonographic refusal through her embodied reproduction of "folk" songs for the record represents a deliberate foregrounding of black cultural notions of exchange, circulation, and temporality despite being invited by Lomax, Barnicle, and the WPA to produce in a future-oriented way for the archive. Thus her embodied, performative representation of "folk songs" for the record introduces a level of deliberate double-consciousness on record.

In the presence of her voice cutting inappropriately into the recording, the future listener (me at the archive) is jolted awake. James Snead's theory of "the cut" picks up just after the theory of repetition above. He continues, "If there is a goal (*Zweck*) in such a culture, it is always deferred; it continually 'cuts' back to the start, in the musical meaning of 'cut' as an abrupt, seemingly unmotivated break (an accidental da capo) with a series already in progress and a willed return to a prior series."[30] Hurston can be heard in numerous recordings in the 1935 Florida expeditions conducted with Mary Barnicle and a young Alan Lomax. At various points on recordings of children's songs one hears a faint "alright," "with feeling," "sing the song" cutting through the ghostly and muffled recordings. Although one might imagine it much more difficult to identify a voice with the same exactitude as an image, I swear I can hear Hurston's voice yelling "Alright" at the end of "Little Sister Wonche Marry Me."[31] Isn't that her corralling the children who are singing out of sync on "Going Down to Richmond" and singing background along with the Zion's Watchman on "Shout-Ho?" And then again, chiming in on "Coming Home Someday?" Once Blue and Group get up to the microphone they have to contend with Hurston's propensity to direct the vocalists as she chimes in on "See Day Dawning." This represents for me Hurston's rejection of what Snead has called the "future-orientation" and antirepetition in "European culture" in place of "the cut." And more specifically, it represents for me a refusal of the archive's desire for fidelity in sound recording offering instead the sound of her infidelity cutting through.

In her later expeditions for the WPA in 1939, Hurston opted to record only herself performing the songs of her interlocutors when it was standard practice among ethnologists, folklorists, and hobby recordists to simply point their microphones at the world out there, collecting or "catching" the sounds produced by the common "folk."[32] One way of interpreting Hurston's performing voice in lieu of making recordings of "folk" in their community settings is to read Hurston's role in the way she cynically does in a letter to her boss, Corita Doggett Corse; Hurston suspected that she was not only Corse's "pet darkey" but also that of the Florida WPA Writers Project.[33] As Carla Kaplan points out, this idea of a "pet darkey" was possibly connected to the theory she develops in the essay "The 'Pet Negro' System."[34] It describes the "petting system" as a cultural formation that has emerged from years of proximal intimacy between blacks and whites in the South. Having herself been reared in the South, minus the intimate proximity to whiteness (having been raised in the all-black town of Eatonville, Florida), Hurston recognizes how she has been interpellated by Corse and the WPA establishment as a "pet negro" who might best guide WPA recordists in the field, much as she had been by Barnicle and Lomax half a decade before.

We can most certainly read Hurston's role in the WPA Florida Folklife Project in such a way, reducing her to the role of native informant; but to end on that conclusion would be to ignore the extraordinary outcomes of the recordings she "collected" for the WPA. Compared to other WPA Florida Folklife recordings, Hurston's are the only ones that are of the "collector" actually performing the songs. What makes this even more curious is that Hurston is credited with having secured the phonograph for the Florida WPA from the Library of Congress.[35] Hurston takes up the songs in the ways described by Snead as "amenable to re-starting, interruption, or entry by a second or third player or to response by an additional musician."[36] This early form of what Dwight Conquergood would later coin "performance ethnography" is unprecedented, leaving me to wonder what influenced Hurston's choices and methodological in-novations, even if we were to assume them to be inadvertent? Is it mere coincidence that she rejected the practice employed by the other Boa-sians, as well as folklorists and ethnomusicologists, as a black woman engaged in phonograph recordings in the prewar period? Regardless of her intentions, the choices she made regarding the representation of subject matter in which she was deeply implicated have resulted in the presence of radical listening relations in the archive.

The WPA employed Hurston to produce the most authentic document of a performance of African American folk songs in Florida. She responded by recording herself singing these songs; she intervened in the archive with her own embodiment. Hurston's use of her own repertoire of forms introduces a "cut" in the archive by refusing the "future-orientation" in place of repetition. As Daphne Brooks has put it, Hurston used her body as a "central instrument . . . of story telling."[37] Rather than perpetuating the mythic representation of authenticity and realism privileged in conventions of continuity editing in both the film and music industries, Hurston employed the practice of inserting her own embodied presence. She has left us with a legacy for the study of sound that is undeniably a radical departure from the practices of her contemporaries and is distinguished in form and content from other recordings contained in the same archives.[38] Hurston's sonic infidelity, or her refusal of the demands imposed on her by the archive, has resulted in a perceptual modality, a way of listening, a listening relation that minoritarian scholars and counterlisteners increasingly desire. What Snead would call the "cut" introduced by her voice and interpretations, denies the listener the aural other, refuses the desire for authentic representation promoted by the ethos of fidelity, and resists the WPA and Lomax archives' desires to filter the aural other through *modernity's ear*. If Mary Barnicle and Alan Lomax asked her to facilitate their encounters with black Floridians so as to record the most fidelous folk songs onto acetate, she interjected with directions to the singers and even with her own voice joining in song. Hurston's voice represents in these recordings a cut that disrupts the continuity of the recording event, what Moten describes in references to Frederic Douglass's aunt Hester's scream as "an irruption of phonic substance that cuts and augments meaning with a phonographic, rematerializing inscription."[39]

Hurston's intrusion on the recording is a symptom of her excessive listening in the real time of the event, her performative and participatory listening. It is compulsive. She knows the machines are running. She knows that the machines are there to record a version of authenticity that she is fully aware she is meant to facilitate for Lomax and Barnicle. But she cannot help it. She cannot *not* chime in. She cannot help but cut into the recording, forgetting (on purpose) what is required of her by *modernity's ear*. I call this Hurston's "radical listening relation" not only toward the recording technologies, not only in reference to the future listener, not only with regard to the archive, not only in terms of her role as anthropologist, not only with regard to her instrumentalization as native informant, but also in terms of me listening to Hurston now. This radical listening relation is only knowable in the present though her presence. This is a thing that has presence that time cannot contain. The collision of forms in Hurston is also the invagination that makes this legible to me now.[40]

In the Barnicle and Lomax recording expeditions Hurston did not defer to the authority of the archive, nor did she honor the codes of silence required of field recordists. Instead she interjected repeatedly, either by singing along to songs, all of which were in her repertoire, or by interrupting the performances to point them in a new direction. In some ways she was acting in a role we would nowadays call the producer of the recording, acting as that individual authorized to arrange the outcome of the final record. Hurston engaged in a sonic infidelity that rejected the authority of the archive. So what, the recording is under way, this did not stop her from chiming in with her own voice, despite the fact that she was not literally of the "folk" being recorded on that particular field expedition. Nor did Hurston honor the fidelity demanded of her by the WPA for whom she set out to conduct recordings with Stetson Kennedy and Herbert Halpert on separate recording expeditions where she can be found singing many of the songs, offering commentary and her interpretations throughout. This sonic infidelity is a cut that disrupts the continuity demanded not only by the recording practices customary among ethnomusicologists of the day but also by the archive for which the audio recordings were being produced. The WPA and Smithsonian archives called for field recordings that were imagined as records of the performance event. Hurston, I would imagine, as a member of the recording expedition and, with the exception of recordings made in Eatonville, Florida, not a resident of the communities being documented, was expected *not* to be present on the record. Hurston's infidelity toward the archive, toward the technology, toward the discipline, and even at times toward the local performers locates her as a sonic infidel.

Hurston's voice, functioning as a cut in the recording event, has caused an invagination of the recording and the archive. This invagination, like the one the WMCI capitalizes on, is made possible by the materiality of the ear; however, in the case of Hurston's invagination of the recordings, hers disrupts, cuts, and creates an opening in the continuity of the recording event, generating novel formations "in the break."[41] Aurality is as critical in this formulation of invagination as in the WMCI's, but it is an aurality that is not produced through a faithful recording of a performance event. Hurston's aurality, her excessive listening in the place and time of the recording event, and her infidelity to the future-orientation of the archive cuts across the recording, intervening in the relationality and temporality it attempts to stage, one that is radical in the way it imagines listening relations.

Conclusion: Modernity's Radical Ear

As Snead has argued, it is the cut; in Hurston's recordings, it is the "sexual cut" that makes a different listening relation possible between her recordings and her future listener. Modernity's radical ear emerges through this sonic sexual cut, audible as Hurston's listening body in performance cutting into the epistemological order of things, refusing the production of Negro folk as archival objects. Moten's "sexual cut," as developed by poet Nathaniel Mackey, is described as "black performance, in improvising through the opposition of earthiness and rapture, immanence and transcendence, enacts a sexual differentiation—a sexual cut in Mackey's words, an invagination in Derrida's—of sexual difference."[42] This sexual difference enables a radical praxis, an ethical listening that rearranges the relations organized by the WMCI. Whereas the WMCI exploits the ideals of mainstream, liberal feminist desire for equality and a subjectivity on par with phallic, masculine subjectivity, Hurston presents the listener with an alternative political desire, radical in its capacity to deliver a non-phallogocentric pleasure-in-listening, a form of feminine *jouissance* that represents a cyclical, participatory, performative, non-object-oriented, non-subject-forming pleasure. It issues from infidelity to sound source and irreverence for authority. Through phonographic refusal, through performative listening, Hurston indexes an alternative genealogy of sound recording and listening relations than the one I have chronicled in the previous five chapters. We are left with a legacy that models an ethical listening praxis in which a nonphallic pleasure in *modernity's ear* is just as possible. *Playing by ear,* I have listened excessively in search of more than a coopted *oto*-eroticism, in pursuit of a queer utopian practice of listening through which I can relate differently to aural pleasure. And, if as Munoz has so effectively put it, "QUEERNESS IS NOT YET HERE. Queerness is an ideality . . . queerness exists for us as an ideality that has been distilled from a past and used to imagine a future." I offer this as a revision upon the aural imaginary in the ongoing search for modernity's radical ear.

NOTES

PREFACE

1 Josh Kun, *Audiotopia: Music, Race and America* (Berkeley: University of California Press, 2005).

2 Kinship Records is a pseudonym for a company whose actual name implies relationality through shared origins. It is also a play on the anthropological fetishization of this very concept. It is an independent record company founded and owned by two seasoned (world) music industry partners. CEO Jamie Alexander and President Jon Cohen started the company in 1996 while heads of Marketing and A & R (Artists and Repertoire) at a successful New Age record label. Initially begun as an imprint of a major label, the partners were able to buy full ownership with the help of venture capital investments in 1998. I began two years of fieldwork there in 2002.

3 Barbara Christian, "The Race for Theory," in *Cultural Critique* 54, no. 6 (1987): 54.

4 For to do so, it seems to me, is to discipline that very undisciplined form of theorizing.

5 Lars Lilliestam, "On Playing by Ear," in *Popular Music* 15, no. 2 (May 1996): 195.

6 Christian, "The Race for Theory," 56.

7 Muñoz, *Cruising Utopia*, 1.

8 Manu Meyer as cited in Smith "Queer Theory," 50.

INTRODUCTION

1 The Kinship Records database at the time of my fieldwork consisted of demographic information volunteered to the label by consumers. During this period, which preceded the standardization of the MP3 format, data was collected in the form of "bounce-back cards" or postcards included with every CD sold. Bounce-back cards solicited simple data (name, sex, address, number of Kinship CDs owned) and were logged in a database for direct marketing purposes. With the popularity of web-based marketing (adopted at Kinship around 2003) came greater emphasis on email addresses and less precise information about each consumer. Additionally, due to the self-selecting nature of participation in the demographics survey, the database only contained information about those consumers who opted to return the bounce-back cards, thus constructing a database of random samples of consumers (thus constituting an unrepresentative sample, in the empirical sense). And while the record company did not collect

demographics data on race I argue that the listener is positioned as white based partly on voluntary comments provided by numerous listeners as well as on the larger claim I am making about the construction of a white, feminized mode of perception in modernity. This is most certainly not an empirically sound, sociological means of demographic data collection; quite the contrary. Rather, I contend that the listener's "actual" race is much less relevant than the way the listener's race is constructed both historically and in relation to the genre of world music. And finally, I have taken great license by inserting the word "[white]" in the context of comments made by Cohen about world music's archetypal listener. Cohen's lack of commentary on the listener's race reiterates what we have long known about whiteness: Its unmarked and hence unremarkable presence is the result of an ideology bolstered by white supremacy generally, and the supremacy of white womanhood in feminism specifically.

2 Customer-generated data was collected during fieldwork in the form of customer-service correspondences, bounce-back cards, and face-to-face interactions at record company sponsored events. Due to the proprietary nature of the information and to the fact that I, like all other record company employees, signed a nondisclosure agreement pertaining to that information, I incorporate as evidence publicly available information like testimonials and reviews written online at sites like Amazon.com, which are exemplary of voluntarily generated user feedback.

3 Sherrie Tucker has also encountered this white woman, this time as jazz fan. See Sherrie Tucker, "'But This Music Is Mine Already!': 'White Woman' as Jazz Collector in the Film *New Orleans* (1947)," in *Big Ears: Listening for Gender in Jazz Studies,* edited by Nicole T. Rustin and Sherrie Tucker (Durham: Duke University Press, 2008), 361–392.

4 Theodor W. Adorno, "The Curves of the Needle," trans. Thomas Y. Levin, in *October* 55 (1990): 50.

5 Ibid., 50.

6 Pekka Gronow, "Ethnic Recordings: An Introduction," in *Ethnic Recordings in America: A Neglected Heritage, Studies in Folklife, no.1* (Washington, D.C.: American Folklife Center, Library of Congress, 1982), 4.

7 Ibid., 1.

8 Joseph Kortarba and Philip Vannini, *Understanding Society through Popular Music* (New York: Routledge, 2009), 134.

9 Steven Feld, "A Sweet Lullaby for World Music," *Public Culture* 12, no. 1 (2000): 146.

10 On the subject of the masculinization of early female anthropologists in the field, see Kamala Visweswaran, *Un/common Cultures: Racism and the Rearticulation of Cultural Difference* (Durham: Duke University Press, 2010), 22.

11 Jonathan Sterne, *The Audible Past: Cultural Origins of Sound Reproduction* (Durham: Duke University Press, 2003), 19.

12 Ibid., 23.

13 Fred Moten, *In the Break: The Aesthetics of the Black Radical Tradition* (Minneapolis: University of Minnesota Press, 2003), 43.

14 Ibid., 45.

15 Susan McClary, *Feminine Endings: Music, Gender, and Sexuality* (Minneapolis: University of Minnesota Press, 1991).

CHAPTER 1. THE FEMALE SOUND COLLECTOR AND HER TALKING MACHINE

1 Peter Rainer, "Love in a Miner Key," *New York Magazine*, June 25, 2001, accessed August 15, 2012, http://nymag.com/nymetro/movies/reviews/4852/.

2 Ibid.

3 Peter Travers, "Songcatcher," *Rolling Stone*, June 7, 2001, accessed August 20, 2012, http://www.rollingstone.com/movies/reviews/songcatcher-20010607?print=true

4 One African American troubadour, played by Taj Mahal, is represented very briefly performing with Aidan Quinn's character in the background of one scene.

5 The first ever phonograph recordings were made by Jesse Walter Fewkes among the Passamquody of Main in 1890. See Erica Brady, *A Spiral Way: How the Phonograph Changed Ethnography* (Jackson: University of Mississippi Press, 1999), 54.

6 Aside from Campbell, however, the phonograph did play a key role in the ethnographic work of comparative musicologists of this period. But it would not make its debut in the Appalachians until after World War I. See Arthur Krim, "Appalachian Songcatcher: Olive Dame Campbell and the Scotch-Irish Ballad," *Journal of Cultural Geography* 24, no. 1 (Fall/Winter 2006): 91–112.

7 A list which was by no means exhaustive would include Laura Boulton, Natali Curtis Burlin, Sidney Robertson Cowell, Constance Goddard Dubois, Alice Cunningham Fletcher, Frances Densmore, Maud Karpeles, Helen Heffron Roberts, Ruth Crawford Seeger, Gertrude Kurath, Barbara Smith, Barbara Krader, Ruth Underhill, and Henrietta Yurchenko.

8 The schoolhouse fire was set by homophobic local men who had recently discovered that the two female teachers were lovers.

9 Throughout the first half of the film, the phonograph stands for all that Penleric will, by film's end, have been liberated from: the trappings of a career in musicology among misogynistic colleagues, the mastery and self-control of Victorian femininity, and a celibate life of the mind. But when her page, Fate Honeycutt (Greg Russell Cook), allows the force of gravity to pull the behemoth machine down the hillside that he had been paid to pull it up, and it smashes into a heap of wood and metal, Penleric is forced into an existential crisis that functions as one of the film's main plot points: She must confront the trauma of her lost object. This crisis sets into motion the predicament of modernity that motivates her professional and personal about-face and begins her gradual metamorphosis from academic to entrepreneur.

10 Kay Shelemay, "Recording Technology, the Record Industry and Ethnomusicological Scholarship," in *Comparative Musicology and Anthropology of*

Music: Essays on the History of Ethnomusicology, edited by Bruno Nettl and Philip V. Bohlman (Chicago: University of Chicago Press, 1991), 280.

11 George Herzog, *Research in Primitive and Folk Music in the United States, a Survey*. (Washington, D.C.: American Council of Learned Societies, 1936), 563.

12 "Women Collectors: American Folklife Center."

13 According to Charlotte Frisbie, there was a supportive and encouraging environment for women within the Society for Ethnomusicology, which had female participants and officers from its inception. She writes, "[T]he climate for women in ethnomusicology was supportive and encouraging." Women interested in the discipline both in the United States and abroad sent news to the newsletters and journals and gave papers at meetings. Frisbie contrasts this with the early years of anthropological professional organizational formation, which she argues were formed through the professional networks of the "founding fathers," none of which included any women. See Charlotte Frisbie, "Women and the Society for Ethnomusicology," in *Comparative Musicology and Anthropology of Music: Essays on the History of Ethnomusicology*, edited by Bruno Nettl and Philip V. Bohlman (Chicago: University of Chicago Press, 1991), 252.

14 Brady, *A Spiral Way*. See marketing text on back cover.

15 Helen Heffron Roberts, *Form in Primitive Music* (New York: Norton, 1933), 157.

16 Thanks to Sora Han for drawing my attention to this.

17 Jacques Lacan, *The Four Fundamental Concepts of Psycho-Analysis*, edited by Jacques-Alain Miller (New York: W. W. Norton, 1981), 157.

18 Eric Wolf, *Europe and the People without History* (Berkeley: University of California Press, 1982).

19 These recordings were studied by American composers in their effort to create a uniquely American art music in the form of opera and "ultra-Modernist" music. On the history of Native American music in opera, see Philip Deloria, *Indians in Unexpected Places (Lawrence: University of Kansas Press, 2004)*. On the importance of Native American music for "ultra-Modernist" music, see Ruth Allen and Elli Hisama, eds., *Ruth Crawford Seeger's Worlds (Rochester: University of Rochester Press, 2007)*.

20 Interestingly enough, 84 percent of American audiologists surveyed by the American Speech Language Hearing Association in 2012 were women. See the audiology survey, http://www.asha.org/uploadedFiles/2012-Audiology-Survey-Methodology.pdf, accessed June 17, 2014.

21 Densmore was actually referred to as a comparative musicologist at the time the photograph was taken. Later, in the 1950s, she would serve in a symbolic role as an early officer of the Society for Ethnomusicology. See Frisbie, "Women and the Society for Ethnomusicology."

22 Those languages are French, German, Spanish, Finnish, Hebrew, Italian, Latin, Turkish, Latvian, Portuguese, Russian, Sanskrit, Vietnamese, and Greek. See "Frances Densmore Recording Mountain Chief," Wikipedia, accessed September

1, 2012. http://en.wikipedia.org/wiki/File:Frances_Densmore_recording_
Mountain_Chief2.jpg.

23 See Featured Pictures, Wikipedia, accessed September 1, 2012. http://en.wikipedia.
org/wiki/Wikipedia:Featured_pictures.

24 See "Frances Densmore Recording Mountain Chief," Wikipedia, accessed
September 1, 2012. http://en.wikipedia.org/wiki/Wikipedia:Featured_picture_can-
didates/Frances_Densmore_recording_Mountain_Chief.

25 http://www.loc.gov/pictures/resource/npcc.20061/

26 After much heated debate, the photo's restorer and nominator to the Wikipedia
"featured picture" category submitted to the likelihood that the photograph was
staged.

27 See "Frances Densmore Recording Mountain Chief," Wikipedia, accessed
September 1, 2012. http://en.wikipedia.org/wiki/Wikipedia:Featured_picture_can-
didates/Frances_Densmore_recording_Mountain_Chief.

28 Alice Fletcher, Francis La Flesche, and John Comfort Fillmore, *A Study of Omaha
Indian Music, volume 1, issue 107 (Omaha: University of Nebraska Press, 1994),* 237.

29 Ibid.

30 Kenney goes on to state: "One study found that 77.3 percent of the time, women
made the final decision in purchases of phonographs. According to this study,
women dominated purchases in large and small cities, department and
specialty music stores; and 95 to 100 percent of these female phonograph
buyers bought machines for domestic use. . . . Women dominated the market
for phonograph records even more completely than that for the machines that
played them." William Howland Kenney, *Recorded Music in American Life: The
Phonograph and Popular Memory, 1890–1945 (New York: Oxford University
Press, 1999),* 89–90.

31 Sterne, *The Audible Past,* 228.

32 Louise Michele Newman, *White Women's Rights: The Racial Origins of Feminism
in the United States* (New York: Oxford University Press, 1999), 21. On the subject
of the female anthropologist's role in reifying the "wildness" of the frontier and,
hence, Native Americans, see Kamala Visweswaran, *Un/common Cultures: Racism
and the Rearticulation of Cultural Difference* (Durham: Duke University Press,
2010), 18-19.

33 Ibid.

34 Ibid., 23.

35 Alice Fletcher, "Among the Omahas," as quoted in Newman, *White Women's
Rights,* 116.

36 Sterne, *The Audible Past,* 27.

37 Ibid., 95.

38 Jacques Derrida, *A Derrida Reader: Between the Blinds,* edited, with an
Introduction and Notes, by Peggy Kamuf (New York: Columbia University Press,
1991), 90.

39 Derrida proclaims, "It is the ear of the other that signs. The ear of the other says me to me and constituted the *autos* of my autobiography. . . . The most important thing about the ear's difference . . . is that the signature becomes effective— performed and performing—not at the moment it apparently takes place, but only later, when ears will have managed to receive the message." I engage Derrida's theory of "the ear of the other" at length in chapter 4. See Jacques Derrida, *The Ear of the Other: Otobiography, Transference, Translation: Texts and Discussions with Jacques Derrida, edited by* Christie McDonald (Lincoln: University of Nebraska Press, 1988), 51.

40 Edward S. Curtis's late nineteenth- and early twentieth-century photographs depicting members of various Native American tribes have been criticized as romantic stagings that are often historically inaccurate (Curtis was said to have traveled with Plains Indian clothing that he would have non-Plains Indians pose in). Although the photographs were staged, they circulated widely as real ethnographic documents. See Gerald Vizenor, "Edward Curtis: Pictorialist and Ethnographic Adventurist," Library of Congress, October 2000, accessed September 12, 2012. http://memory.loc.gov/ammem/award98/ienhtml/essay3.html

41 As film scholars have argued, *point of view* determines with whom the spectator identifies and at whom his or her desires will be directed.

42 Carla Freccero, *Queer/Early/Modern* (Durham: Duke University Press, 2006), 80.

43 Jacques Derrida, *Specters of Marx: The State of the Debt, the Work of Mourning, and the New International (New York: Routledge, 1994)*, quoted in Freccero, *Queer/Early/Modern*, 70.

44 Gayatri Spivak, *A Critique of Postcolonial Reason: Toward a History of the Vanishing Present* (Cambridge, Mass.: Harvard University Press, 1999), 206.

45 Dylan Evans. *An Introductory Dictionary of Lacanian Psychoanalysis (London: Routledge, 1996)*, 211.

46 And while it is beyond the scope of this book to explore this in great detail, a counter-transference can be said to have taken place in processes like "going native" or, as in the case of Alice Fletcher and Francis La Flesche, through adoption and cohabitation as mother and son.

47 Walter Benjamin, "The Work of Art in the Age of Mechanical Reproduction," in *Illuminations*, edited by Hannah Arendt (New York: Schocken Books, 1986), 220–221.

48 Ibid., 220.

49 Brady, *A Spiral Way*, 118.

50 Anjali Arondekar, *For the Record* (Durham: Duke University Press, 2009), 90.

51 Which mimes the clichéd scene of the savage's first encounter with technology that Shari Huhndorf and Michael Taussig have separately discussed regarding the scene in which Flaherty "introduces" the phonograph to Nanook in *Nanook of the North*. See Michael T. Taussig, *Mimesis and Alterity: A Particular History of the Senses (New York: Routledge, 1993)*, and Shari M. Huhndorf, *Going Native: Indians in the American Cultural Imagination (Ithaca: Cornell University Press, 2001)*..

52 "Mountain Chief Listening" not only represents the actual temporality of aurality but it represents Mountain Chief (Nin-Na-Stoko) as the performer, actor, agent, and communicator, with Densmore's rapt attention upon him.

53 Newman, *White Women's Rights*, 122.

CHAPTER 2. LISTEN, INC.

1 This fantasy effectively masks the struggles over labor, compensation, and publishing rights that left countless jazz musicians from this period impoverished by the time they died.

2 2002 was the beginning of the end for the American music industry as we had known it for the previous half century. Countless small independent competitors to Kinship would fold over the next two years. Digital downloads and piracy were on the rise and even the major labels would experience a reshuffling, taking the "Big 5" (Universal, Sony, EMI, BMG, and Warner) down to the "Big 4" (when Sony acquired BMG in 2004) during the period of my fieldwork.

3 While I am not saying that appropriation is no more, I don't believe it is any longer the world music industry business model.

4 Georgina Born and David Hesmondhalgh, *Western Music and Its Others: Difference, Representation, and Appropriation in Music* (Berkeley: University of California Press, 2000), 15. Emphasis mine.

5 Jean Laplanche and J.-B. Pontalis, *The Language of Psychoanalysis* (London: Karnac, 1988), 211.

6 See Boatema Boateng, *The Copyright Thing Doesn't Work Here: Adinkra and Kente Cloth and Intellectual Property in Ghana* (Minneapolis: University of Minnesota Press, 2011); Eric Lott, *Love and Theft: Blackface Minstrelsy and the American Working Class* (New York: Oxford University Press, 1993); Taussig, *Mimesis and Alterity*; Rosemary J. Coombe, *The Cultural Life of Intellectual Properties: Authorship, Appropriation, and the Law* (Durham: Duke University Press); Bruce H. Ziff and Pratima V. Rao, *Borrowed Power: Essays on Cultural Appropriation* (New Brunswick, N.J.: Rutgers University Press, 1997); and Pnina Werbner and Tariq Modood, eds., *Debating Cultural Hybridity: Multicultural Identities and the Politics of Anti-Racism* (London: Zed Books, 1997).

7 On the politics of cultural appropriation in world music, see Andrew Goodwin and Joe Gore, "World Beat and the Cultural Imperialism Debate," *Socialist Review* 20, no. 1 (July–September 1990): 63–80; Feld, "A Sweet Lullaby for World Music"; Veit Erlmann, "The Esthetics of the Global Imagination: Reflections on World Music in the 1990s," *Public Culture* 8, no. 4 (1996):467–487; Louise Meintjes, "Paul Simon's Graceland, South Africa, and the Mediation of Musical Meaning," *Ethnomusicology* (Winter 1990): 37–73; Timothy D. Taylor. "The Commodification of Music at the Dawn of the Era of 'Mechanical Music.'" *Ethnomusicology* 51, 2 (2007): 281–305; John Hutnyk, *Critique of Exotica: Music, Politics, and the Culture Industry* (London: Pluto Press, 2000).

8 See Feld, "A Sweet Lullaby for World Music."

9 This innovation coincides with various forms of what Whole Foods CEO John Mackey has coined "conscious capitalism" such as fair trade capitalism, which promote the production process as a part of the product, thus complicating the classic commodity chain, which imagined production as separate in its aims from consumption.

10 The MP3 format, and more importantly, the wide-scale piracy that it made possible, hurried the obsolescence of the old music industry along, whose unsustainable profit margins and antiquated business practices were already causing it to die slowly. Just to be clear, however, debates over intellectual property and cultural appropriation are in no way dependent on technological irruptions (which have more or less plagued the industry over the entirety of the twentieth century). See Jonathan Sterne, especially his chapter 6, "Is Music a Thing?" on the question of piracy, intellectual property, and the MP3 in his *MP3: The Meaning of a Format (Durham: Duke University Press, 2012).*

11 Boateng, *The Copyright Thing Doesn't Work Here*, 119.

12 Sasha Frere-Jones, "A Paler Shade of White," *New Yorker Magazine*, October 22, 2007, accessed May 9, 2014, http://www.newyorker.com/ magazine/2007/10/22/a-paler-shade-of-white.

13 Jennifer Vineyard, "Vampire Weekend's Ezra Koenig on His Early Influences, the Continued Oxford Comma Debate and the Most Important Hometown Shows," *Vulture Blog*, accessed April 15, 2014. http://www.vulture.com/2014/03/ezra-koenig-new-york-music-scene.html.

14 Vampire Weekend's popularity coincided with the "Great Recession" and the "Occupy" movement that made popular the slogan "We are the 99%," which aimed to draw attention to a statistic that claims that the top 1 percent of the wealthiest Americans owned 40 percent of the wealth in the country in 2011. See http://en.wikipedia.org/wiki/We_are_the_99%25, accessed June 14, 2014

15 Chris Richards, "The Privilege Is Ours: A Review of Vampire Weekend's *Contra*," *Washington Post*, January 10, 2010. Accessed April 24, 2014. http://www.washingtonpost.com/wp-dyn/content/article/2010/01/07/AR2010010704530.html

16 Roshanak Kheshti, "Musical Miscegenation and the Logic of Rock and Roll: Homosocial Desire and Racial Productivity in 'A Paler Shade of White.'" *American Quarterly* 60, no. 4 (December 2008): 1037–1056.

17 http://www.chicagoreader.com/chicago/vampire-weekend-contra-review-indie-rock-appropriation-ezra-koenig/Content?oid=1358299 Accessed 4/24/14

18 See my analysis of the media storm surrounding Frere-Jones's declaration, in Kheshti, "Musical Miscegenation."

19 Ryan Foley, *Seattle Weekly*, "Indie Rock Didn't Lose Its Soul in 2008," December 17, 2008, accessed June 3, 2009, www.seattleweekly.com/2008–12–17/music/indie-rock-didn-t-lose-its-soul-in-2008/.

20 Sigmund Freud, "The Uncanny," in *The Uncanny*, trans. David McLintock (New York: Penguin, 2003), 16.

21 Ibid., 10.

22 Ibid.

23 Kalpana Seshadri-Crooks, *Desiring Whiteness: A Lacanian Analysis of Race* (London: Routledge, 2000), 38.

24 The so-called ocularcentrism of modernity is being challenged by scholars engaging the senses broadly, and through sound specifically. See Alexander G. Weheliye, *Phonographies: Grooves in Sonic Afro-Modernity (Durham: Duke University Press, 2005)*; Sterne, *The Audible Past*; Emily Ann Thompson, *The Soundscape of Modernity: Architectural Acoustics and the Culture of Listening in America, 1900–1933 (Cambridge, Mass.: MIT Press, 2002)*, just to name a few.

25 Kaja Silverman, *Acoustic Mirror: The Female Voice in Psychoanalysis and Cinema* (Bloomington: Indiana University Press, 1988).

26 Joan Copjec, *Imagine There's No Woman: Ethics and Sublimation* (Cambridge, Mass.: MIT Press, 2002), 10.

27 Lacan, *The Four Fundamental Concepts of Psychoanalysis*, 195. The distinction he draws here between the function of the scopic drive as compared to the invocatory drive, when he says, "making oneself heard really goes toward the other," suggests that the *objet petit a* figures more prominently in the production of desire motivated by the invocatory drive.

28 Evans, *Dictionary of Lacanian Psychoanalysis*, 49.

29 Lacan, quoted in Evans, *An Introductory Dictionary of Lacanian Psychoanalysis*, 125.

30 Kofi V. Agawu, *Representing African Music: Postcolonial Notes, Queries, Positions* (New York: Routledge, 2003), 59.

31 Ibid., 59.

32 Ibid., 60.

33 Ibid., 61.

34 Artist, record label, and album names have been changed due to the nondisclosure agreement. However, the names of artists like Cassandra Wilson, whose music was licensed for these compilations, have not been changed.

35 This raises interesting questions about deafness and hearing, which I take up in my essay "Touching Listening." See Roshanak Kheshti, "Touching Listening: The Aural Imaginary in the World Music Culture Industry." *American Quarterly* 63, no. 3 (September 2011): 711–731.

36 See Michel Foucault, *The Archaeology of Knowledge; and, The Discourse on Language (New York: Columbia University Press, 1994)*; Walter Ong, *Orality and Literacy: The Technologizing of the Word (London: Methuen, 1982)*; Donald M. Lowe, *The History of Bourgeois Perception (Chicago: University of Chicago Press, 1982)*; Sterne, *The Audible Past*; Thompson, *The Soundscape of Modernity*; David Suisman, *Selling Sounds: The Commercial Revolution in American Music (Cambridge, Mass.: Harvard University Press, 2009)*.

37 Don Ihde, *Listening and Voice: Phenomenologies of Sound* (Albany: SUNY Press, 2007), 135–136.

38 Lowe, *The History of Bourgeois Perception*, 8.

39 Susan Buck-Morss, *The Dialectics of Seeing: Walter Benjamin and the Arcades Project* (Cambridge, Mass.: MIT Press, 1989), 81.

40 Christian Metz, *The Imaginary Signifier: Psychoanalysis and the Cinema* (Bloomington: Indiana University Press, 1981), 64.

41 Ibid., 59.

42 Sterne, *The Audible Past*, 9

43 Lisa Lowe, "Work, Immigration, Gender: New Subjects of Cultural Politics," in *The Politics of Culture in the Shadow of Capital*, edited by Lisa Lowe and D. Lloyd (Durham: Duke University Press, 1997), 357.

44 Ibid., 360.

45 Silverman, *The Acoustic Mirror*, 81. Silverman painstakingly distinguishes Rosolato's nostalgic longing for the sonorous envelope from Michel Chion's paranoid fear of its return. See her chapter, "The Fantasy of the Maternal Voice."

46 Although Downey is referring to the ear of a capoeirista, I borrow his language to imagine the listener as an active player in the musical event. See Greg Downey, "Listening to Capoeira: Phenemenology, Embodiment and the Materiality of Music," in *Ethnomusicology* 46, no. 3 (Autumn 2002): 489.

47 Both Susan McClary and Timothy Taylor have argued that in tonal music difference is constituted in the musical composition and arrangement, emphasizing difference as gendered female (McClary), and difference as the colonial other (Taylor). See McClary, *Feminine Endings*; and Taylor, *Beyond Exoticism*.

48 Lacan, Four Fundamental Concepts, 104.

49 Seshadri-Crooks, *Desiring Whiteness*, 49. Writing in a Lacanian tradition, she also goes on to state, "Race is a regime of visibility that secures our investment in racial identity. We make such an investment because the unconscious signifier Whiteness, which founds the logic of racial difference, promises wholeness. (This is what it means to desire Whiteness: not a desire to become Caucasian [!] but, to put it redundantly, it is an "insatiable desire" on the part of all raced subjects to overcome difference)." Seshadri-Crooks, *Desiring Whiteness*, 21.

50 Other bands that jumped on the Afro Indie bandwagon circa 2008 are Yeasayer, Gang Gang Dance, Dirty Projectors, Extra Golden, Fools Gold, among others.

51 Thanks to Amy Sara Carroll for engaging me on this point.

52 This is especially the case on world music compilation albums, which accounted for a significant number of the albums the company released during the time of my fieldwork.

53 This emphasis happens in the form of framing devices like liner notes, album biographies (one-sheet descriptions of the album penned by professional copywriters), album artwork, websites, and overall marketing campaigns.

CHAPTER 3. LOSING THE LISTENING SELF IN THE AURAL OTHER

1 Mickey Hart. *Songcatchers: In Search of the World's Music* (Washington, D.C.: National Geographic Society, 2003), 2–3.

2 Ibid., 3.

3 Roland Barthes, "The Grain of the Voice," in *Image-Music-Text,* trans. Stephen Heath, (New York: Hill and Wang, 1977), 179–180.

4 Ibid., 188.

5 Ibid., 189.

6 Barthes argues that the "grain," or the lack thereof, also persists in instrumental music, so it is not simply limited to the domain of the voice. See ibid., 188.

7 Ibid., 188–189.

8 Quoted from company publicity materials.

9 Roland Barthes, *Writing Degree Zero*, trans. Annette Lavers and Colin Smith (New York: Hill and Wang, 1968).

10 Julia Kristeva, "Roland Barthes and Writing as Demystification," in *The Sense and Non-Sense of Revolt: The Powers and Limits of Psychoanalysis* [1996], trans. Jeanine Herman (New York: Columbia University Press, 2000), 199.

11 Barthes, "Translator's Note," in *Image-Music-Text*, 10.

12 Barthes, "The Grain of the Voice," 179.

13 Ibid., 179.

14 Ibid., 180.

15 Ibid., 189.

16 Barthes distinguishes the "pheno-song" from the "geno-song." He defines the former as "everything in the performance which is in the service of communication, representation, expression, [. . .] which forms the tissue of cultural values, [. . .] which takes its bearing directly on the ideological alibis of a period [. . .]." He defines the latter as "[. . .] that apex (or that depth) of production where the melody really works at the language—not at what it says, but the voluptuousness of its sound-signifiers, of its letters—where melody explores how the language works and identifies with that work." Ibid.,182.

17 When Barthes reveals himself as someone who engages in a feminized listening, he names a queer breach otherwise too taboo for a purportedly heterosexual man.

18 Jacques Lacan, Juliette Mitchell, and Jacqueline Rose, *Feminine Sexuality: Jacques Lacan and the ecole freudienne* (New York: W. W. Norton, 1982), 49–50.

19 Roland Barthes, *S/Z* (New York: Hill and Wang, 1974), 118–119, as quoted in Joke Dame, "Unveiled Voices," in *Queering the Pitch: The New Gay and Lesbian Musicology*, edited by Philip Brett, Elizabeth Wood, and Gary C. Thomas (New York: Routledge, 1994), 145.

20 Ibid., 145.

21 All the albums released on Kinship Records include text that frames and curates the listening experience. This text pedagogically guides the listener (who is presumed to be a newcomer to the sounds, genres, regions, artists, or instruments presented on the album) on what to listen for and how to hear it.

22 Quoted from company publicity materials.

23 Barthes, "The Grain of the Voice," 182.

24 Albums (or songs on a compilation) often involve a collaboration between artists from what is imagined by the label to be divergent political and cultural origins.

Kinship, inaugurated in 1996, is built on a model established by artists in the 1980s, as exemplified by Peter Gabriel's Real World record label and David Byrne's Luaka Bop record label and bands like Afro Celt Soundsystem (Real World), Joi (Real World), and Los Amigos Invisibles (Luaka Bop). Kinship, Luaka Bop, and Real World's catalogs consist of some of the same artists. In addition to sharing a sound, all three labels share a "look" employing similar indexical devices and color patterns on album artwork, advertising, and websites.

25 I agree with Joke Dame's critique of Barthes's rigid interpretation of Kristeva's "geno-text/pheno-text" distinction. Dame argues that every text contains elements of "geno-text"; it is the dialectic between these two texts within a performance that elicits interpretation. See Joke Dame, 'Voices within the Voice: Geno-Text and Pheno-Text in Berio's *Sequenza III,*" in *Music/Ideology: Resisting the Aesthetic,* edited by Adam Krims (Amsterdam: Gordon and Breach Publishing Group, 1998), 240.

26 Quoted from company publicity materials.

27 Fred Moten also uses the term "engrain" in the context of theorizing the grain of Billie Holiday's voice, but he does so in a slightly different way. For Moten, "the grained voice engrains" as if to inscribe itself upon the listener, like "lipstick engrained on your temple." I am more interested in how the culture industry systematizes the production of sonic grain and how certain sounds are engrained or fixed within the space of the geno-sonic, thus contributing to the loss of the self through *signifiance.* See Moten, *In the Break,*104.

28 Thanks to Sora Han for helping me to flesh this out.

29 Lalita Sinha, *Unveiling the Garden of Love: Mystical Symbolism in Layla Majnun & Gita Govinda* (Bloomington: World Wisdom, 2008), 145.

30 Avery Gordon, *Ghostly Matters: Haunting and the Sociological Imagination* (Minneapolis: University of Minnesota Press, 1997), 8, 19.

31 See Kristeva, "Roland Barthes and Writing as Demystification," 199.

CHAPTER 4. RACIAL NOISE, HYBRIDITY, AND MISCEGENATION IN WORLD MUSIC

1 Tom Schnabel, *Stolen Moments* (Los Angeles: Acrobat Books, 1988), xi.

2 Ibid., xiii.

3 Peter Bowler, *The Non-Darwinian Revolution* (Baltimore: Johns Hopkins University Press, 1988), ix.

4 Much as Tavia Nyong'o reads the copresence of "the hybrid future and [. . .] mongrel past," I read hybridity and miscegenation as simultaneously signified in world music. Nyong'o writes, "I unpack the relation between the hybrid future and this mongrel past. If the former selects hybridity as a panacea, the latter presents hybridity as a historical alternative to the overly burdened racial identities bequeathed us by slavery, segregation, and ghettoization. Rather than being in contrast or opposed, the two figures often work in tandem insofar as past and future equally leverage a critique of the present." See Tavia Amolo Nyong'o,

The Amalgamation Waltz: Race, Performance, and the Ruses of Memory (Minnesota: University of Minnesota Press, 2009), 7.

5 Quoted from company publicity materials.

6 Charles Darwin, *The Origin of the Species 1859* (Oxford: Oxford University Press, 1985), 131.

7 This queerness emerges specifically in what Porzac periodizes as Darwin's early "barnacle research" phase, which produced a theory of "a radically non-agential, irregular force acting with no teleological aim other than a general tendency toward increasing 'complexity.'" See Simon Porzac, "Inverts and Invertebrates: Darwin, Proust, and Nature's Queer Heterosexuality," *Diacritics* 41, no. 4 (2013): 6–34.

8 Bowler, *The Non-Darwinian Revolution*, 152.

9 Ibid., 153.

10 David Goodman Croly, *Miscegenation: The Theory of the Blending of the Races, Applied to the American White Man and the Negro* (Ithaca: Cornell University Library Digital Collections, 1864), 8–9.

11 Tavia Nyong'o has noted that Croly's parody of the subject of miscegenation walks a fine line that "exposed the theatricality of the science it sought to lampoon, unfolding aggressions, doubts, and ambivalences that its authors could not fully control." See Nyong'o, *Amalgamation Waltz*, 28.

12 Thomas C. Leonard, "Mistaking Eugenics for Social Darwinism," *History of Political Economy* 37, no. 1 (2005): 226.

13 Ibid.

14 Although some scientists have refuted any resemblance between the social application of Darwin's thesis (referred to pejoratively as "social Darwinism") and the theory of natural selection, by the fifth printing in 1869 of his *Origin of the Species* Darwin himself happily embraced Herbert Spencer's recommendation to rename the notion as "survival of the fittest" so that his theory would have wider application. See http://darwin-online.org.uk/content/frameset?viewtype=side&itemID=F387&pageseq=121 (accessed September 21, 2012).

15 Friedrich Engels noted this in his *Dialectics of Nature*: "Darwin did not know what a bitter satire he wrote on mankind, and especially on his countrymen, when he showed that free competition, the struggle for existence, which the economists celebrate as the highest historical achievement, is the normal state of the *animal kingdom*." Frederich Engels, *Dialectics of Nature (1873–86)*, 3rd ed. (Moscow: Progress, 1964), 4.

16 Simon Porzak has argued that "for the evolutionary thought of the late nineteenth century, natural selection appears as constant, regular, and progressive." According to him this is inconsistent with the revolutionary impact of Darwin's theory of natural selection. The Darwin I am describing would be rather what Peter Bowler has referred to as the "nonrevolutionary" Darwin. See Porzak, "Inverts and Invertebrates," 10. Also see Bowler, *The Non-Darwinian Revolution*.

17 Kheshti. "Musical Miscegenation and the Logic of Rock and Roll," 1037–1055.

18 Derrida writes, "The question of the literary genre is not a formal one: it covers the motif of the law in general, of generation in the natural and symbolic senses, of birth in the natural and symbolic senses, of the generation difference, sexual difference between the feminine and masculine genre/gender, of the hymen between the two, of a relationless relation between the two, of an identity and difference between the feminine and masculine." Jacques Derrida, "The Law of Genre," trans. Avital Ronnel, *Critical Inquiry* 7 no. 1 (Autumn 1980): 74.

19 Ibid., 59.

20 I interpret Derrida's slippage between gender and sex not as an uncritical conflation of the two concepts, but instead as an acknowledgement that it is gender (and, I would add, an aural engagement with gender) that discursively contributes to the materialization of sex. See Jacques Derrida, *The Ear of the Other: Otobiography, Transference, Translation: Texts and Discussions with Jacques Derrida, edited by Christie McDonald* (Lincoln: University of Nebraska Press, 1988), 36.

21 Ibid., 49.

22 Ibid., 51.

23 Ibid., 50. Derrida performs close readings of passages from *Ecce Homo* and *Thus Spoke Zarathustra,* where Nietzsche refers both to the deferral of meaning for his writing as well as to the significance of ears and hearing. Here Derrida picks up on Nietzsche's emphasis on the ear and hearing, as for example when Nietzsche writes, "Perhaps the whole of Zarathustra may be reckoned as music; certainly a rebirth of the art of hearing was among its preconditions." Friedrich Nietzsche, *The Genealogy of Morals and Ecce Homo* (New York: Vintage, 1989), 295.

24 Derrida states, "As concerns that obviously deliberate transformation of auto to oto, which has been reversed in a chiasmatic fashion today: Notice that the institution has calculated this reversal so precisely that today we find ourselves in the Great Pavilion [of the ear], whereas yesterday we were somewhere else. . . . If today I am trying to reformulate it, it is because this necessity requires that we pass by way of the ear—the ear involved in any autobiographical discourse that is still at the stage of hearing oneself speak." Ibid., 49.

25 Derrida explicates this point by stating: "The ear of the other says me to me and constitutes the *autos* of my autobiography." Ibid., 51.

26 Laplanche and Pontalis, *The Language of Psycho-Analysis*, 46.

27 Quoted from company publicity materials.

28 It is worth noting here that Djavan da Silva's web and print-based self-representations position him not as a sultry singer, but first and foremost as a hard working producer who spends most days out of the year either in the studio behind a mixing board, or on the road playing guitar for some of Brazil's most successful singers. This is notable because it stands in stark contrast to the feminized representations of him and, in particular, his voice, in the biography for *Essential*.

29 Derrida forms a response to the following question posed by Christie V. McDonald: "[I]n the reading or readings that remain to be done of Nietzsche by

this deciphering ear, and without letting oneself get caught in the trap of what you have called gynegogy, does the "I" have a gender [genre]" (Derrida, 1985: 49). Derrida's translator Peggy Kamuf notes in the passage and at the bottom of the page that "Genre also means 'gender'" (ibid.). Derrida unambiguously interprets McDonald's question as pertaining to gender. He paraphrases her question in the following way: "The most difficult question came at the end of your remarks. It concerns the sexual gender (and not simply the literary genre) of the 'I' whose grammatical form is indeterminate, at least in the languages we are using here." Derrida, *The Ear of the Other*, 52.

30 Ibid.

31 "I'm listening," for example, can be understood as a performative utterance that confirms that which has been doubted by an interlocutor: whether or not auditory attention has been directed at the speaker. Hearing, on the other hand, describes a distinct process from listening, a generic aural mode of perception. "I hear you," is less a performative and more a declarative statement.

32 Alexander Gelfand, "Six Degrees of Accusation: Why Is a World Music Label That Defies Tradition Not Getting More Flak from the Critics?" *JAZZIZ* 19, no. 4 (April 2002): 38, 40–41.

33 See Taylor, *Global Pop;* Taylor, *Beyond Exoticism;* McClary *Feminine Endings.*

34 Jacques Attali, *Noise: The Political Economy of Music* (Minneapolis: University of Minnesota Press, 1985), 9.

35 Ibid.

36 Ibid.

37 Ronald Radano and Tricia Rose have separately written on the notion of "black noise." While each approach this notion differently, they share a common project, which is to point to the attempts at resignifying the pejorative through its reclamation in hip-hop and rap. See Ronald Radano, "Black Noise/White Master," in *Decomposition: Post-Disciplinary Performance,* edited by Sue-Ellen Case, Philip Brett, and Susan Leigh Foster (Bloomington: Indiana University Press, 2000), 39–29. See also Tricia Rose, *Black Noise: Rap Music and Black Culture in Contemporary America* (Hanover, N.H.: Wesleyan University Press, 1994).

38 Fletcher, La Flesche, and Fillmore, *A Study of Omaha Indian Music*, 237.

39 Attali, *Noise,* 6.

40 As a quintessentially modern, utopian theory, Attali's noise fetishizes the primal, pre-modern as the site of liberation.

41 In 2009, for approximately $300, I joined in several listening salons with other world music fans hosted by a popular world music DJ in his home in Southern California. Anybody could participate in these salons, which met once a week over three weeks. I stood out not only as the scholar but also as the younger person of color among the mostly white, middle-aged, well-traveled lawyers and physicians. Many of the participants were not only fans of the music but fans of the DJ, having followed his weekly shows, in some cases for decades. They came to hear host and DJ David Philips play songs and present biographical details

about the artists and minor ethnomusicological details about the musical traditions, peppered with some sociocultural, historical, and/or political details about the nation, culture, or region. This dialogue took place during a listening session focused on Brazilian music. Since I was working on a manuscript about listening to world music, I was very excited by the opportunity to participate in literally that—a salon organized around listening to world music. What I encountered in the discussions, like the one above, were the overt connections drawn by listeners and Philips himself between music and miscegenation.

42 Cesar Braga-Pinto, "Supermen and Chiquita Bacana's Daughters: Transgendered Voices in Brazilian Popular Music," in *Lusosex*, edited by Susan Canty Quinlan and Fernando Arenas (Minneapolis: University of Minnesota Press, 2002), 199.

43 Ibid., 202.

44 Ibid.

45 Quoted from company publicity materials.

46 The legibility of hybridity in world music, like contemporary neoliberal multicultural discourses of "diversity," depends on a hedging against "too much" of the diversifying element. Political scientist and diversity guru Scott Page has referred to the negative outcomes that result from "too much diversity." See Scott E. Page, *Diversity and Complexity* (Princeton: Princeton University Press, 2011), 2.

47 Taylor. *Beyond Exoticism*, 144.

48 Judith Butler, *Bodies that Matter* (New York: Routledge, 1993), 2.

CHAPTER 5. THE WORLD MUSIC CULTURE OF INCORPORATION

1 Entrance into the music industry most often requires participation in an economy of dues in which, no matter one's skill set, one must enter the organization at the bottom rung, performing unpaid work in order to "prove" oneself. Interns are screened and scrutinized and only the most highly skilled applicants are considered. The company seeks out new laborers who have the widest array of talents to offer. Interns are normally hired at twenty hours a week for a three-month period and are unpaid for that time. At the end of three months, if the label deems it prudent, the intern's contract is renewed for another three months or the intern is hired to further perform a specialized task cultivated in the first three months of internship. My willingness to volunteer for the shoot was not unlike what would be expected of any other employee who fit the bill.

2 Frank Wilderson looks to the emergence of the twin libidinal and political economies for the analysis of "dispossession" or its undoing in film theory. See Frank D. Wilderson, *Red, White & Black: Cinema and the Structure of U.S. Antagonisms* (Durham: Duke University Press, 2010), 67.

3 Max Horkheimer and Theodor Adorno, *Dialectic of Enlightenment* (Stanford: Stanford University Press, 2002), 99.

4 Like the photograph of Blackfoot Mountain Chief I discuss in chapter 1, this can also be read as a photograph of the native anthropologist being made absent to herself and being made present for a deferred, future listener.

5 J. M. Bernstein, "Introduction," in *The Culture Industry*, by Theodor Adorno (New York: Routledge, 2003), 4.

6 See Sterne, *MP3: The Meaning of a Format*.

7 Here I refer both to resonance as sound's unique material property moving through space and time as well as to Brian Massumi's notion of "resonation," which helps me to theorize a body's continuity across space and the materializing effect of sound's intensity upon bodies. Brian Massumi, *Parable for the Virtual: Movement, Affect, Sensation* (Durham: Duke University Press, 2002), 14.

8 Buck-Morss, *The Dialectics of Seeing*, xiii.

9 Foucault's oxymoron "incorporeal materialism" helps me to theorize incorporeality as the materialization of fantasy occurring within the aural imaginary that maps onto the listening body. See Michel Foucault, *The Archaeology of Knowledge, and The Discourse on Language* (New York: Pantheon, 1972), 231.

10 However, it is in no way limited to a process that takes place only within the ear. On the subject of listening with one's entire body, see Kheshti, "Touching Listening."

11 Susan Buck-Morss, *The Origin of Negative Dialectics: Theodor W, Adorno, Walter Benjamin, and the Frankfurt Institute* (New York: Free Press, 1977), 147.

12 Ibid., 148.

13 Benjamin, *Illuminations*, 222.

14 Lowe, "Work, Immigration, Gender."

15 Letter from Theodor Adorno to Walter Benjamin, in Buck-Morss, *The Origin of Negative Dialectics*, 85.

16 See Buck-Morss, ibid., 147.

17 The critique of Marxian tendencies for reducing political economy to economics and labor was most forcefully first made by Lukacs, Benjamin, and members of the Frankfurt Institute for Social Research, including Max Horkheimer, Theodor Adorno, and Herbert Marcuse. Otherwise known as "the Frankfurt School," these and other members were generally associated with a critique that gave credence to the dialectical nature of materialism and an emphasis on the social aspects of materialism. For a most relevant study, see as well Herbert Marcuse, *Eros and Civilization: A Philosophical Inquiry into Freud* (Boston: Beacon Press, 1966), as an extended reflection on the liberatory potential of the erotic, fantasy, and sexuality in the Marxist tradition.

18 Benjamin, *Illuminations*, 222.

19 Sterne, *The Audible Past*, 2–3.

20 Ibid., 2.

21 Personal interview with David Philips, October 8, 2009.

22 Foucault, *The Archaeology of Knowledge*, 231.

23 Or, as Brian Massumi has more aptly put it, it resonates. See Massumi, *Parables for the Virtual*, 14.

24 Marx makes this comment in response to an article written in a rival newspaper by Karl Heinrich Hermes, who William Pietz describes as an "anti-Semitic

Catholic who was urging severe censorship of religious criticism." See Emily
Apter and William Pietz, *Fetishism as Cultural Discourse* (Ithaca: Cornell
University Press, 1993), 135. Marx's full quote states: "Fetishism is so far from
raising man above his sensuous desires that, on the contrary, it is 'the religion of
sensuous desire.' Fantasy arising from desire deceives the fetish-worshipper that
an 'inanimate object' will give up its natural character in order to comply with his
desires." Karl Marx, *Early Writings* (New York: Vintage, 1975), 189.

25 Sensuousness was a major concern for the eighteenth-century *philosophes*, such as
Baron d'Holbach and Claude Helvetius, who influenced Marx because, as William
Pietz argues, their ideas and this concept made possible a materialist, nontheo-
logical discourse about religion. See Apter and Pietz, *Fetishism as Cultural
Discourse*, 137.

26 Ibid.

27 Ibid., 139–140.

28 Ibid., 141. There is a very palpable tension in the development of Marx's ideas on
fetishism and sensuality. Take for example the profoundly rich reflection on the
human subject's sensuality taken from his *Early Writings*: "To say that man is a
corporeal, living, real, sensuous, objective being with natural powers means that
he has real, sensuous objects as the objects of his being and of his vital expression,
or that he can only express his life in real, sensuous objects. To be objective,
natural and sensuous, and to have object, nature and sense outside oneself, or to
be oneself object, nature, and sense for a third person is one and the same
thing. . . . To be sensuous, i.e. to be real, is to be an object of sense, a sensuous
object, and thus to have sensuous objects outside oneself, objects of one's sense
perception." Marx, *Early Writings*, 351–357. Here we find Marx delivering a
phenomenological theory of sensuousness, which he determines to be the thing
that essentially makes humanity. His later theories on sensuous desire shed this
compassionate tone and take on a more skeptical position.

29 Theodor Adorno, *The Culture Industry*, Introduction by J. M. Bernstein (New
York: Routledge, 2001), 37.

30 See Pekka Gronow, "The Recording Industry: Growth of a Mass Medium,"
Popular Music 3 (1983): 58.

31 Marx writes, "The mysterious character of the commodity-form consists
therefore simply in the fact that the commodity reflects the social characteristics
of men's own labour as objective characteristics of the products of labour
themselves, as the socio-natural properties of these things. Hence it also reflects
the social relation of the producers to the sum total of labour as a social relation
between objects, a relation which exists apart from and outside the producers.
Through this substitution, the products of labour become commodities, sensuous
things which are at the same time suprasensible or social. . . . As against this, the
commodity-form, and the value-relation of the products of labour within which it
appears, have absolutely no connection with the physical nature of the commodity and the material [*dinglich*] relations arising out of this. It is nothing but the

definite social relation between men themselves which assumes here, for them, the fantastic form of a relation between things" (1975: 164–165).

32 See Apter and Pietz, 1993; Jean-Francois Lyotard, *Libidinal Economy* (Bloomington: Indiana University Press, 1993); Gilles Deleuze and Felix Guattari, *Anti-Oedipus: Capitalism and Schizophrena* (Minneapolis: University of Minnesota Press, 1983).

33 Sigmund Freud, *Sexuality and the Psychology of Love (New York: Touchstone Press, 1963)*, 205.

34 Ibid.

35 Ibid., 206.

36 Taylor, *Beyond Exoticism*, 159.

37 Lyotard *Libidinal Economy,* 108.

38 And despite Lyotard's positioning of "libidinal economy" as antagonistic toward Deleuze and Guattari's "economy of flows," both theories nevertheless engage libidinal and political economy.

39 Personal interview.

40 Emily Apter, *Feminizing the Fetish* (Ithaca: Cornell University Press, 1991), 3.

EPILOGUE

1 Zora Neale Hurston *Mules and Men* (New York: Perennial, 1990), 2–3.

2 I initially developed this idea in response to Hurston's archive of recordings and later discovered the coincidental use of this term in Audra Simpson's work. As I address in my engagement with Simpson's thesis below, this is no mere coincidence but in fact a way of relating to ethnographic knowledge production that I argue both Simpson and Hurston develop as a way of acknowledging and then refusing the archive's desire. See Audra Simpson, "On Ethnographic Refusal: Indigeneity, 'Voice,' and Colonial Citizenship," *Junctures* 9 (2007): 71–72. See her more elaborate theorization on the idea in *Mohawk Interruptus: Political Life Across the Borders of Settler States* (Durham: Duke University Press, 2014).

3 Hurston, *Mules and Men*, 7–8.

4 Robert Hemenway, *Zora Neale Hurston: a Literary Biography* (Urbana: University of Illinois Press, 1977), 101.

5 Ibid., 92, 102.

6 Ibid., 101–102.

7 Gina Dent, *"Flowers and Colored Bottles: The Anthropology of Culture in Twentieth-Century African-American Writing,"* Ph.D. dissertation, Columbia University, 1997, 136.

8 Angela Yvonne Davis, *Blues Legacies and Black Feminism: Gertrude "Ma" Rainey, Bessie Smith, and Billie Holiday* (New York: Vintage Books, 1998): 5.

9 Zora Neale Hurston, "Folklore and Music," *Civilization: The Magazine of the Library of Congress* 2 (January/February 1995), 50.

10 On the prevalence of phonograph recording among the Boasians, see Brady, *A Spriral Way*, 66.

11 Stetson Kennedy, "A Florida Treasure Hunt," Library of Congress, accessed January 3, 2014. http://memory.loc.gov/ammem/collections/florida/ffpres01.html

12 Simpson, "On Ethnographic Refusal," 71–72.

13 Ibid.

14 Ibid., 72.

15 Ibid., 74.

16 Ibid., 78.

17 Sherry Ortner's discussion of ethnographic refusal seems to depart from this. See Sherry B. Ortner, *Anthropology and Social Theory: Culture, Power, and the Acting Subject* (Durham: Duke University Press, 2006). Ortner characterizes ethnographic refusal as a tendency in so-called resistance literature, or studies that attempt to chronicle resistant practices and/or produce resistant outcomes. Ortner describes the refusal to write beyond this point in the resistance literature she reviews as "a kind of bizarre refusal to know and speak and write of the lived worlds inhabited by those who resist" (59). For Ortner, it is bizarre to not want to know and write about the subaltern. She states: "The notion that colonial or academic texts are able completely to distort or exclude the voices and perspectives of those being written about seems to me to endow these texts with far greater power than they have" (59–60). Instead, for Ortner ethnographies seem to be inherently democratic forms through which the lives being represented inevitably make themselves known. She writes, "The final text is a product of our pushing and their pushing back, and no text, however dominant, lacks the traces of this counterforce" (61). She goes on: "Finally, absolute fictionality and absolute silencing are impossible not only because those being written about force themselves into the author's account but also because there is always a multiplicity of accounts" (ibid.).

What distinguishes the Hurston and Simpson praxis of ethnographic refusal from Ortner's characterization of this practice among "resistance scholars" is firslty the utopian faith Ortner seems to have in ethnography as inherently democratic (unlike the dystopian and ambivalent stances taken by Simpson and Hurston, who practice ethnography despite its limits). For Ortner, as long as the ethnography is not deemed to be "thin," it will inherently reflect struggles over meaning between all stakeholders. Ortner's flawed and fundamentally liberal faith in ethnography-as-justice fails to recognize the ethnographic as itself an historically and culturally specific modality of meaning making and knowledge production that is disproportionately dominated by affluent, first-world whites. Ortner imagines that there is an ethical inertia that somehow cleanses anthropology of its racism once ethnographic research is translated into an ethnographic text. Instead of a historically bankrupt and unsupportable faith in ethnography's democratic outcomes, Hurston and Simpson's practices of ethnographic refusal in fact reveal what Ortner claims to be in search of: "the ways resistance can be more than opposition, can be truly creative and transformative " (ibid.).

18 Daphne Lamothe has argued that the distinction between high modernist preoccupations with "civilization and its discontents" and the New Negro modernism was "that New Negro writers interrogate and ultimately critique the colonizing gaze on the racialized subject, intersecting and shifting the presuppositions of both literary modernism and modernist anthropology by making their narratives as much about epistemology as they are about objectivity." Daphne Mary Lamothe, *Inventing the New Negro: Narrative, Culture, and Ethnography* (Philadelphia: University of Pennsylvania Press, 2008), 5.

19 In keeping with my general interest in excavating the sexual etymologies of listening and sound recording I have chosen to stay with the more commonly used *fidelity* and develop upon it in this chapter to think about infidelity as well. Scholars like Michael Chion and Jonathan Sterne have opted for the term "definition" over fidelity to address a particular medium's storage capacity and the degree to which that capacity can adequately convey information to the listener. See Michel Chion, Claudia Gorbman, and Walter Murch, *Audio-Vision: Sound on Screen (New York: Columbia University Press, 1994)*, 98–99; and Sterne, *MP3*, 4, respectively.

20 Fidelity can be said to be a modernist preoccupation. While it is impossible to neatly periodize the beginning and ending of an infatuation with fidelity in recording (just as it is futile to identify a beginning and ending to modernity), digital sampling, music reproduction, and delivery represent a paradigm shift away from the preoccupations with fidelity characteristic of most twentieth-century recording practices. For shorthand, fidelity might be understood as a predigital recording preoccupation characteristic of what we might call old (as opposed to "new") media.

21 Sterne, *The Audible Past*, 218.

22 Ibid., 219.

23 Ibid., 220.

24 How we distinguish the studio from the field seems to also have some relevance here. When we consider the location of certain studios, proximity also seems to matter; a studio is considered more authentic the closer it is to the location of origin for the sounds being recorded. Pekka Gronow has noted of the commercial recording industry of the teens and twenties, "To obtain material for their race and old-time catalogs, the record companies had to go outside New York. Soon they were making regular recording expeditions as far as New Orleans and San Antonio." Gronow, *Ethnic Recordings in America. P. 7* This practice has arguably been in effect throughout the twentieth century, as evident in studios formed around regional sounds like those affiliated with Motown, Nashville's music row, Memphis's Sun Studios, and others.

25 Weheliye, *Phonographics*, 30.

26 Ibid., 32.

27 Ibid.

28 James A. Snead. "On Repetition in Black Culture." *Black American Literature Forum* 15, no. 4 (Winter 1981), pp. 146-154.

29 Ibid., 149–150.

30 Ibid., 150.

31 I am skeptical about a researcher's ability to visually identify a historical figure. For instance, there is a case of mistaken identity regarding a famous photo of Zora Neale Hurston. See Valerie Boyd, *Wrapped in Rainbows: The Life of Zora Neale Hurston (New York: Sribner, 2003),* 437. Also see the notes attached to the digitized version of the photograph: http://www.loc.gov/pictures/collection/lomax/item/2007660326/.

32 These can be heard digitally archived on the Library of Congress site, "Florida Folklife from the WPA Collections," Library of Congress, accessed February 15, 2014, http://memory.loc.gov/cgi-bin/query/S?ammem/flwpabib:@field%28AUTHOR+@od1%28Hurston,+Zora+Neale%29%29

33 See letter from Hurston to Corse dated December 3, 1938, in Zora Neale Hurston and Carla Kaplan, *Zora Neale Hurston: A Life in Letters* (New York: Doubleday, 2002), 418.

34 Hurston and Kaplan, *Zora Neale Hurston*, 181. Zora Neale Hurston, "The 'Pet Negro' System," in *The American Mercury* (Philadelphia: University of Pennsylvania Press, May 1943).

35 "A Florida Treasure Hunt," Library of Congress, American Memory, http://memory.loc.gov/ammem/collections/florida/ffpres04.html

36 Snead, "Repetition as a Figure of Black Culture," 150.

37 Daphne Brooks, "'Sister Can You Line It Out': Zora Neale Hurston and the Sound of Angular Black Womanhood," in *Amerikanstudien* (2010): 624.

38 I found one recording of Mary Barnicle singing "The Bold Young Farmer" but with a more apprehensive and tentative tenor.

39 Moten, *In the Break*, 14.

40 I am grateful to Sora Han for her insights on this critical point.

41 See Moten, *In the Break*.

42 Ibid., 152.

REFERENCES

Adorno, Theodor W. "The Curves of the Needle." Trans. Thomas Y. Levin, in *October* 55 (1990): 48–55.

———. *The Culture Industry: Selected Essays on Mass Culture*. Introduction by J. M. Bernstein. New York: Routledge, 2001.

Agawu, V. Kofi. *Representing African Music: Postcolonial Notes, Queries, Positions*. New York: Routledge, 2003.

Allen, Ruth, and Elli Hisama, eds. *Ruth Crawford Seeger's Worlds*. Rochester: University of Rochester Press, 2007.

Apter, Emily. *Feminizing the Fetish*. Ithaca: Cornell University Press, 1991.

Apter, Emily, and Willliam Pietz. *Fetishism as Cultural Discourse*. Ithaca: Cornell University Press, 1993.

Arondekar, Anjali. *For the Record*. Durham: Duke University Press, 2009.

Attali, Jacques. *Noise: The Political Economy of Music*. Minneapolis: University of Minnesota Press, 1985.

Barthes, Roland. *Writing Degree Zero*. Trans. Annette Lavers and Colin Smith. New York: Hill and Wang, 1968.

———. *Image, Music, Text*. Trans. Stephen Heath. New York: Hill and Wang, 1977.

Benjamin, Walter. "The Work of Art in the Age of Mechanical Reproduction." In *Illuminations*. Edited by Hannah Arendt. New York: Schocken Books, 1986.

Bernstein, J. M. "Introduction." In *The Culture Industry*, by Theodor Adorno. New York: Routledge, 2003.

Boateng, Boatema. *The Copyright Thing Doesn't Work Here: Adinkra and Kente Cloth and Intellectual Property in Ghana*. Minneapolis: University of Minnesota Press, 2011.

Born, Georgina, and David Hesmondhalgh. *Western Music and Its Others: Difference, Representation, and Appropriation in Music*. Berkeley: University of California Press, 2000.

Bowler, Peter. *The Non-Darwinian Revolution*. Baltimore: Johns Hopkins University Press, 1988.

Boyd, Valerie. *Wrapped in Rainbows: The Life of Zora Neale Hurston*. New York: Scribner, 2003.

Brady, Erica. *A Spiral Way: How the Phonograph Changed Ethnography*. Jackson: University of Mississippi Press, 1999.

Braga-Pinto, Cesar. "Supermen and Chiquita Bacana's Daughters: Transgendered Voices in Brazilian Popular Music." In *Lusosex*. Edited by Susan Canty Quinlan and Fernando Arenas, 187–207. Minneapolis: University of Minnesota Press, 2002.

Brooks, Daphne. "'Sister Can You Line It Out': Zora Neale Hurston and the Sound of Angular Black Womanhood." *Amerikanstudien* (2010): 624.

Buck-Morss, Susan. *The Origin of Negative Dialectics: Theodor W. Adorno, Walter Benjamin, and the Frankfurt Institute.* New York: Free Press, 1977.

———. *The Dialectics of Seeing: Walter Benjamin and the Arcades Project.* Cambridge, Mass.: MIT Press, 1989.

Butler, Judith. *Bodies That Matter.* New York: Routledge, 1993.

Carby, Hazel. *Race Man.* Cambridge, Mass.: Harvard University Press, 1998.

Chion, Michel, Claudia Gorbman, and Walter Murch. *Audio-Vision: Sound on Screen.* New York: Columbia University Press, 1994.

Christian, Barbara. "The Race for Theory." *Cultural Critique* 54, no. 6 (1987): 51–63.

Coombe, Rosemary J. *The Cultural Life of Intellectual Properties: Authorship, Appropriation, and the Law.* Durham: Duke University Press, 1998.

Copjec, Joan. *Imagine There's No Woman: Ethics and Sublimation.* Cambridge, Mass.: MIT Press, 2002.

Croly, David Goodman. *Miscegenation: The Theory of the Blending of the Races, Applied to the American White Man and the Negro.* Ithaca: Cornell University Library Digital Collections, 1864.

Dame, Joke. "Unveiled Voices." In *Queering the Pitch: The New Gay and Lesbian Musicology.* Edited by Philip Brett, Elizabeth Wood, and Gary C. Thomas, 139–154. New York: Routledge, 1994.

———. "Voices within the Voice: Geno-Text and Pheno-Text in Berio's *Sequenza III.*" In *Music/Ideology: Resisting the Aesthetic.* Edited by Adam Krims, 233–246. Amsterdam: Gordon and Breach Publishing Group, 1998.

Darwin, Charles. *The Origin of the Species 1859.* Oxford: Oxford University Press, 1985.

Davis, Angela Yvonne. *Blues Legacies and Black Feminism: Gertrude "Ma" Rainey, Bessie Smith, and Billie Holiday.* New York: Vintage Books, 1998.

Deleuze, Gilles, and Felix Guattari. *Anti-Oedipus: Capitalism and Schizophrenia.* Minneapolis: University of Minnesota Press, 1983.

Deloria, Philip. *Indians in Unexpected Places.* Lawrence: University of Kansas Press, 2004.

Dent, Gina. *"Flowers and Colored Bottles: The Anthropology of Culture in Twentieth-Century African-American Writing."* Ph.D. dissertation, Columbia University, 1997.

Derrida, Jacques. "The Law of Genre." Trans. Avital Ronnel. *Critical Inquiry* 7, no. 1 (Autumn 1980): 55–81.

———. *The Ear of the Other: Otobiography, Transference, Translation: Texts and Discussions with Jacques Derrida.* Edited by Christie McDonald. Lincoln: University of Nebraska Press, 1988.

———. Derrida, Jacques *A Derrida Reader: Between the Blinds.* Edited, with an Introduction and Notes, by Peggy Kamuf. New York: Columbia University Press, 1991.

———. *Specters of Marx: The State of the Debt, the Work of Mourning, and the New International.* New York: Routledge, 1994.

Downey, Greg. "Listening to Capoeira: Phenomenology, Embodiment and the Materiality of Music." *Ethnomusicology* 46, no. 3 (Autumn 2002): 487–509.

Engels, Frederich. *Dialectics of Nature (1873–86).* 3rd ed. Moscow: Progress, 1964.

Erlmann, Veit. "The Esthetics of the Global Imagination: Reflections on World Music in the 1990s." *Public Culture* 8, no. 4 (1996): 467–487.

Evans, Dylan. *An Introductory Dictionary of Lacanian Psychoanalysis.* London: Routledge, 1996.

Feld, Steven. "A Sweet Lullaby for World Music." *Public Culture* 12, no. 1 (2000): 145–171.

Fletcher, Alice, Francis La Flesche, and John Comfort Fillmore. *A Study of Omaha Indian Music, volume 1, issue 107.* Omaha: University of Nebraska Press, 1994.

Foucault, Michel. *The Archaeology of Knowledge, and The Discourse on Language.* New York: Pantheon, 1972.

Freccero, Carla. *Queer/Early/Modern.* Durham: Duke University Press, 2006.

Freud, Sigmund. "Fetishism." In *Sexuality and the Psychology of Love.* New York: Touchstone Press, 1963.

———. *The Uncanny.* Trans. David McLintock. New York: Penguin Books, 2003.

Frisbie, Charlotte. "Women and the Society for Ethnomusicology." In *Comparative Musicology and Anthropology of Music: Essays on the History of Ethnomusicology.* Edited by Bruno Nettl and Philip V. Bohlman, 244–265. Chicago: University of Chicago Press, 1991.

Gelfand, Alexander. "Six Degrees of Accusation: Why Is a World Music Label That Defies Tradition Not Getting More Flak from the Critics?" *JAZZIZ* 19. 4 (April 2002): 38, 40–41.

Goodwin, Andrew, and Joe Gore. "World Beat and the Cultural Imperialism Debate." *Socialist Review* 20, no. 1 (July–September 1990): 63–80.

Gordon, Avery. *Ghostly Matters: Haunting and the Sociological Imagination.* Minneapolis: University of Minnesota Press, 1997.

Gronow, Pekka. "Ethnic Recordings: An Introduction." In *Ethnic Recordings in America: A Neglected Heritage, Studies in Folklife, no.1.* Washington, D.C.: American Folklife Center, Library of Congress, 1982, 1–50.

———. "The Recording Industry: Growth of a Mass Medium." *Popular Music* 3 (1983): 58.

Hart, Mickey. *Songcatchers: In Search of the World's Music.* Washington, D.C.: National Geographic Society, 2003.

Hemenway, Robert E. *Zora Neale Hurston: A Literary Biography.* Urbana: University of Illinois Press, 1977.

Herzog, George. *Research in Primitive and Folk Music in the United States, a Survey.* Washington, D.C.: American Council of Learned Societies, 1936.

Horkheimer, Max, and Theodor Adorno. *Dialectic of Enlightenment.* Stanford: Stanford University Press, 2002.

Huhndorf, Shari M. *Going Native: Indians in the American Cultural Imagination.* Ithaca: Cornell University Press, 2001.

Hurston, Zora Neale. "The 'Pet Negro' System." In *The American Mercury*. Philadelphia: University of Pennsylvania Press, May 1943.

———. *Mules and Men*. New York: Perennial, 1990.

———. "Folklore and Music." *Civilization: The Magazine of the Library of Congress 2* (January/February 1995): 50.

Hurston, Zora Neale, and Carla Kaplan. *Zora Neale Hurston: A Life in Letters*. New York: Doubleday, 2002.

Hutnyk, John. *Critique of Exotica: Music, Politics, and the Culture Industry*. London: Pluto Press, 2000.

Ihde, Don. *Listening and Voice: Phenomenologies of Sound*. Albany: SUNY Press, 2007.

Kenney, William Howland. *Recorded Music in American Life: The Phonograph and Popular Memory,1890–1945*. New York: Oxford University Press, 1999.

Kheshti, Roshanak. "Musical Miscegenation and the Logic of Rock and Roll: Homosocial Desire and Racial Productivity in 'A Paler Shade of White.'" *American Quarterly* 60, no. 4 (December 2008): 1037–1056.

———. "Touching Listening: The Aural Imaginary in the World Music Culture Industry." *American Quarterly* 63, no. 3 (September 2011): 711–731.

Kortarba, Joseph, and Philip Vannini. *Understanding Society through Popular Music*. New York: Routledge, 2009.

Krim, Arthur. "Appalachian Songcatcher: Olive Dame Campbell and the Scotch-Irish Ballad." *Journal of Cultural Geography* 24, no. 1 (Fall/Winter 2006): 91–112.

Kristeva, Julia. *Desire in Language: A Semiotic Approach to Literature and Art*. European Perspectives. New York: Columbia University Press, 1980.

———. "Roland Barthes and Writing as Demystification." In *The Sense and Non-Sense of Revolt: The Powers and Limits of Psychoanalysis*. Trans. Jeanine Herman. New York: Columbia University Press, 2000.

Kun, Josh. *Audiotopia: Music, Race, and America*. Berkeley: University of California Press, 2005.

Lacan, Jacques. *The Four Fundamental Concepts of Psycho-Analysis*. Edited by Jacques-Alain Miller. New York: W. W. Norton, 1981.

———. *Feminine Sexuality: Jacques Lacan and the école freudienne*. Edited by Juliet Mitchell and Jackqueline Rose. New York: W. W. Norton, 1982.

Lamothe, Daphne Mary. *Inventing the New Negro: Narrative, Culture, and Ethnography*. Philadelphia: University of Pennsylvania Press, 2008.

Laplanche, Jean, and J.-B. Pontalis. *The Language of Psycho-Analysis*. London: Karnac, 1988.

Leonard, Thomas C. "Mistaking Eugenics for Social Darwinism." *History of Political Economy* 37, no. 1 (2005): 226.

Lilliestam, Lars. "On Playing by Ear." *Popular Music* 15, no. 02 (May 1996): 195–216.

Lott, Eric. *Love and Theft: Blackface Minstrelsy and the American Working Class*. New York: Oxford University Press, 1993.

Lowe, Donald M. *The History of Bourgeois Perception*. Chicago: University of Chicago Press, 1982.

Lowe, Lisa. "Work, Immigration, Gender: New Subjects of Cultural Politics." In *The Politics of Culture in the Shadow of Capital*. Edited by Lisa Lowe and D. Lloyd, 354–374. Durham: Duke University Press, 1997.

Lyotard, Jean-Francois. *Libidinal Economy*. Bloomington: Indiana University Press, 1993.

Marcuse, Herbert. *Eros and Civilization: A Philosophical Inquiry into Freud*. Boston: Beacon Press, 1966.

Marx, Karl. *Early Writings*. New York: Vintage Books, 1975.

Massumi, Brian. *Parables for the Virtual: Movement, Affect, Sensation*. Durham: Duke University Press, 2002.

McClary, Susan. *Feminine Endings: Music, Gender, and Sexuality*. Minneapolis: University of Minnesota Press, 1991.

Meintjes, Louise. "Paul Simon's Graceland, South Africa, and the Mediation of Musical Meaning." *Ethnomusicology* (Winter 1990): 37–73.

Metz, Christian. *The Imaginary Signifier: Psychoanalysis and the Cinema*. Bloomington: Indiana University Press, 1981.

Miller, Karl Hagstrom. *Segregating Sound: Inventing Folk and Pop Music in the Age of Jim Crow*. Durham: Duke University Press, 2010.

Moten, Fred. *In the Break: The Aesthetics of the Black Radical Tradition*. Minneapolis: University of Minnesota Press, 2003.

Muñoz, Jose Estaban. *Cruising Utopia: The Then and There of Queer Futurity*. New York: New York University Press, 2009.

Newman, Louise Michele. *White Women's Rights: The Racial Origins of Feminism in the United States*. New York: Oxford University Press, 1999.

Nietzsche, Friedrich. *The Genealogy of Morals and Ecce Homo*. New York: Vintage, 1989.

Nyongó, Tavia Amolo. *The Amalgamation Waltz: Race, Performance, and the Ruses of Memory*. Minneapolis: University of Minnesota Press, 2009.

Ong, Walter J. *Orality and Literacy: The Technologizing of the Word*. London: Methuen, 1982.

Ortner, Sherry B. *Anthropology and Social Theory: Culture, Power, and the Acting Subject*. Durham: Duke University Press, 2006.

Page, Scott E. *Diversity and Complexity*. Princeton: Princeton University Press, 2011.

Porzak, Simon. "Inverts and Invertebrates: Darwin, Proust, and Nature's Queer Heterosexuality." *Diacritics* 41, no. 4 (2013): 10.

Radano, Ronald. "Black Noise/White Master." In *Decomposition: Post-Disciplinary Performance*. Edited by Sue-Ellen Case, Philip Brett, Susan Leigh Foster, 39–49. Bloomington: Indiana University Press, 2000.

Rainer, Peter. "Love in a Miner Key." *New York Magazine*, June 25, 2001. Accessed August 15, 2012. http://nymag.com/nymetro/movies/reviews/4852/.

Roberts, Helen Heffron. *Form in Primitive Music*. New York: Norton, 1933.

Rose, Tricia. *Black Noise: Rap Music and Black Culture in Contemporary America*. Music/Culture. Hanover, N.H.: University Press of New England, 1994.

Schnabel, Tom. *Stolen Moments*. Los Angeles: Acrobat Books, 1988.

Seshadri-Crooks, Kalpana. *Desiring Whiteness: A Lacanian Analysis of Race*. London: Routledge, 2000.

Shelemay, Kay. "Recording Technology, the Record Industry and Ethnomusicological Scholarship." In *Comparative Musicology and Anthropology of Music: Essays on the History of Ethnomusicology*. Edited by Bruno Nettl and Philip V. Bohlman, 277–292. Chicago: University of Chicago Press, 1991.

Silverman, Kaja. *The Acoustic Mirror: The Female Voice in Psychoanalysis and Cinema*. Bloomington: Indiana University Press, 1988.

Simpson, Audra. "On Ethnographic Refusal: Indigeneity, 'Voice,' and Colonial Citizenship." *Junctures* 9 (2007): 71–72.

———. *Mohawk Interruptus: Political Life Across the Borders of Settler States* Durham: Duke University Press, 2014.

Sinha, Lalita. *Unveiling the Garden of Love: Mystical Symbolism in Layla Majnun & Gita Govinda*. Bloomington: World Wisdom, 2008.

Snead, James A. "On Repetition in Black Culture." *Black American Literature Forum* 15, no. 4 (Winter 1981): 146-154.

Smith, Andrea. "Queer Theory and Native Studies: The Heteronormativity of Settler Colonialism." *GLQ: A Journal of Gay and Lesbian Studies* 16, no. 1–2 (2010): 41–68.

Spivak, Gayatri Chakravorty. *A Critique of Postcolonial Reason: Toward a History of the Vanishing Present*. Cambridge, Mass.: Harvard University Press, 1999.

Sterne, Jonathan. *The Audible Past: Cultural Origins of Sound Reproduction*. Durham: Duke University Press, 2003.

———. *MP3: The Meaning of a Format*. Durham: Duke University Press, 2012.

Suisman, David. *Selling Sounds: The Commercial Revolution in American Music*. Cambridge, Mass.: Harvard University Press, 2009.

Taussig, Michael T. *Mimesis and Alterity: A Particular History of the Senses*. New York: Routledge, 1993.

Taylor, Timothy D. *Global Pop: World Music, World Markets*. New York: Routledge, 1997.

———. "The Commodification of Music at the Dawn of the Era of 'Mechanical Music.'" *Ethnomusicology* 51, no. 2 (2007): 281–305.

———. *Beyond Exoticism: Western Music and the World*. Durham: Duke University Press, 2007.

Thompson, Emily Ann. *The Soundscape of Modernity: Architectural Acoustics and the Culture of Listening in America, 1900–1933*. Cambridge, Mass.: MIT Press, 2002.

Travers, Peter. "Songcatcher." *Rolling Stone*, June 7, 2001. Accessed August 20, 2012. http://www.rollingstone.com/movies/reviews/songcatcher-20010607?print=true.

Tsing, Anna Lowenhaupt. *In the Realm of the Diamond Queen: Marginality in an Out-of-the-Way Place*. Princeton: Princeton University Press, 1993.

Tucker, Sherrie. "'But This Music Is Mine Already!': 'White Woman' as Jazz Collector in the Film *New Orleans* (1947)." In *Big Ears: Listening for Gender in Jazz Studies*. Edited by Nicole T. Rustin and Sherrie Tucker, 361–392. Durham: Duke University Press, 2008.

Visweswaran, Kamala. *Un/common Cultures: Racism and the Rearticulation of Cultural Difference*. Durham: Duke University Press, 2010.

Vizenor, Gerald. "Edward Curtis: Pictorialist and Ethnographic Adventurist." Library of Congress, October 2000, accessed September 22, 2012. http://memory.loc.gov/ammem/award98/ienhtml/essay3.html

Weheliye, Alexander G. *Phonographies: Grooves in Sonic Afro-Modernity*. Durham: Duke University Press, 2005.

Werbner, Pnina, and Tariq Modood, eds. *Debating Cultural Hybridity: Multicultural Identities and the Politics of Anti-Racism*. London: Zed Books, 1997.

Wilderson, Frank B. *Red, White & Black: Cinema and the Structure of U.S. Antagonisms*. Durham: Duke University Press, 2010.

Wolf, Eric. *Europe and the People without History*. Berkeley: University of California Press, 1982.

"Women Collectors: American Folklife Center." American Memory. Library of Congress. Available at http://memory.loc.gov. Accessed August 12, 2012.

Ziff, Bruce H., and Pratima V. Rao. *Borrowed Power: Essays on Cultural Appropriation*. New Brunswick, N.J.: Rutgers University Press, 1997.

INDEX

Adorno, Theodor, 3, 30, 37, 51, 55–56, 109–111, 113, 118–120

Afro pop, 46–47, 49; Afro-Indie genre, 12, 152n50

Agawu, Kofi, 52–54

Alpert, Herb, 95

ambivalence, 24, 34–36, 43, 112, 119, 127–128

Appalachian music. *See* Campbell, Olive Dame; *Songcatcher* (film)

appropriation,7, 11–13, 15, 38, 40–44, 46, 51, 58–59, 63, 100, 106, 123, 150n10. *See also* incorporation; world music; world music culture industry (WMCI)

archive: aurality and, 2–3; fidelity and, 130, 137, 141; future orientation of, 33, 35, 133, 137, 139; power of, 133; production of, 18, 21; radical listening relations in, 138–141, 161n2; subjectivity and, 46; world music culture industry, 5

Arondekar, Anjali, 35

Asian underground music, xvi

Attali, Jacques, 96–97, 157n40

audiotopia, xv

aurality, xviii, xix, 37–38, 115–116; aura and, 34, 36–37, 51, 113–115, 123, 135; aural fantasies, 2–3, 7, 55–56; aural imaginary, 5, 7, 11, 12–13, 22, 45, 50, 55–56, 61, 67–68, 70, 78, 81, 87, 111, 116–117, 124–125, 159n9; aural incorporation, 13, 40–41, 44, 51, 83–84, 112; aural intelligibility, 96; aural other, 5, 7–8, 12, 32, 45, 61, 64, 66,

69, 84, 101, 105, 111, 125–126, 132, 139 (*see also* hybridity; miscegenation); aural trace, 1–2, 7, 12, 29–33, 34–35; commoditization of, xviii, 10, 106 (*see also* listening); erotic aspect of, 93; phonograph as site of, 31; queer, 10–11, 142; white women and, 1–4, 12, 31–33, 115. *See also* appropriation; incorporation; listening; *significance*

authenticity. *See* fidelity

Barthes, Roland, 13, 70–72, 74–75, 77, 81, 153n6; as feminized listener, 71–73, 153n17; geno-song, 70, 74–76, 78, 80–81, 153n16; "grain of the voice," 66–69, 80; pheno-song 74, 76–78, 80–81, 153n16. See also *significance*

Benjamin, Walter, 33–34, 57, 112–114

Bernstein, J. M., 110

biopolitics: aural incorporation as, 13; hybridization and, 105; incorporation and, 44; invagination and, 83; listening and, 3, 8–9; miscegenation and 87; somatic hearing and, 57; world music culture industry and, 38. *See also* hybridity; miscegenation

"Blackfoot Chief, Mountain Chief making phonographic record at Smithsonian, 2/9/1916," 24, 23–27, 35–36

Blackfoot Mountain Chief, 20, 23–27, 33, 35–36, 133

blackness, 46–47, 91

Boas, Franz, 127, 129, 134

Boateng, Boatema, 43

Born, Georgina, 40–41
Bowler, Peter, 88, 155n16
Brady, Erika, 34–35
Braga-Pinto, Cesar, 99–100
Breuer, Josef, 22–23
Brooks, Daphne, 139
Buck-Morss, Susan, 112
Bureau of American Ethnology, 3–4, 12,
    17, 19
Butler, Judith, 107
Byrne, David, 82–83

Campbell, Olive Dame, 16
Christian, Barbara, xix, "a race for
    theory," xvii-xviii
Conquergood, Dwight
Copjec, Joan, 50
country music, xv-xvi; as American
    music, xvi
Croly, David Goodman, 88–89, 155n11
Croly, Herbert, 89–90
The Culture Industry (Adorno and
    Horkheimer), 110
Curtis, Edward S., 31, 148n40
Curtis-Burlin, Natalie, 19

Dame, Joke, 73, 154n25
Davis, Angela, 128
Darwin, Charles, 13, 88, 90, 105, 155n7,
    155nn14–16
Darwinism, 88–90; social Darwinism,
    28–29, 88, 155n14
Decade for Women (UN), 58–59
Densmore, Frances, 18, 19, 20, 23–27, 33,
    36, 133, 146n21
Dent, Gina, 128
Derrida, Jacques, 1, 30, 32, 51, 59, 91–93,
    95, 141, 148n39, 156n18, 156n20,
    156nn23–25, 156–157n29. *See also*
    invagination
difference, 6
Downey, Greg, 60
Dubois, W. E. B., 48

Engels, Friedrich, 155n15
ethnography: capitalism and, 9; whiteness
    and, 19. *See also* Hurston, Zora Neale;
    Simpson, Audra
ethnomusicology, 4, 5–6; popular
    recording industry and, 17–18; Society
    for Ethnomusicology, 11, 146n13. *See
    also* Densmore, Frances; Blackfoot
    Mountain Chief
eugenics, 89–90

Feld, Steven, 5–6
female masculinity, 8
fetishism, 117–119, 160n28: aesthetics and,
    112; castration anxiety and, 72, 121;
    commodity, 107, 111, 113, 117–118, 123,
    160–161n31; as false consciousness,
    113, 118, 122–123; libidinal economy
    and, 122–123; miscegenation and, 106;
    modernity and, 57–58; musical, 119–120;
    post-fetishism, 122–123; psychoanalytic,
    118, 120–121; sensuality and, 159–160n24,
    160n28; temporality of, 33; world music
    and, 2–3, 7, 13–14, 44, 121–122
fidelity, 35, 163nn19–20; hybridization
    and, 77; sonic infidelity, 125–126, 130–
    131, 133–137, 139–141. *See also* Hurston,
    Zora Neale
Fletcher, Alice B., 18, 19, 26–27, 29, 37, 96
Foley, Ryan, 47
Foucault, Michel, 116, 159n9
Freccero, Carla, 32
Frere-Jones, Sasha, 44, 47, 91
Freud, Sigmund, 7, 22, 33, 41, 48–49,
    51, 118, 120–122. *See also* fetishism;
    incorporation; invagination;
    transference; uncanny
Frisbie, Charlotte, 146n13

Galton, Francis, 89
gender: aural imaginary and, 7; exchange
    value of, 11; female masculinity, 8;
    genre/gender, 91–92, 95, 156n18, 156n20,

ABOUT THE AUTHOR

Roshanak Kheshti is Associate Professor of Ethnic Studies and affiliate faculty in the Critical Gender Studies Program at the University of California, San Diego.